"Alpesh gives you a rare glimpse into]
rules to investment the professionals d(
packed full of good advice for all leve
Managing Director, The Information I   *?nt*
Conference Company)

"With the media playing an increasingly important role in investment decision-making, find out how one of the UK's best known traders and broadcasters uses the wealth of information out there." – **Michael Foulkes**, *President and Chief Executive, TD Waterhouse Europe*

"Alpesh's ability to communicate in an entertaining and thought-provoking way makes this a must-read for anyone interested in the financial markets; from novice to professional." – **Clem Chambers**, *CEO, ADVFN.com*

"Alpesh's proven track record speaks for itself. Learning from him will help ordinary people match the results of market professionals." – **Clive Cooke**, *CEO, City Index (part of ICAP one of the world's largest bond dealers)*

"Once again Alpesh Patel produces an outstanding guide that will capture the attention of beginners and professional investors alike." – **Robin Houldsworth**, *CEO, Tradition (one of Europe's largest brokers)*

"Alpesh shares his valuable insight into the financial media industry – what news really means and how to profit from it. I wish that I had read this book years ago." – **Paul Basham**, *MD, Sharescope (major stockmarket data provider)*

"Alpesh's great book from the backstage of the world of investment helps us to trade on wiser grounds." – **Michele Raris**, *former Chief Executive Officer IMIWeb (fastest growing broker in 2001, 2002 & 2003)*

"A fascinating, insightful look at improving your investment returns from a knowledgeable professional." – **David Bearman**, *CEO, Eden Group Plc (leading City stockbrokers)*

"A fascinating inside view on the secrets of the investment world." – **John Spooner**, *CEO, Quester Venture Capital Trusts managing $400m*

"*Investing Unplugged* does a masterful job of blending the theoretical and the practical. It's an insight with many implications and it offers a set of useful tools to make better decisions and thereby create wealth." – **Sonjoy Chatterjee**, *CEO ICICI Bank UK Limited*

"Patel does it again – condenses and simplifies the world of investing into an easy-to-understand, indispensable handbook." – **James Bateman**, *Head of Marketing, ODL Securities*

"Busy people like me do not get the time to manage investments – so we pay 'professionals'. Eventually, having got fed up with getting angry every time a valuation statement arrives, we get around to taking control. If prior to reading this book you were thinking of taking control of your own finances, by the end of Chapter 1 you will be convinced of the need to make that move." – **Kevin Ashby,** *CEO Patsystems*

"Insightful and challenging, *Investing Unplugged* looks at what's under the gloss of financial news and how financial reporting influences the investment process." – **Max Butti,** *euronext.LIFFE (world's second largest derivatives exchange)*

"One of the few books I have seen that genuinely attempts *and* succeeds in giving the tools to convert a private investor in to a professional investor for today's 'Holy Grail' obsessed market." – **Dan Moczulski,** *IG Index*

"Revealing insights are peppered throughout this book, illustrated with real anecdotes, laced with alarming irony and brought to our attention in a typically humorous manner … the truth is truly disturbing and you want to read it here!" – **Guy Cohen,** *CEO, InvestorEasy*

"When Alpesh speaks, investors should listen. As both an active investor and former journalist, I know this book offers a unique experience and view to the art of trading." – **Andy Yates,** *Director of leading financial website DigitalLook.com*

"Alpesh's track record speaks for itself. This book offers incisive, thought-provoking reading for all active investors, whether they be short or long-term traders." – **Chris Cole,** *Technical Editor, Company REFS*

"Takes a no-holds-barred approach to uncovering stock market secrets, and searches for the truth that most financial TV coverage keeps well hidden … a brave guide that will help any stock market investor navigate the muddy waters of financial reporting – a sort of Columbo meets Warren Buffet." – **Polly Fergusson,** *Shares Magazine*

"Full of useful insights for private investors, particularly on risk, Alpesh blends his wealth of experience with that of real market experts." – **Neil Jamieson,** *condirect*

INVESTING
Unplugged

Secrets from the Inside

ALPESH B. PATEL

Dear Sean

Wishing you wealth

Yours Alpesh Patel

palgrave
macmillan

First published 2005 by
PALGRAVE MACMILLAN
Houndmills, Basingstoke, Hampshire RG21 6XS and
175 Fifth Avenue, New York, N.Y. 10010
Companies and representatives throughout the world

PALGRAVE MACMILLAN is the global academic imprint of the Palgrave Macmillan division of St. Martin's Press, LLC and of Palgrave Macmillan Ltd. Macmillan® is a registered trademark in the United States, United Kingdom and other countries. Palgrave is a registered trademark in the European Union and other countries.

ISBN 13: 978–1–4039–4620–1 (hardcover)
ISBN 13: 978–1–349–52345–0 (softcover)

This book is printed on paper suitable for recycling and made from fully managed and sustained forest sources.

A catalogue record for this book is available from the British Library.

A catalog record for this book is available from the Library of Congress.

10 9 8 7 6 5 4 3 2 1
14 13 12 01 10 09 08 07 06 05

For my niece Chandni,
born the year I completed this book

From your "favorite uncle"!

Because thou art dearly loved by Me,
I will relate what is beneficial to thee.
Bhagavad Gita: Chapter XVIII, Verse 64

For a complimentary multi-media audio-visual "Investing Better" CD-ROM for all purchasers of this book please email alpesh@tradermind.com with your name and address and quoting *Investing Unplugged*.

The CD-ROM educates readers about top investment mistakes, investment strategies, money and risk management techniques and much more. It is narrated by Alpesh Patel and leads you step-by-step through his trading techniques.

The book's website is located at www.investingunplugged.com

CONTENTS

Contents

LIST OF FIGURES

List of tables

Alpesh B. Patel (alpesh.patel@tradermind.com)

Founder Director, Agile Partners Asset Management Hedge Fund

Chairman, Aranca (Independent Financial Research from India)

Founder, TraderMind Limited, consulting to some of the world's largest brokers on customer acquisition and strategy

Director, AHM Inc (online casino and betting)

Board Member, Indo-British Partnership

Member, UK-India Roundtable

Trustee, Royal Institute of International Affairs

Columnist, *Financial Times*

Global stock markets contributor for BBC, CNBC, CNN

Author, nine investment books translated into six languages

Visiting Fellow, Business & Industry, Corpus Christi College, Oxford (2002)

Previously interviewer on Bloomberg Television for three years, "CEO in the HotSeat" – cross-examining CEOs of listed companies on their company performances

Advisor to world's second largest derivatives exchange on market penetration and competitive strategy and reaching 1.6m UK investors on US and European companies worth investing in (2000–2003)

Member of the Board, The Indus Entrepreneurs, a global organization of businesspeople (www.tie-uk.org)

ACKNOWLEDGEMENTS

First and foremost, thank you to my editor Stephen Rutt for making this whole process painless, for sound advice, and for understanding the project.

Thanks also to all the people behind the scenes at Palgrave Macmillan and Aardvark Editorial, who authors rarely meet, but owe a great debt.

Many thanks, too, to all the people who have offered me an insight and breaks into financial journalism, especially Simon London, my first editor at the *Financial Times*, Katherine Oliver, who offered me the three-year Bloomberg contract, C.B. Patel who published my first ever piece and gave me a taste for seeing my name in print, and all my editors at all the magazines and financial portals for which I have written over the years.

Do not believe in anything simply because you have heard it. Do not believe in anything simply because it is spoken and rumored by many. Do not believe in anything simply because it is found written in your religious books. Do not believe in anything merely on the authority of your teachers and elders. Do not believe in traditions because they have been handed down for many generations. But after observation and analysis, when you find that anything agrees with reason and is conducive to the good and benefit of one and all, then accept it and live up to it. **Buddha**

I am a trader. My life as a trader meant I could take up an offer from the head of TV at Bloomberg TV to present shows, which I did for three years. I cross-examined CEOs from around the world, analysts of the biggest banks and fund managers. I am a columnist for the *Financial Times*. My columns are read around the world. All this put me at the centre of market events. I saw the rise and fall of the dot-com boom and the day-trader craze into saner times where the internet, TV and print influence millions of private investor decisions.

As a trader I have won stock-picking competitions held by Bloomberg and the *Financial Times*. Clients of my company have included Goldman Sachs, American Express, Charles Schwab, Barclays and many other financial firms who have asked me to talk about investing to their clients.

Pick the right stock tomorrow and you could be a multimillionaire next year. That is the lure for many of the markets. They may not state it so crassly, but they treat it like a lottery.

When I won the *Financial Times* competition to predict the FTSE 100 over a 12-month period. I came within 0.5% of the final value. The person who came last was 50% out, had a first class degree from Cambridge University and was a markets commentator for the newspaper. So I had to write this book; where the media meets the markets.

I was also the best performing stock picker on Bloomberg TV as analyzed by them over a six-month period; beating every single one of their other pickers. I also won a competition to pick the best performing stock – beating 45 other analysts on Channel 4. That is also why I had to write this book.

Consider that you have more information today about the markets, more quickly available than at any point in history. You have more computing power trying to solve the problem of where a price will go next. Surely if supercomputers can absorb all the information about the environment to tell us that it will rain tomorrow afternoon, then they can tell us that next week the price of Microsoft will be higher than it is today?

And so the seduction of the markets continues. Within this alluring dance financial journalism plays a pivotal role. *If the markets are a whore taking payment for seductive promises of great pleasure, then financial journalism is the pimp setting the price and guiding you to the best on offer.*

Why?

Private investors relate to financial TV; it's accessible, hundreds of thousands watch it. But they fail to become great investors no matter how much financial news they digest. We on the financial TV side can't tell you what will make you money: that would be dull TV.

Having received thousands of viewer and investor emails over the years, I have an idea of what investors don't know that costs them money.

My constant contact with the entire financial services industry (brokers, journalists, fund managers, traders, analysts, CEOs, academics) through Bloomberg and the *Financial Times* and as a professional trader myself, revealed the "secret" of distinguishing great from good investments and why private investors never get to hear about them.

From why some financial products are simply better than others to why we can't talk on TV about asset allocation, money management and what will really make you money, this books reveals the inside view of financial investments from the most powerful market-influencing medium: financial TV. Through that quirky, fast-paced and often humorous angle, the book guides the reader through the neglected 20% essentials of great investing and avoiding the 80% rubbish out there.

But there is a story that needs telling. It's a story about why private investors do not invest well – why we buy the financial products we do, lose the sums we do. And it seeks to right those wrongs and make better investors. It's a story that could only be written by someone who has worked in the financial media and is a professional investor. So if not me, then who? If not now, then when?

I worked at Bloomberg throughout the dot-com boom when every private investor thought he was a financial genius. I also worked through the collapse when the viewer realized he wasn't a financial genius and he would not mistake a bull market for skill again. Well, not until the next boom.

But it is also a story about why, despite some of the best-paid journalists in the world, Enron, Global Crossing and other scandals were not uncovered by financial journalists.

If a government was corrupt, which journalist from CNN, *Time* magazine or *60 Minutes* would not reproach himself for not getting the scoop? Why do we not expect the same of our financial journalists when the damage of a corrupt company can be in the millions, if not billions?

At every level it is a story about the power of the financial media from someone who works within it. It is a fascinating world of mini-celebrity.

Subject

Lesser known essentials include outstanding investment practice from the most diverse collection of financial sources, including Nobel laureates, explained in plain language, even where the sources of know-how are market boffins, academics and fund managers.

But the difference with this book is the angle of why these topics are not covered on financial TV and media. That adds an interesting dimension and lets the investor know they are getting unique access to top advice from multiple credible sources.

Equally, in the few cases when I did cover these topics, the thousands of positive emails led to congratulations from the overall editor of the *Financial Times* and a media award. But it is not just financial TV that I use as a platform for education. I have also been a financial magazine editor as editor of "e-Shares" which was a pullout section of *Shares* magazine, and editor of "Financial Voice", part of the *Asian Voice* newspaper. I will use my financial print journalism expertise too.

As legendary trader Ed Seykota put it:

> when magazine covers get pretty emotional, get out of the position. There's nothing else in the magazine that works very well, but the covers are pretty good. This is not an indictment of the magazine people, it's just that at the end of a big move there is a communal psychological abreaction which shows up on the covers of magazines.

Typical subjects covered in detail in this book are:

- Asset allocation (why it is more important than stock picks)

- Diversification (how much is right)

- Market neutral trading (its uniqueness)

- Risk management (what risk really means and how professionals reduce it)

- Track an index or beat it?

- Exchange traded funds (why they offer great advantages)
- Single stock futures (why the product is underutilized)
- Analysts' ratings (how they really work)
- Dollar cost averaging (does it work?)
- Technical analysis (to what extent it works)
- Psychological investment biases (or why your mind messes you up)
- Investing shortcuts – the five best sites to reduce your research time by 80%
- Money management: how professional profitable fund managers reduce risk and maintain reward
- Investment styles, what they are and how to find one for you
- Ten mistakes Bloomberg TV viewers and all investors make.

Market

The market for this book is the same as the millions who have read my weekend *Financial Times* column for the past five years and those who read me on various online financial portals and magazines, and also those viewers who watch me now on BBC TV and have watched me for three years on Bloomberg TV, that is, mainstream people concerned about investments.

Until recently the typical readers would have been male, graduate, professional, over 30 years old. Today, they are homemakers, retirees, teenagers, as well as the professionals.

To date I have eight other books translated into German, French, Spanish, Polish, Chinese and Russian.

But I leave you with a word of caution, in the words of John W. Henry:

There is no Holy Grail. There is no perfect way to capture [the] move from $100/ounce to $800/ounce in gold ... We cannot be profitable every month; we don't try; we're not that smart ... but we feel that we can rely upon a philosophy that has worked very well over the last 17 years, and only pay attention to what the markets are saying currently, and don't ask why the dollar is going up or why interest rates are going down. Our philosophy is that if something is going down, we want to be short. Period.

ALPESH B. PATEL

CHAPTER 1

Why we can't tell you what Buffett and Soros know and what will make you money

There's something very reductive about the stock market. You can be right for the wrong reasons or wrong for the right reasons, but to the market, you're just plain right or wrong. **John Allen Paulos**

- Fund managers in the financial press ... dirty little secrets
- Stock picks and why we really offer them
- The knowledge that will make you money but why financial TV can't tell you
- What the presenter does not know and why it costs you money
- How to really read the financial news as a trader or investor

Fund managers can't keep it up

When I used to cross-examine fund managers on Bloomberg TV I reserved a special vitriol. Why? It wasn't personal. It's just that I was fed up with getting emails from private investors who saw their investments entrusted to fund managers whittled away year after year in poor performance.

And just because you're on TV you have the added credibility of "as seen on TV." But we never looked at their fund performance, we only knew they were fund managers. The program "booker" who takes the bookings doesn't vet the quality. It's 5pm, we're on air in a couple of hours. Who'll come on? They're on!

We should have got monkeys to give their stock views. Actually, looking back, sometimes we did.

Since you are reading this book, you are probably someone unwilling to let a fund manager burn your cash. Consider the fund management industry. Here is a profession which gets paid irrespective of results; even if they lose you money. It's guaranteed.

But what do you do if you are too busy to manage your money. Surely you give it to a fund manager? No.

They're supposedly the best equipped to manage your funds. Billions of dollars are entrusted to them, and they have global resources at their disposal. So should you assign some of your money to fund managers?

After all, there's been a recent proliferation of fund supermarkets. The hearings of the case brought by Unilever's pension fund against Merrill Lynch's Mercury Asset Management (MAM) subsidiary alleging fund manager negligence because of underperformance are groundbreaking. If Unilever can be so unhappy, what hope has a private investor, even with novel online tools, of picking a good fund manager?

Not much, according to ample evidence. "The deeper one delves, the worse things look for actively managed funds; 99 percent of fund managers demonstrate no evidence of skill whatsoever," says William Bernstein in a study of the fund industry published in 2004.[1]

Investment legend Peter Lynch in *Beating the Street* confirms: "All the time and effort people devote to picking the right fund, the hot hand, the great manager, have in most cases led to no advantage."[2]

Warren Buffett, in his 1996 letter to his Berkshire Hathaway shareholders, advocated recourse to a passive index tracker rather than fund managers: "The best way to own stocks is through an index fund ..."

But the strongest argument against trying to pick a fund manager is performance. Only 9 out of 355 funds analyzed by Lipper and Vanguard beat their market benchmarks from 1970 to 1999. Analysis by http://www.ifa.com/ of the Morningstar database of equity funds found "no discernible pattern of persistence in superior manager performance."

What about picking the best performers using tables? Unfortunately, all the top 10 performing funds in any year drop from first place to nearly last place among all funds within two to four years, according to a 26-year study by the Dalbar rankings agency.[3]

Updated in 2001, the study found that from 1984 to 2000, the average stock fund investor earned returns of only 5.23% a year while the S&P 500 returned 16.29%.

Yet in spite of this, 75% of mutual fund inflows follow last year's "winners," according to fund researcher www.morningstar.com. And Lipper Europe at www.lipper.com confidently claims that European fund assets will grow to more than $10,000bn before 2010 from the current $3000bn.

Even Nobel laureates agree on the hopelessness of picking top performing fund managers. Prizewinner Merton Miller observed in a documentary last year about funds:

> If there's 10,000 people looking at the stocks and trying to pick winners, one in 10,000 is going to score, by chance alone, a great coup, and that's all that's

going on. It's a game, it's a chance operation, and people think they are doing something purposeful ... but they're really not.

All is not lost for fund investors. Research published in October 2001 by Jay Kaeppel of eCharts.com indicated that a simple fund investing strategy can be lucrative. By buying at the start of each month the top five best performing sector funds of the past 240 days, and then starting over again the subsequent month, he turned $50,000 invested on the last day of 1989 to $692,384 by December 31 2001; an annual 27% rate of return. He used Fidelity's sector funds. Of course this is a ridiculously simple test and only goes back to 1989.

So what is to be done? If fund managers can't beat market benchmarks, then we could invest in index trackers and be assured of at least matching the benchmarks. If only it was that easy. Tracker funds can diverge from the index they're tracking by up to 30%, according to a survey by Chartwell Investment Management. For tracking the FTSE 100 they recommend the Prudential U.K. Index Tracker Trust.

Meanwhile, what about Unilever and MAM? With so much evidence about poor fund manager returns, little wonder that no pension fund has ever before tried to claim negligence against a fund manager for under-performance. After all, the fund managers could turn around and say: "What did you expect?"

Some useful quotes about fund managers

1. Skepticism about past returns is crucial. The truth is, much as you may wish you could know which funds will be hot, you can't – and neither can the legions of advisers and publications that claim they can. That's why building a portfolio around index funds isn't really settling for average. It's just refusing to believe in magic. (Bethany McLean, "The Skeptic's Guide to Mutual Funds," *Fortune*, March 15, 1999)

2. By day we write about "Six Funds to Buy NOW!" ... By night, we invest in sensible index funds. Unfortunately, pro-index fund stories don't sell magazines. (anonymous, *Fortune*, April 26, 1999)

3. Statisticians will tell you that you need 20 years worth of data – that's right, two full decades – to draw statistically meaningful conclusions [about mutual funds]. Anything less, they say, and you have little to hang your hat on. But here's the problem for fund investors: After 20 successful years of managing a mutual fund, most managers are ready to retire. In fact, only 22 U.S. stock funds have had the same manager on board for at least two

decades – and I wouldn't call all the managers in that bunch skilled. (Susan Dziubinski, university editor with Morningstar.com)

4. There is one final problem in selecting a winning manager. According to Richard A. Brealey, "you probably need at least 25 years of fund performance to distinguish at the 95% significance level whether a manager has above average competence." Another commentator accepted the 25-year time frame, "but only if the pension executive is using the perfect benchmark for that manager. Using a less than perfect benchmark may increase the observation time to 80 years." (p. 177, *Bogle on Mutual Funds*, John C. Bogle, founder, The Vanguard Group)

5. Former Oakmark Fund manager Bob Sanborn, Yackman Fund's Don Yackman, and former Internet Fund manager Ryan Jacob; these once-revered fund managers have fallen to earth. (Susan Dziubinski, university editor, Morningstar.com: *Five Lies About Fund Manager Talent*)

6. People exaggerate their own skills. They are overoptimistic about their prospects and overconfident about their guesses, including which [investment] managers to pick. (Professor Richard Thaler, University of Chicago quoted in *Investment Titans*, Jonathan Burton, 2001)

7. a. Studies show either that most managers cannot outperform passive strategies, or that if there is a margin of superiority, it is small. (p. 372)
   b. It will take Joe Dart's entire working career [calculated to be 32 years] to get to the point where statistics will confirm his true ability. (p. 821)
   c. In the end, it is likely that the margin of superiority that any professional manager can add is so slight that the statistician will not easily be able to detect it. (Zvi Bodie, Alex Kane and Alan J. Marcus, *Investments*, 5th edn, McGraw-Hill, p. 374)

8. Most depressing of all, the "superstar" fund managers I encountered in the early 1990s had a disconcerting habit of fading from supernova to black hole: Rod Linafelter, Roger Engemann, Richard Fontaine, John Hartwell, John Kaweske, Heiko Thieme. I soon realized that if you thought they were great, you had only to wait a year and look again: Now they were terrible. (Jason Zweig, "I don't know, I don't care, Indexing lets you say those magic words," CNNMoney.com, August 29, 2001)

9. Yet even the smartest, most determined fund-picker can't escape a host of nasty surprises. Next time you're tempted to buy anything other than an index fund, remember this – and think again. (Robert Barker, "It's Tough to Find Fund Whizzes," BusinessWeek.com, December 17, 2001)

10. None of us is as smart as all of us (anonymous quote hanging in the office of James Vertin, Head of Wells Fargo Management Sciences Department and backer of the first equally weighted S&P 500 index fund in 1971). After twenty years of watching investment practitioners dance around the fire shaking their feathered sticks, I observe that far too many of their patients die and that the turnover of medicine men is rather high. There must be a better way. And there is!" [index funds] (Also from James Vertin in *Bogle on Mutual Funds*, John C. Bogle, founder, The Vanguard Group)

11. Santa Claus and the Easter Bunny should take a few pointers from the mutual-fund industry [and its fund managers]. **All three are trying to pull off elaborate hoaxes.** But while Santa and the bunny suffer the derision of eight year olds everywhere, actively-managed stock funds still have an ardent following among otherwise clear-thinking adults. This continued loyalty amazes me. **Reams of statistics prove that most of the fund industry's stock pickers fail to beat the market.** For instance, over the 10 years through 2001, U.S. stock funds returned 12.4% a year, vs. 12.9% for the Standard & Poor's 500 stock index. (Jonathan Clements, "Only Fools Fall in ... Managed Funds?," *Wall Street Journal*, September 15, 2002)

12. Contrary to their oft articulated goal of outperforming the market averages, investment managers are not beating the market; the market is beating them. (Charles D. Ellis, "The Loser's Game," *Financial Analysts Journal*, July–Aug 1975)

13. The evidence on mutual fund performance indicates not only that these 115 mutual funds were on average not able to predict security prices well enough to outperform a buy-the-market-and-hold policy, but also that there is very little evidence that any individual fund was able to do significantly better than that which we expected from mere random chance. ("The Performance of Mutual Funds in the Period 1945–1964," Michael C. Jensen, Harvard Business School, *Journal of Finance*, 1967, **23**(2): 389–416)

Consistency of performance – what consistency?

The top 30 mutual funds for sequential five-year periods from 1970 to 1994 (twenty-five years) are charted in Table 1.1, along with those same top 30 funds' performance for the five-year subsequent period up to 1998. You will note a lack of consistency of performance.

Tables 1.2 to 1.6 show that *fund managers "just can't keep it up."* Maybe that is why they come on financial TV.

TABLE 1.1 Subsequent performance of top 30 mutual funds, 1970–98		
	Return 1970–1974	**Return 1975–1998**
Top 30 funds 1970–1974	0.78%	16.05%
All Funds	–6.12%	16.38%
S&P 500 Index	–2.35%	17.04%
	Return 1975–1979	**Return 1980–1998**
Top 30 funds 1975–1979	35.70%	15.78%
All Funds	20.44%	15.28%
S&P 500 Index	14.76%	17.67%
	Return 1980–1984	**Return 1985–1998**
Top 30 funds 1980–1984	22.51%	16.01%
All Funds	14.83%	15.59%
S&P 500 Index	14.76%	18.76%
	Return 1985–1989	**Return 1990–1998**
Top 30 funds 1985–1989	22.08%	16.24%
All Funds	16.40%	15.28%
S&P 500 Index	20.41%	17.81%
	Return 1990–1994	**Return 1995–1998**
Top 30 funds 1990–1994	18.94%	21.28%
All Funds	9.39%	24.60%
S&P 500 Index	8.69%	32.18%
Source: DFA.		

TABLE 1.2 2000 top 10 managers and subsequent performance			
Fund name	**Manager name**	**Annual rankings**	
		2000	**2001**
Schroder Ultra Inv	Unschuld, Ira L.	1	2
Evergreen Health Care A	Chen, Liu-Er	2	2360
Deutsche European Eq Insti	Brody/Knerr/Kratz	3	5360
Nicholas-Applegate Glb Hth I	Management Team	4	5795
Exeter Life Sciences A	Management Team	5	313
Munder Framlington Health Y	Milford, Antony	6	4890
American Eagle Capital App	Jundt/Jundt	7	4562
State St Res Glb Resource A	Rice, III, Daniel J.	8	2828
Dresdner RCM Biotechnology N	Dauchot M.D., Michael et al.	9	5185
Eaton Vance Wldwd Health A	Isaly, Samuel D.	10	3252
Total number of mutual funds		5283	6058
Source: Morningstar Principia; Universe limited to "Distinct Portfolios" and Indexes, 2002.			

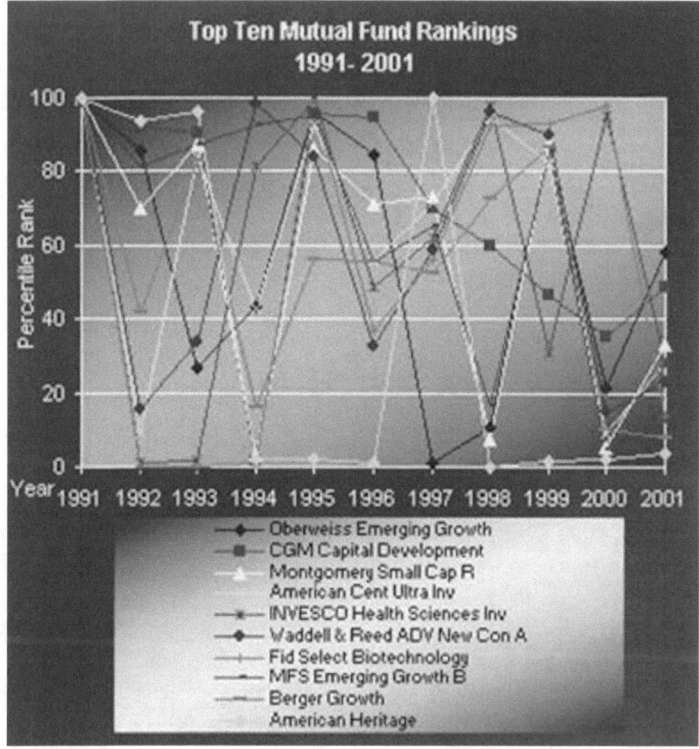

Figure 1.1 What performance?

Source: Morningstar Principia, Feb 2002.

TABLE 1.3 1999 top 10 managers and subsequent performance				
Fund name	Manager name	Annual rankings		
		1999	2000	2001
Nicholas-Apple Glb Tech I	Management team	1	5183	355
Credit Suisse Jpn Sm Adv	Management team	2	5279	5235
Morgan Stan Ins SmGr	Armstrong/Chu/Chulik	3	4704	4837
Van Wagoner Emerging Growth	Van Wagoner/Garrabrandt	4	4794	5838
Nevis Fund	Wilmerding III/Baker	5	4946	5755
Driehaus Asia Pacific In MS Grth	Ritter, Eric J.	6	5083	4762
Credit Suisse Jpn Gr Adv	Management team	7	5277	4743
Amerindo Technology D	Vilar/Tanaka	8	5275	5803
PBHG Tech & Communic PBHG	Ma, Michael K.	9	5243	5813
Fidelity Japan Smaller Co	Mizushita, Kenichi	10	5258	4793
Total number of mutual funds		4868	5283	6058

Source: Morningstar Principia; Universe limited to "Distinct Portfolios" and Indexes, 2002.

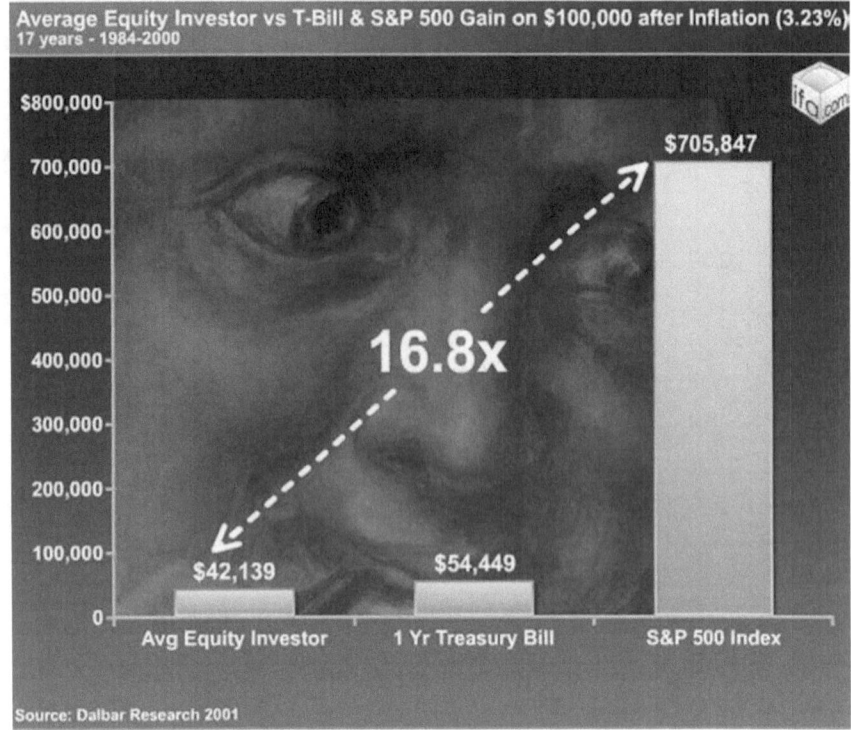

Figure 1.2 So we watch a bit of financial
TV and think we can perform
Source: Dalbar Research 2001.

TABLE 1.4 1998 top 10 managers and subsequent performance					
Fund name	**Manager name**	**Annual rankings**			
		1998	**1999**	**2000**	**2001**
Kinetics Internet	Tuen/Doyle/Larsson	1	4756	365	3562
ProFunds UltraOTC Inv	Management team	2	12	5281	5848
Fidelity Adv Korea A	Chung, Hokeun	3	73	5273	25
Grand Prix A	Zuccaro, Robert	4	52	5139	5833
Potomac OTC Plus Inv	Management team	5	86	5256	5737
Berkshire Focus	Fobes III, Malcolm R	6	62	4509	5852
Dreyfus Premier Tech Gr A	Herskovitz, Mark	7	41	5038	5628
Munder NetNet A	Management team	8	31	5266	5790
Fidelity Sel Computers	Bertsekas, Telis	9	308	5115	4890
Matthews Korea	Matthews/Headley	10	151	5265	3
Total number of mutual funds		4418	4868	5283	6058
Source: Morningstar Principia; Universe limited to "Distinct Portfolios" and Indexes, 2002.					

TABLE 1.5 1997 top 10 managers and subsequent performance						
Fund name	Manager name	Annual rankings				
		1997	1998	1999	2000	2001
American Heritage	Thieme, Heiko H.	1	4427	4875	5120	5829
Munder Micro-Cap Equity Y	Management Team	2	4023	351	4340	177
FMI Focus	Kellner/Lane	3	207	601	269	2328
Pilgrim Russia A	Saler/Derks/Schwartz/oubadia	4	4428	40	4644	1
Pilgrim Financial Services A	Kloss/Rayner	5	3898	4860	191	319
Fidelity Sel Brokerage&Invmt	Spencer, Joshua	6	2802	1181	190	3476
FBR Small Cap Financial A	Ellison, David	7	4222	4608	111	79
Turner Fut Finan Services	Management Team	8	4129	1911	133	4448
Alpine U.S. Real Estate Eq Y	Lieber, Samuel A.	9	4305	4856	293	65
Hartford Cap Apprec A	Pannell, Saul J.	10	3625	432	2021	3281
Total number of mutual funds		3883	4418	4868	5283	6058

Source: Morningstar Principia; Universe limited to "Distinct Portfolios" and Indexes, 2002.

TABLE 1.6 1996 top 10 managers and subsequent performance							
Fund name	Manager name	Annual rankings					
		1996	1997	1998	1999	2000	2001
State St Res Glb Resource A	Rice, III, Daniel J.	1	3616	4424	2077	8	2828
Van Kampen Growth A	New/Maly/Davis	2	765	756	532	3285	4767
Firsthand Technology Value	Landis, Kevin M.	3	3335	732	24	4047	5751
State St Res Aurora A	Burbank, John	4	23	4238	1077	78	197
First Amer Micro Cap A	Frohna/Randall	5	1819	3932	70	1156	1411
Phoenix-Goodwin Emerg Bd A	Lannigan, Peter	6	1811	4384	887	2904	1297
PBHG Tech & Communic PBHG	Ma, Michael K.	7	3581	614	9	5254	5824
Phoenix-Engemann Sm-Mid Gr A	Lipsker/Holtz	8	822	1375	281	4412	5473
Needham Growth	Trapp, Peter J.R.	9	1665	937	316	2237	307
Morgan Stan Ins EmMkDb A	McKenna, Abigail L.	10	1483	4399	1263	789	356
Total number of mutual funds		3445	3883	4418	4868	5283	6058

Source: Morningstar Principia; Universe limited to "Distinct Portfolios" and Indexes, 2002.

It's not about the stocks you pick

"Ten stocks you must own now;" "Companies that grow in good times and bad." These are just some of the investment magazines headlines you will have read.

On financial TV we know we have to bring you stock pickers, fund managers and analysts with stock ideas – otherwise you will not watch and even more importantly advertisers will not advertise. In financial TV we have even started using the techniques of tacky mainstream entertainment shows. For instance, have you heard the financial TV presenters say, "after the break we will tell you Alpesh's top three picks for the year ahead … don't go away, we'll be right back."

There is only one thing wrong about all this. Market success has next to nothing to do with the stocks you pick. It has everything to do with money management – how much you stand to lose, when you increase your winning positions and exit your losing ones. Research proves it, and professional traders confirm it. Yet our obsession with stock picks continues. So, what are the most important investment questions you need answered?

"How much money should I put in any one trade?" Professional traders will tell you success is about "the 2×2 rule." Ensure your upside is twice your downside and never lose more than 2% of your trading capital in a single trade.

For instance with $20,000 capital, if you think Microsoft will go from $100 to $130 (30% gain), then you should equally not expect the stock to fall beyond $85 (15% loss). And that worst loss should total no more than 2% of your $20,000 capital, which is $400. So, you should only buy $2670 of stock at $100 ($400 is 15% of $2670).

The formula (yes there is one, you don't think professionals trade by the seat of their pants do you?): $T = PR/(E–X)$ where T is the size of the trade, P is the portfolio size (cash plus holdings), R is 2%, E is the entry price and X is the predetermined stop-loss exit price.

But surely if you are a good stock picker you don't need to worry about money management. Not true. If you gain 30% through stock picking, it only takes a 23% loss to bring you back down to where you started. But if you lose 30%, it takes a much greater 43% through stock picking to just break even.

The same percentage loss and gain have unequal impact on your portfolio. Losses hurt more than gains benefit. The same percentage gain in the next trade from stock picking will not bail you out.

Why only 2%? Any more and you get too close to precipitous irrevocable losses from just a few trades. Let's say you have four consecutive losing trades, which is feasible for even the best stock pickers; a read of George Soros's trading diary in his *The Alchemy of Finance* confirms that.[4]

And say you lose 5% of your portfolio on each trade. With the remainder of your portfolio you now need to make a gain greater than the world's second richest man and investor Warren Buffett achieves on average each year (23%). That's why it's not about the stocks you pick – whichever ones you pick, with poor money management you will suffer.

Imagine two traders. Both make identical trades with their portfolio of

$20,000. One bets $2000 per trade and the other $10,000. Their results after five trades are +20%, –25%, –25%, +5% and –5%. A typical set of trades. After just four trades, the second trader has underperformed the first by 22%. It was not the stocks they picked, after all both picked the same ones. It was down to money management.

If money management is so important, why are there not more internet sites devoted to it? Expert investor Gibbons Burke puts it best:

> Money management is like sex: Everyone does it, but not many like to talk about it and some do it better than others. But whilst sex sites on the web proliferate, sites devoted to the art and science of money management are somewhat difficult to find.

Put another way, you don't think a CEO of an online brokerage is a trader, do you?

Still looking for a hot stock tip? Then I leave you with legendary investment academic William Bernstein who put it most honestly:

> A decade ago, I really did believe that the average investor could do it himself. After all, the flesh was willing, the vehicles were available, and the math wasn't that hard. I was wrong. Having emailed and spoken to thousands of investors over the years, I've come to the sad conclusion that only a tiny minority, at most one percent, are capable of pulling it off. Heck, if the nation's largest pension funds can't get it right, what chance does John Q investor have?[5]

Me? I believe I'm in the top 1%. After all, George Soros is, why not me? How about you?

My sites: Money management
www.turtletrader.com *****
www.moneymaximizer.com ****
www.seykota.com/tribe/risk/ ****

But I didn't say that ...

You know it is not only the tabloid newspapers who mangle what celebrities say into falsehoods. "George W Bush converses with Imam in Mosque" turns into "George Bush converts to Islam in Mosque." Well, maybe not that bad, but a similar thing happens in financial broadcasting. Our stock

---

Key to my sites: * = Adequate   ** = Fine   *** = Good   **** = Very good   ***** = Outstanding
This grading system is used throughout the book

ideas, our well-thought-out, detailed reasoning about which stocks we like, why, at what prices we would suggest investors buying them, under what circumstance, when they should exit – all these very important things get mangled into "Alpesh says buy Yahoo."

Let me show you a real life example. Below is an exact transcript of my recommendations which were sent to one of the world's largest stockbrokers for their client newsletters.

I then reveal how it got mangled for publication. Wouldn't be a problem except it reaches 800,000 readers.

What I sent:

From Alpesh Patel's Trading Desk

Small Cap Market Overview – *The Alpesh Patel Perspective*

"Elephants don't gallop" goes the market saying, referring to the fact that the large blue chip stocks often do not provide the kinds of healthy returns many private investors seek. Of course with rewards come risks too. The Small Cap index looks like it's overcome its falls between March and May and is set to continue building its healthy upward trend since then.

The key drivers continue being an increased interest in merger and acquisitions (albeit expect this to be a bit slower over summer – even lawyers, chief executives and bankers go on holiday), "bored money" (money looking for returns which is fed up of waiting on the sidelines), and improving results.

These 340 odd small cap stocks represent companies outside the 350 largest FTSE stocks. Companies range in market capitalisation from a mere £20m to £370m. Since the start of 2004 the Small Cap index has outperformed the FTSE 100.

Alpesh's Small Cap One To Watch

Peacock Group (Market Cap: £275m, 52week high: 240.5p, 52 week low: 131p)

The value fashion group – which trades from 397 own-brand stores and 314 bonmarche outlets – continues its upward price trend helped by full year results reported in June which showed a 56% increase in full year underlying pretax profit. The purchase of the discount fragrance store, "The Fragrance Shop" will add to earnings probably in the second year.

The stock should reach 300p by year end. Any drop below 200p however would mean an exit. With a volatility, or "riskiness", around the market average, yet it having outperformed 89% of stocks, the company has a good reward to risk profile.

Technology Stocks Overview – The Alpesh Patel Perspective

"Please don't ask me to relax, it's only the tension that is holding me together"– and so it must be for the holders of technology stocks who might be thinking of relaxing now

Risers and fallers

	TABLE 1.7 Heroes and villains 1	
Name	Expectations	52 Week Hi-Low (Market Cap)
Lookers	**UP:** The new and used car dealer reported a record March performance. It has also received a £15m VAT rebate. If only we were all so lucky. Despite an expected weakness in the price until August, as long as the stock stays above 280p and breaks above 300p then we would expect a 20% return by year end.	331.5p–213p (£103m)
ROK Property Solutions	**UP:** Despite strong share price performance the company continues to be fairly well valued. As long as the stock remains above the recent low of 337p, then the upward price trend suggests a target of 420p by year end.	409.5p–201p (£92m)
Warner Estate Holdings	**UP:** Despite concerns about the property sector, Warner's exposure to the office market and also shopping centres, which in many parts of the U.K. continue doing well, means the company looks likely to reproduce fair results such as those in June which revealed profits of £15.7m. If the stock remaining on the present uptrend, and certainly above 480p, then a 20% return to year end is not extravagant.	520p–367.5p (£265m)
Bookham Technology	**DOWN:** The story in May, "Bookham still unable to give guidance beyond current quarter" sums up the uncertainty around the company. Whilst in the past the stock has tripled in months after sharp falls, I consider any fall below price support at 50p will see even further drops.	179.5p–47p (£152m)
Ultraframe	**DOWN:** A 58% interim profit slump partly due to increased competition in the conservatory business means the market continues to lack confidence in the company.	355p–110p (£112m)
Vanco	**DOWN:** Despite attempts by the share price to make some resuscitation in June, the 25% drop for the first 6 months of the year looks likely to continue in this overvalued stock. A drive back down to 150p would seem likely by year end. Any rise above 280p however would suggest the market has changed from negative to positive on the stock.	348.5p–150p (£131.7m)

that the the FTSE TechMARK 100 index is up 16% in the first 6 months of the year – not too bad given the FTSE managed an anaemic 3%.

Indeed the TechMARK has doubled since its low point in March 2003. This rally which the media only belated picked up upon has also occurred in the U.S., with dot-com villains coming back in vogue, such as Yahoo, EBay and Amazon.

The drivers seem to be growing revenues – if you have survived this long as your competition died a slow painful death then surely profits must be close, indeed for some, profits are here, such as Lastminute.com (depending on how you measure profits of course). Another important share price driver is the interest in technology companies coming to market – if Google can raise millions then it lifts technology stocks generally.

Alpesh's Technology One To Watch

CML Microsystems (Market Cap: £57.5m, 52 week high: 397.5p, 52 week low: 192.5p)

"Now turning the corner" after two years of difficult trading – this is the typical IT story. In June this designer, manufacturer and distributor of semiconductor products said exactly that and announced increased sales, from £12m to £16m and turning the previous year's loss into a profit for this year. A few days later a director bought some shares in the company – always makes the City happy that does.

Risers and fallers

TABLE 1.8 Heroes and villains 2		
Name	**Expectations**	**52 Week Hi-Low (Market Cap)**
Hansard Group	**UP:** Although a small volatile stock, its relentless climb upwards this year has been reinforced by results showing a doubling in sales over the previous twelve months and swinging into profit from a loss.	27.5p–10p (£3.5m)
Fundamental-e Investments	**UP:** Another higher risk, but major performer. Although it has tripled since the start of the year the momentum behind the stock remains in place. Any dips would be a warning to exit.	11.25p–2.75p (£29.2m)
Corin Group	**UP:** A developer, manufacturer and distributor of a wide range of reconstructive orthopaedic devices, the company sells in 70 countries. Whilst it is too early to make this a long-term purchase, the short-term trend should see a 20% gain to year end as long as the current trend is not broken by a dip below 200p.	281p–142.5p (£111m)
Mondas	**DOWN:** After an April profit warning there is little reason to suppose a turnaround yet.	51.5p–21.5p (£6.3m)
Parity Group	**DOWN:** After comments in June that it expects profits in the first six months to be lower than the preceding six months, investor confidence dictates moving money somewhere safer. Only a move above 13p would show investors are willing to back the company with cash.	16p–9.25p (£30.3m)

The recovery like all technology companies is fragile and dependent on business investment by buyers so I focus very much on the price trend too, which continues for now to be steady and rising.

Small Caps

"Elephants don't gallop" goes the market saying, referring to the fact that the large blue-chip stocks don't often provide the kind of healthy returns many private investors seek. Of course, with rewards come risks too. The Small Cap Index looks like it's overcome its falls between March and May and is set to continue building its healthy upward trend.

The key drivers continue to be: an increased interest in M&As (although we can expect this to be a bit slower over the summer – even bankers, CEOs and lawyers go on holiday): 'bored money' (money sat on the sidelines that is looking to invest back in the market); and improving results.

These 340-odd small cap stocks represent companies outside the 350 largest FTSE stocks. Companies range in market cap from £20 million to £370 million. Since the start of 2004, the Small Cap Index has outperformed the FTSE 100.

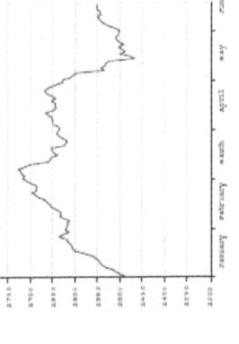

FTSE Small Cap Index

ALPESH'S ONE TO WATCH

Peacock Group

Market Cap: £275 million; 52-week high/low: 240.5p/131p

The value fashion group – which trades from 397 own-brand stores and 314 Bonmarché outlets – continues its upward price trend, helped by full-year results reported in June which showed a 56% increase in full-year underlying pre-tax profit.

The purchase of discount perfume store, The Fragrance Shop, will add to earnings probably in the second year.

The stock should reach 300p by the year end. Any drop below 200p, however, would mean an exit. There is volatility or 'riskiness' around the market average, but having outperformed 89% of all stock, the company has a good reward-to-risk profile.

BUY ▲

Lookers

ROK Property Solutions

Warner Estate Holdings

SELL ▼

Bookham Technology

Ultraframe

Vanco

Figure 1.3 First part of what I said, "translated"

Technology

"Don't ask me to relax, it's only the tension that's holding me together." And so it must be for the holders of tech stocks who might be thinking of relaxing, now that the FTSE TechMARK 100 Index is up 16% in the first six months of the year – not bad given that the FTSE 100 managed an anaemic 3%.

Indeed, the TechMARK has doubled since its low point in March 2003. This rally, which the media only belatedly picked up on, has also occurred in the US, with dotcom villains such as Yahoo, eBay and Amazon coming back in vogue.

The drivers seem to be growing revenues – if you survived while your competition died a slow death, then profits must be close. Indeed for some, such as Lastminute.com, profits are here (depending on how you measure profits). Another important driver is the interest in tech companies coming to market – if Google can raise millions then it lifts technology stocks generally.

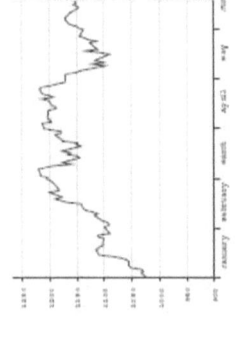

FTSE TechMARK 100 Index

BUY ▲

Hansard Group
Corin Group
Fundamental-e Investments

SELL ▶

Mondas
Jasmin
Parity Group

ALPESH'S ONE TO WATCH

CML Microsystems
Market Cap: £57.5 million; 52-week high/low: 397.5p/192.5p

Now 'turning the corner' after two years of difficult trading – this is the typical IT story. In June this designer, manufacturer and distributor of semiconductor products announced exactly that, along with a sales uplift from £12 million to £16 million, and the fact that it turned the previous year's loss into profit this year. A few

days later, a director bought some shares in the company, which always makes those folks in the City happy.

The recovery, as with all tech companies, is fragile and dependent on business investment from buyers. So I focus very much on the price trend too, which, for now, continues to be steady and rising.

Figure 1.4 Second part of what I said, "translated"

What they published:

Figures 1.3 and 1.4 show what they actually published.

So the omissions were significant. Because Tables 1.7 and 1.8 were reduced to "buy" and "sell", you, the poor investor, were not told when I would suggest buying Hansard Group, what the share price would have to do, whether it is a high-risk or low-risk stock, over what time I consider it a "buy", what the target price is and so on. None of it, not a thing. No wonder private investors lose money.

You could easily buy the "right" stock, one which rises, and still lose money because:

1. you bought it too early

2. you bought it too late

3. you held on too long

4. you sold too soon.

Any good stock picker will tell you must know all these other things. I keep a notebook with a fresh page for each stock. It lists:

1. entry price

2. why I liked the stock (for example price/earnings, chart patterns and so on)

3. exit price

4. exit conditions

5. what I learned from the trade. (Did I follow my system, did I learn anything about the markets?)

Now, which of the above comes from a TV comment about buying a particular stock?

The Bloomberg way – "What's your buy and sell?"

On Bloomberg, as a stock picker, I had the ability to script my whole session. So, on those slots on Wednesday evenings, as Sally, my co-presenter, asked me for my "buy" and my "sell" of the week, I would have a list of criteria each week I would go through in my preparation.

Now, some background, the way it worked was that each week, I would pick a stock which I thought would rise over the next six months (my "buy") and which I thought would fall over the next six months (my "sell"). The program went out live from 8pm–9pm. I would come in at around 11am to prepare for my noon slot and the evening show. For the stock picking I had a set of criteria to make life easier.

But don't forget, each week I am putting my head on the block. Make no mistake, if you get it wrong, you're costing people money and they aren't too forgiving. And don't forget the bulletin boards. Investors on there can kill your reputation in a few anonymous keystrokes.

Those criteria and that stock picking meant for one six-month period I had a 100% track record on each week's buy and each week's sell for some three months. In other words, each week the two stock picks from six months ago had both done what they were supposed to: the "buy" had gone up and the "sell" had gone down.

In fact, over the only six-month period we had analyzed my stock picks, outperformed those of every single other analyst, guru and pundit on Bloomberg.

Later in the book I describe those criteria. Here the point is that, although I could put more detail into a stock pick, such as when to enter, exit points, and stop-losses, even then I couldn't, because I knew in Sally's book, sitting on her lap, all that would be written down would be "Vodafone – buy." And rightly so. That was the job at hand.

And that's the problem. What was the point of saying: "buy Vodafone if the share price rises above 120p, but any fall below 115p would be an exit. If you do buy keep up a trailing stop-loss so that you exit on a 1 week low." All that the viewers were interested in six months later were the scores. The superficiality of it all! But that grabs people's attention.

Your average investor does not want to make money, he just likes the idea of it. To actually make money takes effort. And there isn't anyone, not least the average person, who ever wants to know about stop-losses, trailing stops, resistance levels, price supports and so forth. These are all things we cover in this book.

Now, you dear reader may be different. Maybe the act of buying this book makes you above average. Well, there is only one way to find out. Will you take the advice in its pages, or flick it to one side looking for the easy answer; the next magazine cover proclaiming "ten stocks you must own now"?

What the presenter does not know

But there is another problem. No presenter, whether it was Sally, Sara, Kavita, Philip or whoever, was ever going to probe on the finer details of investing. How could they? They weren't allowed to invest. Five minutes investing and you soon learn a lot more than 1000 hours conducting investor interviews. But they also only had a few minutes anyway.

Sally knew more about investing than any nonprofessional investor. And she would ask probing questions. It was like a tennis match. I would say, "I like this stock because earnings have been improving and sales are up" and she would hit back with, "yes but they said costs are up and the price is already up 30% this year."

Now, I used to be an attorney, so I like asking questions, I don't like answering them. Answering Sally was sometimes tough. I would, however, use a trick I learnt as an attorney, but is useful for investing too.

You write down in one column why you like a stock, and in the next one the reasons why your reasoning could be challenged (or what Sally might say) and in the final column, your reply to that criticism.

What that does is to force you to think hard about why you like a stock. And it makes for good TV, but that's by the by.

Actually, again I'll come to the defence of Bloomberg, they were outstanding financial journalists. But that says more about the state of the financial journalism elsewhere. Remember in political journalism you had the likes of Woodward and Bernstein. In financial journalism, no one picks up on Enron or Global Crossing or all the other stock travesties which cost investors money. Investigative financial journalism sticks to personal finance not stock trading.

Don't shoot the messenger ... or the message

Don't get me wrong – I don't blame the Bloomberg way. It's television that's to blame. Television is good for conveying many things, including complex pieces of information. But, when you have 60 seconds before the break, a producer in your ear giving you a countdown and advertisers wanting viewers, awards to be won – you have little choice but to make sacrifices. We have to play the game. The viewer can lose out if he doesn't know how the game is played.

When the tables are turned

Of course I was also the interviewer not just the interviewee. On the lunchtime show and also in the evening show we would sometimes have fund managers who would swagger in with their latest "house" stock ideas (those their funds or investment banks or brokers companies recommend).

Funny thing about financial television, you can basically conduct advertising for your company – not because its name appears on screen, but because the stock your company has just told its clients to buy, now appears on TV and guess what – that doesn't half help its share price if it is a small company. That is exactly what happened in the dot-com boom, but it still goes on.

I recall one session of CNBC where the share price flew up on air and the presenter pointed out to the broker/stock pundit that he just made a 10% return by appearing on the show. Darn right he did. Why do you think he's there? To impress the opposite sex? No, to drum up advertising for the stock so his clients will be happy.

So what did I do when I was conducting the interviews? Well I would try to ask, in the time I had, the tough questions: over what time-frame is it a buy; what price target, when should they get out and how do they know the stock price is irrecoverable?

So what are you supposed to do?

Where do you get your stock ideas? CNBC, Bloomberg, BBC, *Fortune* magazine? News is important. It allows us to get a feel for why the market is moving, then why a sector may be moving and downward onto an industry then into a stock. News has many functions for the trader.

The problem is no one ever teaches us how to properly use the news. And ignorance is bliss if you're watching financial TV for pleasure. But most of us aren't. We're watching it to earn.

TABLE 1.9 News you can use	
Type of News	**Uses**
Market news	▪ Is the market in trouble? ▪ Is there much negative news that will stop stocks soaring? ▪ Are there economic problems in the economy, such as high inflation, low growth, strikes, political uncertainty, low productivity, all of which will impact stock price rises?
Sector	▪ Which sectors are rising and which falling? ▪ Is there sector rotation, that is, some sectors accelerate while others fall? ▪ Is there growth in certain sectors, for example technology, and trouble with others, for example consumer goods?
Industry	▪ More specifically, which industries in a sector are going through good growth? ▪ Is there news about positive telecoms development or negative tobacco issues?
Company	▪ Is the company generating a sound, positive stream of news? ▪ Or is it warning of earnings problems. Good newsflows should be reflected in strong upward price moves. How is the price faring?

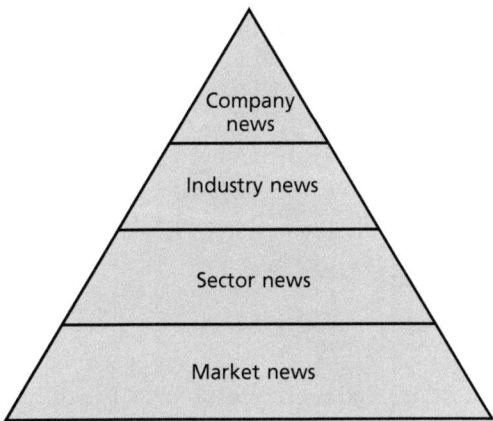

Figure 1.5 Pyramid of news

There is a lot of information on financial TV and you have little time. Therefore, you'll have to know where to go to get the knowledge you need and how to use it once you have it.

General news

As a trader, at the outset you must have a general idea of what parts of the economy are doing well. Your aim as an online trader is to invest into those projects that will present you with the highest possible return relative to the plethora of other available investment projects, over a given period of time. But, "there are so many different areas to invest in", I hear you retort.

Therefore you need to have a starting point, otherwise you will be swamped. A good starting point is to ask general questions about the markets and stocks and then proceed to answer those questions. As you proceed through the chapter answer the following questions:

- Which markets am I interested in?
- Is the general economy doing well?
- Which sectors am I interested in?
- Is the U.S. telecoms sector (or other sector you may be interested in) suffering?
- Which telecoms stocks have been popular?

All this questioning – what purpose does it serve? Questioning is the first stage of analysis. It helps to focus your thoughts so that you can create an efficient plan of action.

It's not enough to ask questions. Here is where the general market news comes in. Financial and market news is crucial because it answers your queries and encourages further questioning.

Also, if you wish to trade on a market index, for example the FTSE 100 or the Nasdaq, rather than any particular company, general market news is, of course, directly important.

Types of news

All news is not the same. And each type of news has different uses for the trader. We need to appreciate the different types of news and how to use it.

TABLE 1.10 News to use		
Type of news	**What it provides**	**How to use it**
Newswire (also called market pulse)	A quick-fire summary of news items. Limited analysis. Mainly just describes what has happened. We have to do most of our own analysis.	Can give us advance warning of impending price moves. Most useful to short-term active trader because of its likely impact in the short term on prices.
Column (commentary)	A regular writer writes a daily or weekly piece on a particular issue such as telecoms stocks, emerging market stocks.	The columnist is usually taking the recent newswires and adding a bit more analysis and opinion to them; explaining their significance to us. They give us a clearer, better picture of which stocks we should investigate further.
Feature	An infrequent, very detailed special feature on a sector.	For the longer term trader, as usually identifying longer term prospects. Often identifies value stocks whose present stock price does not yet accurately reflect future prospects, or will gradually rise over time as the company "proves itself."

Where to look

Here are some of the best news sites. The sites listed in the next section on researching individual companies will also be useful for general news.

■ **Bloomberg*****
www.bloomberg.com
An abundance of news and commentary in a no-nonsense format. Excellent reporting, sharp presentation and speed for top-notch coverage of

industry, markets, high-tech stocks and the global economy. The site is cleanly designed. Valuable information delivered well.

- **CBS Market Watch*****
  www.cbs.marketwatch.com
  Front page packs essential breaking stories on the market and companies. The information is well organised and easy to navigate, with keyword searches. Links in articles are well thought out. Free tools include company research, charts and delayed quotes.

- **The *Financial Times* ****
  www.ft.com

- **CNN*****
  www.cnnfn.com
  With its worldwide reporters, the site is able to break news and offer a very fast newswire.

Should I listen to the commentary?

But how do you know if that one commentator on that one site should be listened to? Easy:

1. Is it a well-respected site such as the ones I have listed here? If it is not listed above, is it one whose brand you have come across before?

2. Scan a few other sites, do any of them pick up a similar theme, for example tobacco stocks likely to rally?

3. Make a note of the stock names, and the reasons the site gives, then use them later for when we do our own research and confirm for ourselves whether we agree these stocks are a good buy or a good-bye. *A good trader doesn't take anyone's word for it but his own.*

Starting with news to research individual companies

Let's presume you have heard about a company and are interested in it as a potential investment – you may have heard about it on one of the sites above, in the newspaper, or from a friend.

How do you gauge whether *you* should invest into this company? The news is a starting point; but it's time for you to think whether the company looks good enough for *you*.

More questions: what kinds of things would you want to know about a potential investment?

Here are a few suggestions:

- What exactly its business is, how big is it?

- Any major items of recent news about it

- How much profit analysts think it will make in the future, the firm's business strategy

- What other investors have thought of it

- How its share price has performed in the last few years

- How its accounts look – how profitable it is and how profitable it can be

To find out news about a specific company using any of the excellent sites mentioned above is relatively easy as they all follow a similar format.

The story

Often however, whenever a company is mentioned in a story, the company name is underlined, meaning that if you click on it you will be taken to more information about the company including news (see the examples below).

This is what we are looking for in company newsflow:

- Positive news items about the company:
  - Winning new orders
  - Increasing orders
  - Entry into new sectors
  - New product developments
  - Good strategic alliances
  - Accelerations in current business model

- What the analysts are forecasting upcoming profits to be. This is worth knowing because they receive regular private briefings from the company on how things are going and so are usually on the mark with their estimates

- Finding out what other investors have thought of the company through chat rooms and "share picks" is interesting since you gauge other people's opinion. If there is some aspect of the company you are wondering about or cannot understand, other people's opinions will be helpful. However, there are various warnings that are stamped on these sorts of prescriptions.

> REMEMBER: an investor's opinion is just one estimation, one outlook, not the last word.

How to scan newsflow

Since there are many news items – and we want to be as efficient as possible so we can make our money and actually have time to spend it instead of being in front of the computer all the time – we need to know how to scan these news headlines.

The general rule is that news companies try to tell as much as possible in the headline. Consequently I tend to focus on those headlines which common sense tells me are likely to include some information of the above type I am looking for.

In the example below I have highlighted the ones I consider in that category out of a series for Sun Microsystems. However, I may examine some of the others too, if I think I need to, on the basis that I need more information about a stock.

The following newsflow for Sun Microsystems shows some headlines which merit further investigation (I have put them in bold italics):

headlines for: sunw

11:56 PM   Startup Axient Bets On Private Fiber Network – WITH A 60-CITY NETWORK, AXIENT GETS DEAL FROM NBC TO DELIVER BROADBAND OLYMPIC COVERAGE – *CMP Media*

11:56 PM   Vendors As VCs – Money And Influence – As the biggest technology vendors increasingly act as venture capitalists, what are they getting in return? – *CMP Media*

11:56 PM   Finding Components On The Web – DEVELOPMENT PORTALS OFFER TESTED, CERTIFIED, REUSABLE CODE THAT HELPS SPEED PROJECTS – *CMP Media*

11:52 PM   The New Developer Portals – BUYING, SELLING, AND BUILDING COMPONENTS ON THE WEB SPEEDS COMPANIES' TIME TO MARKET – *CMP Media*

11:51 PM Vendors Partner With Venture Capitalists To Fund Startups – CMP Media

11:50 PM   The Two Faces Of E-Biz Management – *CMP Media*

11:50 PM Sun teams with vignette – CMP Media

11:50 PM   Stealing Java's Thunder – Microsoft's upcoming Visual Studio.net offers an integrated development interface, a new programming language, and programming shortcuts that should result in more-efficient Web development. A secondary, unstated aim is to slow Java's progress. – *CMP Media*

11:39 PM   AMD, Intel draw 64-bit battle lines – *CMP Media*

11:37 PM   XML GAINS MOMENTUM – ebXML emerging as EDI alternative for B2B transactions – *CMP Media*

6:05 PM   GSA Awards FirstGov Contract to GRC International – *PRNewswire*

4:14 PM   *WRAP: Dell shares fall 11% on concerns about future sales growth (Update1) – Futures World News Select*

3:46 PM   LinuxWorld Conference & Expo Exhibitor Profiles A to Z; Conference and Expo to Start Next Week in San Jose, Calif. – *BusinessWire*

2:47 PM   Stock picks of the week: EMC, Pfizer, Sun, Johnson & Johnson and H-P – *Deborah Adamson*

12:54 PM   First Ecom.com Inc. Announces Second Quarter Financial Results – *BusinessWire*

11:02 AM Robinson-Humphrey Analyst Interviews On RadioWallStreet.com – *BusinessWire*

9:45 AM   Planet City Software Teams With CRD Capital – *PRNewswire*

Thursday, August 10, 2000

11:01 PM Sun, Microsoft Java Battle Delayed – Unknown (cmtx-pc)

8:23 PM   James J. Whitney Named Forsythe Solutions Group's E-Business Solutions Technologist – *BusinessWire*

8:13 PM   PVI, Sportvision, Inc. Named Winners Success Story Receives Recognition from Sun Microsystems, Computerworld Competition – *PRNewswire*

The point is that with so much news, the canny investor starts being able to spot the keywords – the stories that may move markets. We are not looking for the hidden story that everyone may have missed and trying to profit from that. Instead, I recommend looking for the story everyone will have seen.

For instance, look at Figure 1.6. It is a picture of the share price of Research in Motion, the makers of Blackberry. In late December 2003 the company announced earnings which were received well by financial journalists. The stock then leapt to $30.

So as you watch financial TV, you probably think you missed the price

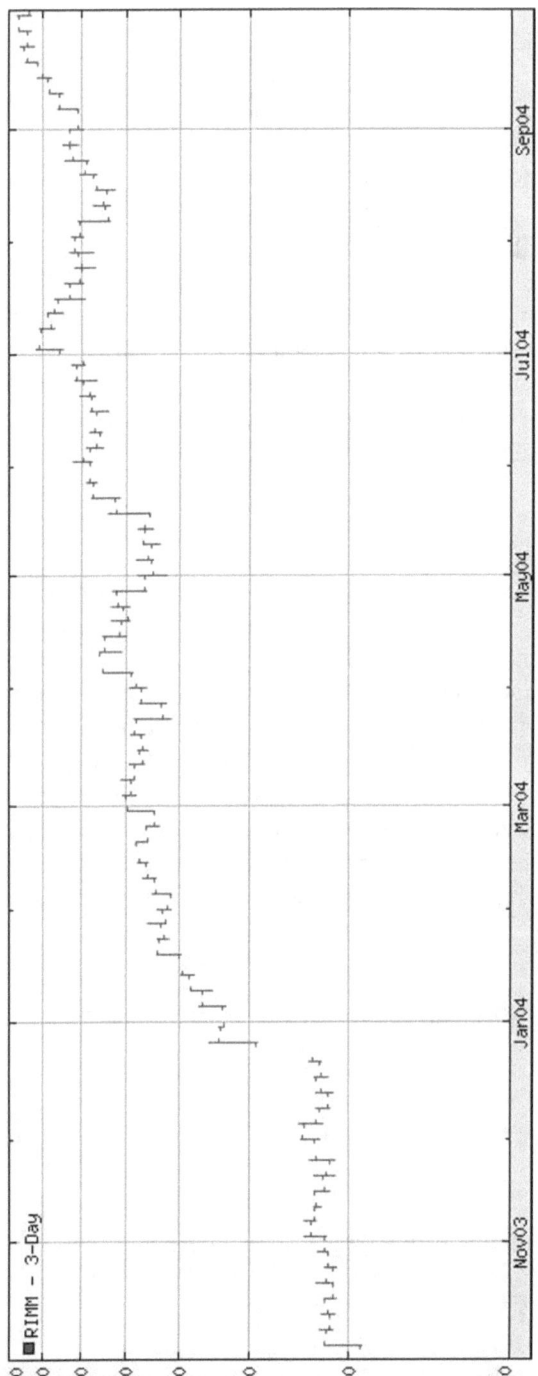

Figure 1.6 Profiting from what everyone knows!

move and should hunt for some ingenious insight not seen by anyone else. In fact the ingenious insight is right in front of you because if you got in *after* the news hit the market you would still achieve a 30% rise before the next set of earnings results.

In other words, forget *efficient market hypothesis*, that the market has all the information out there at any one time and so you cannot profit. Even if the first part of the last sentence is correct, the second part does not necessarily follow. Different investors get in at different times.

So, why do prices sometimes fall after seemingly good earnings results? And am I really saying that you should invest by only looking at news? Of course not. But we will deal with both these issues later in the book. The point for now is that there is a way to use financial news rather than being used by it – it's about being "street smart."

Are they all bad on TV?

My point is not that commentators on TV do not get stock picks right. My point is that they are often poor, and in any event, as we see later in the book, without an explanation of risk, they are pointless.

So who are apparently good? Some results are presented in Table 1.11. Stock picks comprise those made by guests appearing on CNBC TV. Performance of active picks is calculated from the price on the date recommended. Unless otherwise specified by the stock picker, each recommendation expires after one year. Performance of expired, or closed, picks is calculated between the date the recommendation was made and when it expired. Stock pickers are ranked by their average performance on closed picks.

But do we report share price moves or make them?

Below are some self-explanatory bulletin board postings.

JANUARY 23, 2004

THOM CALANDRA CALLS IT QUITS

Wow. Interesting revelation – CBS MarketWatch's Thom Calandra *has resigned* after reports have come out that the SEC is investigating his trading history and his alerts and writings to investors.

This would be a big blow to the stock pundits, as Calandra was pretty well respected and followed. MarketWatch seems to be following all the rules and

Symbol	Company name	Date picked	Price when picked	Date dropped	Price when dropped	Performance
TABLE 1.11 Stock pickers' performance						
Kevin Jones: past performance						
GLW	Corning	10/18/2002	1.55	10/18/2003	11.09	+615.48%
VSH	Vishay Intertch	10/18/2002	9.46	10/18/2003	19.43	+105.39%
ACI	Arch Coal	10/18/2002	16.25	10/18/2003	24.64	+51.63%
UCO	Univ Compression	10/18/2002	17.46	10/18/2003	23.20	+32.88%
SCRI	Sicor	10/18/2002	16.17	10/18/2003	20.52	+26.90%
EP	El Paso Corp	10/18/2002	5.72	10/18/2003	7.13	+24.65%
Doug Sease: past performance						
PSUN	Pacific Sunwear	08/06/2002	12.17	08/06/2003	29.81	+145.01%
KROL	Kroll Inc	08/06/2002	18.75	08/06/2003	21.94	+17.01%
David Sowerby: past performance						
NCI	Navigant Consult	08/05/2002	5.36	08/05/2003	13.36	+149.25%
NCI	Navigant Consult	07/22/2002	6.18	07/22/2003	12.90	+108.74%
PRGO	Perrigo Co	08/05/2002	9.47	08/05/2003	15.64	+65.15%
AAPL	Apple Computer	08/05/2002	14.01	08/05/2003	20.37	+45.40%
GMH	GM Hughes Elctr	08/05/2002	9.28	08/05/2003	13.37	+44.07%
AAPL	Apple Computer	07/22/2002	14.95	07/22/2003	20.90	+39.80%
PRGO	Perrigo Co	07/22/2002	11.30	07/22/2003	15.61	+38.14%
GMH	GM Hughes Elctr	07/22/2002	9.66	07/22/2003	13.08	+35.44%
OMC	Omnicom Group	11/08/2002	61.70	11/08/2003	80.99	+31.26%
MAS	Masco Corp	11/08/2002	21.39	11/08/2003	26.88	+25.67%
REY	Reynolds & Reynolds	11/08/2002	24.96	11/08/2003	27.05	+8.37%

crossing the t's to make sure it's not as implicated as Calandra could possibly be. They'll take a big brand hit if Calandra is guilty of any of the potential charges, methinks. Will shareholder suits arise from this? Hopefully not, but in our over-litigious society, you never know.

Posted by: djspicerack at January 23, 2004 12:46 PM | TrackBack

COMMENTS

This was the guy who, in October of 2002, predicted the Dow would freefall to 4000 by the summer of 2003 … that's all I have to say about Mr. Calandra.

Posted by: Stephen Blythe at January 29, 2004 08:10 PM

What a fraud. By using a respectable medium such as CBSMarketWatch.com, Mr. Calandra pumped and dumped stocks he was charging people to read about in his newsletter. First of all, anybody paying $250 for his recommendations was a complete fool. Secondly, I hope the SEC nails his ass to the wall.

Posted by: Calandra is a crook at March 30, 2004 04:47 PM

First of all for the previous poster. You are ignorant and it shows. Thom Calandra didn't USE CBSMarketwatch … He STARTED it. Second for those of us who know how to trade, his report was just another piece of information to trade with. No one was forced into paying for the subscription or trading his picks. He fully disclosed his holdings and trading. I paid the $250 for his report and made $400,000 on his calls. Seems like a good deal to me. He probably is a crook and traded his picks but there is no doubt that his newsletter moved stocks. If you can't stand the heat stay out of the kitchen.

Posted by: pepe at March 31, 2004 05:28 PM

Exactly, pepe. I made a killing with Calandra's picks. Bottom line – i'm –26% since he stopped. He wasn't hurting anybody.

Posted by: mizax at August 2, 2004 02:41 PM

Does anyone know the whereabouts of Calandra? or the SEC investigation?

Posted by: Blue Moose at August 6, 2004 04:41 PM

I have to echo Mizax and Blue Moose. I made MONEY with Calandra's picks. Lost on some of 'em as well, but the guy worked hard and let you know what he found out and you made your own decision.

WHERE IS CALANDRA NOW THAT MY PORTFOLIO NEEDS HIM?

Please let me know of his whereabouts.

I know Thom and as of December 2003 he was a very well-respected journalist. *Forbes* wrote in January 2003:

Calandra, who recommended Ivanhoe Energy and Ivanhoe Mines in his newsletter, numerous Internet columns and on the CBS Marketwatch television program, said he had fully disclosed the junkets and his share ownership in Ivanhoe Energy. "The last time we asked him about this before the investigation was after *Forbes* wrote the story," Kramer said in an interview. "We asked him if he had been disclosing everything and he said 'yes'."

As *Forbes* pointed out in the same piece in January 2004:

> The volatile stocks have both more than doubled in the last year, but Ivanhoe Energy has tumbled 57% and Ivanhoe Mines is down 43% since the stocks reached their peak in early November.

I can certainly reveal I receive anonymous press clippings about how certain small caps are bound to do well in the future. Clearly there are some desperate people out there desperate for me to cover their favored stocks.

Conclusion: what you don't know about great investing

1. Beware whenever you got a stock tip – you MUST know the following from the tipster, or decide it yourself:
   a. Where is the entry price? Is it conditional on the share price first moving higher or lower?
   b. Where is the exit price?
   c. What was the time-frame for the price target?

2. Where was the stop-loss – the point at which you know you are wrong and must exit?

Take a Nobel prize winner's view:

THE PARABLE OF THE MONEY MANAGERS
William F. Sharpe (Nobel prize winner)

Some years ago, in a land called Indicia, revolution led to the overthrow of a socialist regime and the restoration of a system of private property. Former government enterprises were reformed as corporations, which then issued stocks and bonds. These securities were given to a central agency, which offered them for sale to individuals, pension funds, and the like (all armed with newly printed money).

Almost immediately a group of money managers came forth to assist these investors. Recalling the words of a venerated elder, uttered before the previous revolution ("Invest in Corporate Indicia"), they invited clients to give them money, with which they would buy a cross-section of all the newly issued securities. Investors considered this a reasonable idea, and soon everyone held a piece of Corporate Indicia.

Before long the money managers became bored because there was little for them to do. Soon they fell into the habit of gathering at a beachfront casino where they passed the time playing roulette, craps, and similar games, for low stakes, with their own money.

After a while, the owner of the casino suggested a new idea. He would furnish an impressive set of rooms which would be designated the Money Managers' Club. There the members could place bets with one another about the fortunes of various corporations, industries, the level of the Gross National Product, foreign trade, and so on. To make the betting more exciting, the casino owner suggested that the managers use their clients' money for this purpose.

The offer was immediately accepted, and soon the money managers were betting eagerly with one another. At the end of each week, some found that they had won money for their clients, while others found that they had lost. But the losses always exceeded the gains, for a certain amount was deducted from each bet to cover the costs of the elegant surroundings in which the gambling took place.

Before long a group of professors from Indicia U. suggested that investors were not well served by the activities being conducted at the Money Managers' Club. "Why pay people to gamble with your money? Why not just hold your own piece of Corporate Indicia?" they said.

This argument seemed sensible to some of the investors, and they raised the issue with their money managers. A few capitulated, announcing that they would henceforth stay away from the casino and use their clients' money only to buy proportionate shares of all the stocks and bonds issued by corporations.

The converts, who became known as managers of Indicia funds, were initially shunned by those who continued to frequent the Money Managers' Club, but in time, grudging acceptance replaced outright hostility. The wave of puritan reform some had predicted failed to materialize, and gambling remained legal. Many managers continued to make their daily pilgrimage to the casino. But they exercised more restraint than before, placed smaller bets, and generally behaved in a manner consonant with their responsibilities. Even the members of the Lawyers' Club found it difficult to object to the small amount of gambling that still went on.

And everyone but the casino owner lived happily ever after.

(*The Financial Analysts' Journal* **32**(4), July/August 1976)

Notes

1   William Bernstein (2004) *The Birth of Plenty*, McGraw-Hill.
2   Peter Lynch (1994) *Beating the Street*, Simon & Schuster.
3   "Quantative Analysis of Investor Behavior". Reports 2001. www.dalbarinc.com.
4   George Soros (2003) *The Alchemy of Finance,* Wiley.
5   "The Probability of Success", www.efficientfrontier.com/ef/103/probable.htm.

CHAPTER 2

Why the programs for private investors are kept different to programs for the professional viewer

Profits, like sausages ... are esteemed most by those who know least about what goes into them. **Alvin Toffler**

Now that you are fed on a diet of getting your financial news secondhand through the prism of journalists, isn't it about time you knew how those journalists change things? At least that way you can improve your investing. As for the guru, the pundit and the expert on financial TV – believe me when I say it is only because they are on TV that they are a "guru." The proof will be revealed as you read on.

They say the difference between a lawyer and a layman is not that the lawyer knows the law, but that the lawyer knows where to find the law. The same is true of financial journalists and private investors. I want to level the playing field more in your favor in this chapter.

- This is why the media stops you investing like a professional: the analyst, fund manager and the company director
- Psychological investment biases (or why your mind messes up your investments)
- Dollar cost averaging
- Mistakes all Bloomberg TV viewers and other investors make
- Investing shortcuts – some great websites to cut your research time in half

This is why the media stops you investing like a professional

Financial media is short term and it's late and it is only partially informed. End of story. No, you've paid good money for this book. Let me expand.

We appear on screen all morbid after a day's drops on the major indices and you think it is the end of the world. So you get spooked out of your longer term positions which you should have held.

The presenter or guest then adds some ex post facto hypothesizing: "yes stocks were due for a fall and the market is weak." Why? "Ummm, because it has fallen!"

Or, we tell you about how a stock has risen – so what? What do you do? Buy because it might rise more or sell because it has risen enough? Quite useless aren't we? We're about as useful as reading about yesterday's weather. That is why both Bloomberg and the *Financial Times* independently told me they wanted me for the added value that a trader brings. Someone who uses and sees information differently to a journalist.

In the spirit of the BBC's recent National IQ test, here's a spot quiz to measure your trading IQ. You have three doors. Behind one is a car and behind the other two a donkey. You pick, say, door one, and the host, who knows what is behind the other two doors, opens door three, which has a donkey. He then asks you if "you want to pick door number two." Is it to your advantage to switch? Most people get the answer wrong, reasoning it makes no difference whether or not you switch your choice. It is in fact beneficial to switch.

What's it got to do with online trading? Everything. The lack of even a rudimentary understanding of probabilities leads to poor trading decisions. It's tests like the above that investment bankers should use in selecting naturally talented traders, argues the Centre for the Study of Financial Innovation, a London think tank.

If you got the wrong answer, you will be relieved to know there are several online trading sites to assist you calculating the probabilities of success when making an investment.

Handling probabilities is not the only area where your trading IQ may be below par. Reading corporate news is another worrying area. Try this one. You are told that a pack of cards has letters on one side and numbers on the other. Imagine that someone makes the following statement: "If there is a vowel on one side, there is an even number on the other." There are four cards drawn, on which A, B, 2, 3 respectively are facing up. Which cards would you need to turn over to decide if the statement is true or false?

A card problem with no relevance to trading? Try telling that to George Soros, the legendary trader. According to him, most traders would say A and 2, whereas the correct answer is A and 3.

Most get it wrong because they seek confirmation of a statement, instead of disconfirmation (turning over 2 and finding a vowel would at best only confirm the statement, you need to turn over 3 to disconfirm and disprove it). The ability of traders to look for disconfirmation is rare and profitable, argues Soros.[1] It relates directly to trading because other experiments[2] too show that when traders are presented with market news, their trading decisions tend to be based on merely confirming their pre-existing views.

The lesson is clear, our trading IQ is improved if in reading financial news sites we look for evidence of our pre-existing views being incorrect. Look for reasons not to buy a stock.

The ability to forecast future price ranges is central to any form of investment. Yet it is another area where traders' IQ appears deficient. For instance, imagine you are asked to make a range prediction such that you are 90% sure that the price of, say, Vodafone will be within that range in 12 months.

The chances are you will be wrong and the price will be outside your range – even though you were asked for 90% certainty. We know traders would get it wrong because research shows that over 80% of traders wrongly forecast the price range of certain equities 12 months hence, even when asked for a range which was so wide that they felt 90% sure the price would fall within it.[3] And that's the professionals!

So how can we improve our trading IQ when it comes to price forecasting? Consider RiskGrades.com and Metastock software which calculate the likelihood of price ranges based on historic volatility not intuition.

The solution to more accurate forecasting isn't to look at more information about the security whose price you are trying to forecast either. More information only boosts your confidence in your ability to make an accurate forecast not your accuracy.[4] Information is the trading equivalent of Dutch courage.

Armed with our revitalized trading IQ, the next time opportunity knocks on our door, at least we won't make an ass of ourselves – probably.

My sites: Probability of price moves
www.riskgrades.com
Metastock software: www.equis.com
www.optionvue.com
www.quicken.com

How were your budget forecasts? If the computing power of a calculator was behind the *Apollo* spacecraft in 1969 taking man to the moon, surely by the twenty-first century computing power allows us to forecast stock prices, even if it is fleetingly? And surely the internet means private investors can access such power?

After all, computers allow us to forecast the weather, well most of the time, and surely the stock market is no more complex? Equally, with information passing around the globe in milliseconds, it must mean we know instantly which individuals are forecasting consistently well. Well, I have already said I don't trust the experts on financial media for their stock ideas.

From fundamentalists to chartists to astrologers there are websites dedicated to the serious and the seriously weird stock picker. Which seems to work?

Statistical forecasting such as "neural networks" have been around for several years. Increasingly used by hedge fund managers, these "artificial intelligence" systems claim to simulate the processes of the brain. Neural networks learn by picking up complex patterns in the price data.

The most one can say is that the companies offering them remain in business after several years in the litigious U.S., apparently have endorsements from real investors, some have won awards from reputable publications, the products are cheap, often with one-off fees as little as $80, and offer free trials or money back guarantees. NeuroSignalXL, one such stock forecaster, gives a record of performance: annual returns between 40% and 172% with between 50% to 80% profitable trades.

The incomprehensible is alluring for private investors when it comes to stock market forecasting. "It sounds complicated, do you think it works" is the suspicion. Just check the postings on MotleyFool.co.uk or Trade2Win.com.

It doesn't necessarily mean you should bet the house on them. Many of these systems predict the future by calculating mathematical rules that closely explain past price moves. But these rules can "overfit" the past and so not forecast the future.

From statistical forecasting let's move to company fundamentals, like profits. Valuengine.com calculates how undervalued a stock is and forecasts future returns based on the likelihood that it achieves its proper value.

Valuengine.com for instance calculated for me several months ago that Microsoft, then trading at $25, was 30% undervalued. The stock was up 25% nine months later.

The problem with forecasts based on undervalue is that the price may never reflect the inherent value because the rest of the market simply chooses not to push prices higher.

Nevertheless, Valuengine.com says its portfolio has returned on average just under 30% annually since 1999. Hedge funds and even the Bank of New York use its reports. So again, a forecasting model with money manager support.

What about price charts? Again, prestigious institutions add validity to these forecasting methods. Cambridge University research finds one can consistently profit when applying combinations of charting indicators.[5] But it does take skill. Detractors of chart patterns usually pick a pattern and point out that it does not work on all instances. Forecasters such as Recognia.com seek to replace the need for human skill with that of computers.

What about forecasters of the human variety? Surely, you would love to be a fly on wall in the Warren Buffett household. Validea.com creates portfolios based on the forecast methods of legendary investors such as Buffett and Peter Lynch.

Hulbert Financial Digest ranks and profiles more than 160 investment newsletters and the over 500 portfolios it recommends, telling you their performance over several years. That should avoid one-year wonders. The best 2003 portfolio was up 146%. Computing power means we can know which stocks are common to the portfolios with the best track records too.

But why then do these forecasters not simply start their own investment funds? Perhaps the answer is not the cynical one – that the systems don't stand scrutiny – but that it is far harder to raise $50m for a small fund than it is to sell stock ideas for $100 a year. Consider that a 1% annual fund charge produces the same returns as 5000 newsletter subscribers on the above figures.

But what do you do if you want U.K.- not U.S.-based forecasts? The best you can hope for is to track fund manager performance as a proxy for who is the best forecaster. Thankfully, investing in U.S. stocks is as cheap and easy as investing in U.K. ones.

As for stock forecasting based on astrology and planetary movement (apparently as the Sun moves into Aries each 20th March, the Dow-Jones industrial average is highly likely to decline over the next five days, according to one site!) – not in a million lunar cycles will I find such ways of stock forecasting convincing.

If you want specifics, here's one. Christeen Skinner, an astrologer, reported on the BBC in November 2003 that:

> the technology sector – including 3G mobile phone operators – could get a New Year boost thanks to a rare alignment between Pisces and Uranus on 30 December. This is because Uranus is associated with technology, while Pisces is linked to visual entertainment.

She also forecast $400 for gold in 2004 and a fall in the dollar. Hmmm.

My sites: Stock picking
http://www.billmeridian.com/pst.htm
http://www.neuroshell.com/
www.e-mastertrade.com
www.validea.com
http://cbs.marketwatch.com/Hulbert
www.alyuda.com/trading-software.htm
www.recognia.com

Profiting from profits warnings

One thing financial TV is great at is stuffing you full of earnings announcements. As they pontificate, trying to look all serious, as if anyone really
knows what "earnings before interest, tax, depreciation and amortization
(EBITDA)" really means, you might think profits warnings are bad.

A "profits warning" by a company would seem to be a good reason to
steer clear of its shares. After all, the subsequent price fall can be both swift
and costly. Indeed, stocks fall on average 16% on the day of a warning
itself, according to one study.[6]

But where there's fear in the market, there's money to be made. And
profits warnings are no exception. So what should you do if you're unfortu-
nate enough to hold shares in a company that issues a profits warning? Buy
some more it seems – but not straightaway.

Stocks of U.K. companies that issued profits warnings deliver returns
that are on average 22% more than the FTSE All Share index in the
year beginning *12 months after* the warning. That is the key finding of the
above study.

What about the short term? What's the best way to beat the market
immediately following a profits warning? Unsurprisingly there are two
opposing views.

One group believes stocks will rebound after a profits warning; the other
believes stocks will fall even further. Who's right and where's the money to
be made?

The first group argues that the market overreacts to news and so following a profit warning the market drives a share price too low in the short
term. They therefore buy stocks after bad news They are the "contrarians."

The second group believes that the market underreacts to news and is
slow to revise its existing views on a company. They buy stocks on good
news on the assumption that the stocks will rise even further in the short
term. Conversely, they stay clear in the short term of stocks issuing profits

warnings. My experience puts me in this group. These are sometimes called "momentum traders."

According to the study, it seems momentum traders will do better than contrarians because over the six months following a warning, a company's stock price falls on average a further 5%.

The apparent contradiction between shorter term trades and longer term investments (where following a profits warning stocks fall in the short term and rise in the long term) is supported by other studies too.[7] This study found a portfolio constructed by buying stocks which were losers five years up to one year ago is profitable so is buying winners over the last 12 months.

So in the short term steer clear of companies issuing profits warnings and get in at the start of their second year after the profits warning. But what explains the striking returns in the second year after the profits warning?

As traders we're reluctant to cut our losses, often holding on in hope of a turnaround.[8] Perhaps this is partly from the shock of a profits warning and a drop of around 16% in a day. Unfortunately, by the time we give up hope of a rise and decide to ditch the stock, it may be just about to turn around.

Profits warnings presage improved stock performance after 12 months. Hemscott published figures showing that the total of profits warnings issued by British firms in the first half of 2001 had quadrupled. A year on, things indeed improved.

You can find U.S. stock profit warnings on http://money.cnn.com and www.whispernumber.com. For U.K. stocks you can find profits warnings covered on www.ftinvestor.com and www.digitallook.com

One note of caution: The studies were performed on a relatively narrow sample, and it seems foolhardy to buy stocks solely on the basis of a profits warning a year earlier. Prior to buying stocks you should still look for evidence of improved performance by the company. Nevertheless, we need not fear profit warnings as much as we might have done.

Asking directors the right questions

Another favorite of the financial media is the company director. Again, surely he is a person to be trusted, relied upon. If we don't get him or the fund manager, whom do we get? Private investors? God forbid.

Did you know that each time Paul Little, a director of Direct Focus Inc., has bought stock in that company, its share price has risen on average 75% within six months? Or that when Ellis Earl has bought stock in Exco Resources, a company in which he is a director, the share price has risen

67% on average in six months. Of course you didn't know this. And most investors never would. That's because they ask the wrong questions about directors' dealings.

The theory behind directors' dealings is simple: directors should know more about their own companies than outsiders. Therefore, if the directors are buying shares, this should signal that the company is doing well and the share price will rise. But it's the wrong question to ask – "In which companies have the directors themselves been buying stock?" That's too simplistic.

Directors could be buying shares not because of faith in a rising share price, but because the company expects new directors to do this (just as a new worker is expected to "volunteer" overtime). It could also be that the share price has fallen sharply and they're buying stock as a public statement of confidence in the company. Equally, it could be part of their estate planning, tax reorganization, or an exercise of options. These purchases are hardly calculated moves based on the director's belief in a share price rise.

An equally wrong question to ask is: "In which companies are directors selling shares?" Wharton's Andrew Metrick and Harvard's Leslie Jeng constructed a hypothetical portfolio of all "insider" (the U.S. term for high-ranking corporate officers including directors) sales over a 10-year period ending in 1996. The portfolio merely performed in line with the market. You might as well have ignored directors' sales altogether.

If directors' dealings do work as a signal, they don't work in an obvious, easy or straightforward way. That's why www.thompsonfn.com's insider scores is invaluable – it implies we've been asking the wrong questions about directors' dealings all along.

Instead of asking "Are the directors of this company buying or selling its stock", we should have asked: "How accurate a predictor of share price movements are this director's transactions?" Prior to the internet such information would not only have been inaccessible to the private investor, it certainly would never have been free. Such data reveals that most directors' purchases have little impact on price. But a few purchases consistently seem to precede price rises. It's those that the site allows us to quickly pinpoint.

But be careful, it could simply be coincidence that out of the previous ten occasions a particular director bought stock in his own company, the share price rose within six months; there is no certainty it will happen again.

Nevertheless, for my longer term investments I will in future check there isn't any recent directors' selling which in the past has predicted price falls.

What other questions should we ask about directors dealings? How about: "Are there out of the ordinary directors' dealings for an individual company – perhaps signifying a fundamental shift in a firm's future prospects?" Or what about: "Which sectors show the highest levels of directors' purchasing?" By tracking which sectors are showing concentrated pockets of director buying and selling, you should have insight into potential broader market shifts.

A further useful question is: "Which companies show the largest ever director purchases and ones with the first director purchase in over six months?" Or how about: "Which companies are near their year high share price and the directors are nevertheless buying (implying that despite share price rises the stock may still have further to go)?"

Answers to all these questions are at last available for free to online traders. Whilst, unsurprisingly, they only cover U.S. stocks, at least all major U.K. online brokers offer trading in U.S. shares. For U.K. stocks you'll have to sift through company data yourself such as on www.hemscott.net. City-wire.co.uk tries to discern this information too.

Finally, what if we aggregate the actions of the most predictive directors? Surely if their purchases and sales are accurate predictors of how they feel about their own companies, then in aggregate that gives us a clue to market sentiment for the following few months? Sadly, market sentiment is bearish on this measure, according to Thompsonfn.com. That's the problem with asking questions – you may not like the answers.

Enter the analyst

Yet another favourite for financial TV is the analyst. But he looks so grown up, that 25 year old. *This category of pundit dresses the part, uses all the right words, "EBITDA, pre-tax, earnings enhancing, M&A, profit margins, competitor analysis" – sometimes he even uses them in the right order.*

There's just one small problem: there is nothing more useless to the private investor than an analyst's stock upgrade or downgrade.

You would be wrong to think an upgrade heralds a price rise. If it were that simple, why did Logica, Cable & Wireless, and Vodafone all slump within six weeks of an upgrade?

Maybe the price rise comes later? It certainly didn't when investment bank McDonald Investment upgraded Amazon to a "strong buy" when the stock was at $70. It fell to $40 in 9 months and $15 in 18 months. Just one rotten apple? There comes a point where there are so many rotten apples that the whole barrel needs dumping.

Surely, upgrades can give us an advance notice of good corporate earnings announcements? No, upgrades regularly come belatedly after bumper results. Thanks, but I know how to read bumper earnings.

What of downgrades? Maybe they give net traders advance warning of trouble ahead? If they do, it's impossible to discern. Where were the downgrades before British American Tobacco's recent weak results (heralded with the headline "BAT results at bottom end of forecasts")?

Sure sometimes analysts do upgrade to a strong buy and the stock rises. But if you throw enough strong buys, some are bound to be correct. Consider that, according to investment researcher Multex, one-fifth of 1% of all stock recommendations were "sells" in March 2000.

So who follows analyst upgrades? Maybe fund managers do. After all 82% of fund managers failed to beat the stock market over the past 20 years, according to Virgin Money.

Does this mean all institutional research is without value? No of course not. It needs to be handled with care. My recommendations are:

■ Ignore positive news. Look for reasons not to buy a stock. Such reasons are a scarcity. Look for negatives in an analyst's report. You can find reports on http://quote.yahoo.co.uk and www.companiesonline.com and www.hemscott.net.

■ Use institutional research for short-term trading. Analysts upgrades are of value not for their accurate prescience but for their short-term influence. Witness for instance the recent sharp rises in WPP as upgrades following their strong results reinforce gains. One strategy is to buy immediately after unexpectedly positive earnings announcements *if the share price also rises*, as analysts upgrades usually take a couple of days to follow and result in another boost to the share price.

Do the opposite of what the analysts are doing

Research[9] shows that you could forecast the earnings growth of a particular company more accurately by ignoring the analysts' forecasts; instead companies with high or low forecast growth will typically just grow at the same rate as the average company.

Bulkley and Harris show it is possible to earn excess returns by buying shares for which earnings growth is forecast to be low and holding them for five years. Over that period of time, the excessive pessimism should become apparent.

Consequently, between 1982 and 1993, you could on average have earned an excess return of 5% a year (over and above the average return on all shares) by this strategy. Over the same period, shares with the highest forecast earnings growth underperformed the market by an average of 5% a year.

But be warned: low earnings forecast shares do not deliver excess returns over holding horizons of a year or less. The profits on low forecast growth shares are only realized over a five-year holding horizon as the mistakes in the earnings forecasts become apparent.

So if there is pressure on fund managers to show the success of their share selection strategy over such short periods, they have no incentive to use the criterion for identifying stocks – which in turn may well explain their poor performance.

Psychological investment biases (or why your mind messes up your investments)

I am not suggesting that if you watch too much financial TV, you will need to see a psychiatrist. No, work in financial TV and you will definitely need to see one. But watching it from a safe distance is harmless. Just remember to take regular breaks, no more than two small portions a day and watch something healthy in between. Oh, and don't swallow.

Bernard Oppetit and risk aversion

As part of my endeavors to discover the traits of the leading traders in the world and what they can teach the rest of us, I interviewed Bernard Oppetit when he was global head of equity derivatives at Paribas. He went on to create his own hedge fund, Centaurus Capital, now one of the most success-ful in the world, managing over $2 billion of clients' (and his own) money. This part of the interview focuses on risk and money management – two essential components to trading success.

Great traders tend to be risk averse
The public perception of traders, propagated by trading scandals, is that they are attracted to wild risks and take massive gambles. Of all the traders I interviewed for this book, not one claimed to be risk loving.
Oppetit details the contrary view:

> I am very risk averse. I would definitely take the certainty of making $10,000 dollars than the 10% chance of making $100,000. In terms of economics, my personal utility function is very much concave.

When we speak of risk in trading we are, of course, discussing price volatility. Price volatility cannot be discussed without an idea of probabil-ity. The probability of a stock's price reaching your target can be derived from the historic price volatility of the particular stock. Consequently, risk, price volatility, and probability go hand in hand. Good traders wait until the probability of a favorable move is the greatest and the risk of an unfavor-able move the lowest. Moreover, unlike nonprofessional traders, the great trader knows that risk and reward are not always directly proportional. There are very low risk and yet high reward trades.

Oppetit continues:

The important thing is to look at risk in a rational way, and an imaginative way. A good trader knows how and when to take risk and how and when to avoid risk. There are risks which should be taken and risks which should not be taken. The game is to distinguish between the two. You do not need to risk a lot to profit a lot. There are a lot of trades where you can make a lot of money which are not particularly risky. You may have to invest a lot of your time to do research and discover what is going on, but the actual money you invest may not be at much risk.

There is a joke about an economics professor who is walking in New York with a friend. His friend notices a $100 bill on the sidewalk and points to the bill and says, "Look professor, a $100 bill." The economics professor replies, "No that cannot be so, if that was a $100 bill somebody would have picked it up already." Still I believe there are opportunities to make money with very little risk.

Analyzing risk and probability

So, how does Bernard Oppetit analyze risk and probability when he examines a position?

Even though I know I will get out after a certain loss, I consider the amount I have risked as the whole amount invested. Also, I look to see what percentage probability there is of a certain percentage rise and I compare that to the risk I am taking. I would look at some kind of distribution of possible outcomes, such as a 50% chance of doing something special, or a 50% chance of doing nothing in particular, or a 50% chance of a small loss against a 50% chance of a great gain. There has to be some idea of the distribution of outcomes.

What Bernard Oppetit does when analyzing a potential trade is to consider at risk the whole amount he is trading with. This is even if he knows that he will exit the position if the price falls by, say, 15% and, therefore, he would only risk losing 15% of his stake.

He then examines the reward. He measures reward by examining the probabilities of various outcomes. You can only gain an idea of the reward if you examine the probability of it occurring.

Bernard Oppetit would then compare the risk with the reward. For instance, an options position opened with $10,000 would place $10,000 at risk. To get an idea of his risk and reward ratio, Bernard Oppetit would then examine the likely outcomes and their probabilities. This would give him some idea of the reward he may get for the risk he is taking. (If he were being very mathematical he would sum the products of all the outcomes and their corresponding probabilities, and compare this figure to the amount risked.)

Money management

Good risk analysis and management is not only about volatility and probability, it is also about good money management.

As Oppetit explains:

> You have to have good money management. You have to ensure you are not going to be hopelessly underwater. You can have rules like maximum drawdown or value at risk or limits. You can also have your own internal rules like "this is too much money to lose." You must have that in your mind and that you are not going to risk more than that at any one time. You have to make sure you are left in the game. That is very important. Once this is clearly established you need fear, you need to feel that things can very quickly go wrong.

In devising a money management plan, you should consider the following:

- What is the most money I will risk on any single trade at any one time, that is, what is too much to be lost?

- What amount must I avoid losing on a trade, given that I might lose on a consecutive number of trades, so that I do not become in serious danger of being out of the game?

- Once in the trade, what is the maximum percentage I am prepared to lose before exiting? Some decide this based on "value at risk," that is, a mathematical calculation based upon the probabilities of various outcomes of all open positions, and hence the value of money at risk of the positions.

Facing a loss

When sitting on a paper loss a trader will indubitably experience immense pressure and fear.

Oppetit continues:

> It is very important to experience this fear to ensure you do not end up in that situation again. Fear is also a bad thing in that it will affect your judgment, in the same way elation would affect your judgment. You have to take a very neutral approach.

So, experience the fear when faced with a loss, do not deny it. But use the fear as a means of loss prevention in future, not as a cause of ever-increasing losses. When looking at a new price, you do not focus on the fear of how much you have lost, or the hope it may turn around:

> You have to ask, if you are a buyer at this new price, if you didn't own it already, would you buy it? If the answer is no, then I sell it. You have to look at the position with an open mind, and ask if you would put it on today if you did not already have it. If new information came in while I had an open position, I would change my expectations. But you have to be honest with yourself. It is a question of attitude. It is an easy trap to fall into to kid yourself that you are holding onto something because you believe things have changed and it will now rise. It comes back to being honest with yourself.

Handling a profit

As well as hope, another damaging emotion surrounding open positions which prevents an honest analysis, is that an unrealized profit may vanish:

> It is a cliché that you cut your losers and ride your winners – but it is very true. Most people and many traders do the opposite. There is a desire to take profits, sometimes encouraged by accounting rules. Many people look at their unrealized gains as nonexistent. They think taking profit is making real profit and it is unreal before then. They feel taking a loss is an admission of being wrong.

Again, this emotional attitude to profits has to be eradicated.

Instead of focusing on whether he was right or wrong, Bernard Oppetit focuses on his expectations regarding a position, in order to maintain objectivity:

> If what I had expected to happen does not happen then I know to get out. Whether I get out at a profit or loss does not matter. As soon as I realize my scenario was wrong I get out. Another easy case is when everything I expected happened, so I take my profits. Those are the two easy cases, and everything in between is difficult.

What Bernard Oppetit is discussing is that all open positions have to be viewed objectively. That means you have to focus on certain questions and reasons and ignore others.

You need to focus on these points:

- Has what you expected to happen happened?

- Are you a buyer or a seller at this price?

- Is the probability of what you expected to occur still the same as when you placed the trade?

You have to ignore:

- How much of a loss you are sitting on.

- How much of a profit you are sitting on.

- How much you paid for the position.

- The fact that the position may turn around.

Risk advice from Pat Arbor

Risk taking is older than literature. As far back as 3500 BC the *Mahabharata*, the holy scriptures of the world's oldest religion, Hinduism, describes a game of chance played with dice on which kingdoms were wagered. Little wonder then, as Peter Bernstein states in *Against the Gods*: "The modern conception of risk is rooted in the Hindu-Arabic numbering system that reached the West seven to eight hundred years ago."

Dealing with risk is part and parcel of being a trader, and many traders great and small will have their own ideas about risk management. But what precisely is the relationship of the great trader to risk? What would an experienced trader such as Pat Arbor, former chairman of the Chicago Board of Trade, the world's largest derivatives exchange, have to say about risk?

Risk: Why take it?

"Nobody ever achieved greatness by doing nothing. You have got to step out and do something and take a chance and get your teeth kicked in. A good trader has to engage in some acts which are considered risky," says Arbor.

As Pat Arbor explains, great traders take risks and manage risks:

> I think a great trader certainly has to have a psychological stability about themselves, but not too much stability, because one has to have a certain flair for risk. It is a fine psychological blend you have got to look for in a trader; the ability to take risk, the ability to have some courage, coupled with stability in the psychological makeup. I think the great traders have to have a greater appetite for risk than the normal person or the poorer traders. Then the question is how they manage that risk, the discipline they impose on themselves to manage that risk.

In most cases the risk is balanced. In my own trading I have always tried to be a spreader or arbitrageur. If I am long one month soybeans then I am generally short another month soybeans. And I generally do soybeans or bond spreads. If I am long bonds then I am short 10-year notes. Sometimes if I am long a commodity outright, then I might be long corn and short soybeans or long soybeans and short corn.

You also spread because you may not be prepared for the straight position. You may like the position, you may be bullish on the position, and it may not be going well. You would like to maintain your position, possibly moderate it a little, by selling something against it. You may be long soybeans outright, and you can neutralize it a little by selling soybean meal, or soybean oil or some corn against it. Your S&P position may not be going so well and you may want to sell bonds against it. You are keeping your position but cutting your profit potential. Of course, you could just take the loss. But where you may not do that and have a spread instead is where you think you are right and like the position then you tend to neutralize it a little bit to mitigate the loss.

Spreading or hedging as a form of risk management is not necessarily suited to everyone, as Pat Arbor explains.

Finding a style to fit

As a trader you must decide what you are. You are either a speculator, spreader, or local scalper. You have to fit into one of those categories. Me, I am suited to spreading.

To find what suits his personality, he just has to see whether or not he makes money at what he's doing. I have had people come into the office, saying, "I am a great trader," I say, "You're right," they say, "I know how to trade." I say again, "You're right" and they say, "I predicted that the market was going to go up or down," and I say again, "You are right. But the bottom line is whether you make any money."

So, while hedging can be a good way to manage risk, whether or not you wish to be a hedger depends on what trading style makes money for you given the type of trading personality you are.

From small acorns: progressive trading

Progressive trading is the name I have given to the idea that the best trading results and long-term profitability are assured through a "slow and steady" style of trading. I have yet to meet a great trader that advocates wild risks in order to make spectacular home runs.

As Pat Arbor continues:

> The best traders I think are those who try to make a little bit every day. You surely have your success stories; those that hit home runs, but if you take a record or study of the home run hitters against those that try to hit singles every day, the success rate of the former is a lot less than the latter. So a good trader ends up being one who accumulates capital over a period of time.

> I remember once explaining this to a young Italian trader and I said to him, it's una fagiola (one bean) a day. If you try to put one bean in a bag per day, then at the end of the month you are going to have 31 beans in the bag. But if you try to put all 31 beans through the mouth of the bag you will spill a few, and in some cases you will not get any of them in. So, it is better to build it up one day at a time, in a small manner, slowly. It's tempting not to do that when you see George Soros, but if you live by the trading sword, you die by the trading sword.

Implicit in Pat Arbor's advice about "progressive trading" is the idea that it is all right to be out of the market:

> The discipline not to trade, that's a big one. A lot of people don't realize that. A lot of people think you should stand there all day long and be in the market all day long. There are times when the market is so dead or so illiquid that you should not be trading. There are times when the market is terribly volatile and makes no sense and you should not be trading. It is generally the former, though. I have seen people stand there all day long when there is nothing going on, just a few locals in the pit. They will put a position on out of boredom. Then they can't get out of it easily. I say to them, "Well, you shouldn't be trading. There's nothing going on. Take it easy. Take a walk. Go off to the coffee shop."

I think I'll go for a coffee now.

Risk aversion: risk not thine whole wad

Trading is about risk. Risk can be bought and sold like any other commodity. Derivatives are one instrument through which risk is transferred. The great trader has a deep understanding of the nature of risk, but, perhaps most surprisingly, is risk averse; he takes out insurance against being wrong. Moreover, he balances risk with his own personality to produce a harmony between the two; never being so exposed as to feel uncomfortable and let it affect his trading.

Six feet tall, a muscular physique and bald save for a pony tail – that is Jon Najarian by appearance. In 1989 Jon Najarian formed Mercury Trading, a designated primary market maker, responsible for maintaining a market in stocks for which it had been designated. Two years later, it reported a return on capital of 415%. Today it is the second most active market maker on the CBOE (Chicago Board Options Exchange).

As he is a highly profitable trader, I wanted to know what he would have to advise other traders about risk.

Perceptions of trading risks

As Najarian explains:

> I am very risk averse. You have probably seen on people's walls, "Risk not thine whole wad." We always try to position ourselves so that we can always trade tomorrow. That is the single most important thing. Not making money today, making money today is not more important than being able to come back tomorrow. If I want to be short the market, because I think they are going to raise rates and that will pressure the market, will I be naked short? No, we are long puts and every day that goes by and the market drops, we buy a ton of calls so that if the market turns and goes up we do not lose all the money that we made by being right. You only get so many times a year to be right. But we always want to lock in the profits so we are constantly rolling down our hedge and never just one way long or short.

> Many days when placing a spread or a hedge, we think, "god, if someone had tied me up in a closet we would have made a fortune, because as the stock was falling we were taking profits all the way down." Well that is just the curse of being a hedger. It is also the reason why we sleep the way we sleep every night.

Because Najarian knows he has disaster protection insurance, he can be more at ease:

> When you come in after a weekend where the market was down 148 points, it looks ugly, they were having trouble finding buyers all day, then if I am stuck in a position I could be very panicked. But we sleep like babies.

Any temptation to go for home runs?
It is comforting to know that the top traders have the same bad trading temptations as the rest of us:

> Sure, there are times when we wished that we were not as disciplined. But more times than not we were glad that we were disciplined. We see so many people bet for home runs by putting all their marbles on a big shot. When we bet on a big move we do it with a controlled amount of risk even though we are betting for a home run. We are buying a lot of out-of-the-money puts and we are selling out-of-the-money puts as well as a hedge against the puts we are buying. If we say we are buying some puts for $4 and selling other puts for $2 then we only have $2 worth of risk. So I can stay at the table twice as long. The other guy, who is unhedged, is starting to gag when the market is going against him, but we can stay with the trade longer.

Since the hedge provides Jon Najarian with a comfort zone, he can be free to exercise clearer judgment. Imagine the last time you were panicked by an adverse price move. Did it ruin your day? Did it plague your mind? Did it affect other trading decisions? If so, have you considered hedging your position? You will, of course, have to examine the cost elements of hedging and the extent you may wish to be hedged. Risk is a beautiful thing; with ingenuity you can purchase or sell just the precise amount of risk:

> The other thing we look at is the buyers and sellers. Again, on the derivatives side we see Salomon, Morgan Stanley, Lehman, NatWest buying, buying, buying a certain stock and we know they are betting on the upside, too. So, we are reading all these tea leaves as well. We see that the chart pattern looks good, institutional buyers are coming in – is there anything in the news? Are there earnings coming up, has anybody commented on it favorably, is there a new product coming out, is there a lawsuit pending? We look at all those things so that by the time we actually place the bet we probably have a huge edge because of all those factors we looked at, that our winning percentage is off the charts. Most people do not have the benefit of seeing all that information so what they have to do is give themselves the chance of being as right as possible.

It follows from this that when Jon Najarian does enter a trade he wants the upside to be far greater than the downside, even if the downside move is highly improbable:

> The worst I do is a 1:1 risk reward ratio. Most of the time I want a 2:1 or 3:1 reward to risk ratio. So if I think it could go to $35 then I sell at a loss, if I am

wrong at $29 or $28 so that I have a multiple risk reward ratio on the upside. If I am wrong I cut the trade and move on.

You cannot be willing to say I am going to ride this stock down to $20 if I am wrong, but I am going to make $5 if I am right. If you do that kind of thing you are just not going to be in business very long.

I would never put a multiplier on the risk to the downside. I would never say that although there is $5 on the upside, I am so confident that I am willing to take a $10 risk to the downside. It would not be acceptable risk.

Few people would associate such a risk-averse, belt and braces approach with a trader, let alone a great trader. However, risk aversion and caution are the hallmarks of great traders. While many of us may have a strong appreciation of this, it can never hurt to be reminded.

The equation using other people's funds

Many traders dream of going it alone and managing money. So what are the pitfalls that a private trader working for himself should be aware of when competing against the institutions?

Bill Lipschutz is an institutional investor who went it alone and set up his own company. Lipschutz was global head of currency trading at Salomon Brothers at the end of the 1980s. If ever there were a right time and a right place for a trader, that was it – then and there.

Over the eight years he was there, Bill Lipschutz earned for his employer an average of $250,000 profit each and every trading day. Here is a man who knows his trading.

It's not all the same money: source and effect
Bill left Salomon in 1990 and currently has a company called Hathersage Capital Management, focusing on foreign exchange trading.

It is often not realized that the source of trading funds can affect one's trading style and performance. As Bill Lipschutz explains, this fact is something even the most able traders do not appreciate until they experience it:

I was unaware that there were these differences. Seven years ago, I had a naive view that you get the money from here, or from Salomon Brothers' proprietary capital, whether it is ten high net worth individuals or a fund of funds I felt it was all the same; let me see how much I can extract from the market.

The whole money management game is a difficult game. It has not only to do with how well you perform, but what kinds of results people are looking for in their portfolios. Absolute performance is a real misleading thing. I can say to you, "We were up 600%" over five years in our most aggressive program, and you might say, "Wow, 600%." But that does not necessarily mean that much in and of itself, without knowing how well other currency-only managers performed. For example, say a guy is managing $200 million, and $120 million of it is a fund that he runs with a very specific mandate. If he made 600% over four years in that particular fund, he may have people pulling money out from that particular fund, because they are nervous, because that really was not the kind of variance they were looking for. So, it is very complicated.

As Lipschutz explains, one way the source of funding can affect your trading style is through the motivation of the lender and the terms on which the funds were granted. We all, as traders, seek more capital with which to trade. Whatever the source of money, you must be aware that since it can affect your trading style it may also affect your trading performance. The worst time to have a deterioration in your trading performance is when the money is not your own:

But, now when you have to charge clients, the client says to you, "I know you are a speculative guy, or you can be a speculative guy, I am willing to lose 20%." I have sat with clients, and we try to talk with our clients and really understand what they want. If a guy looks me in the eye and says, "I can be down 20%, no problem," I know he really means 5%, because if you call him in three days and say, "You know what, you're down 18%, I just wanna know how you feel, so we can discuss what to do from here," he's going to forget he ever said he was comfortable with a 20% loss.

Regardless of what they say, because they are not traders, they don't understand, they certainly do intellectually, I am not trying to take anything from them, but they don't understand it emotionally, necessarily, what they are getting into. When you are charged with other people's money you have to help them and not let them get into something they are not emotionally ready for yet.

Sometimes, being wrong, even if there is a 5% chance of that happening, is a whole lot worse than being right, even if there is a 95% chance of that. It's the old, "Gee, if I make 25% for these guys, they'll be really happy, and they'll think I am a great trader and I'll earn big fees. But you know what, if I lose 5% for these guys they're going to pull that money out and I am going to be close to being out of business." But that is not the probability of the trade succeeding or failing. So you have to lay this on top of the probability of the trade succeeding or failing. It is very complicated. It's a whole set of simultaneous constraints that you have to solve at once.

Therefore, trading with other people's money becomes far more complicated than trading with one's own. You have to consider both the likely
outcome of the trade and the likely reaction of the investor to a positive and
a negative trading outcome. The decisions you can make are restricted by
the likely responses of your client. That, in turn, could impinge upon your
trading performance.

A checklist
So, before taking on new funds, ask yourself the following questions:

1. What does the lender *say* he expects?

2. What does he *really* expect?

3. Have I traded successfully in the past *in the manner required* by the
   lender's expectations?

4. Can I *deliver* what the lender really expects?

5. What are the consequences for me if I *fail* to deliver?

6. How much *control* does the lender want?

7. How *frequently* is the lender going to inquire about the performance?

8. What type of *personality* has the lender? Is he likely to pester and
   aggravate?

9. Can some *ground rules* be set?

There are three key areas to trading success, shown in Figure 2.1. What if
the great online trading boom actually might reduce trader returns and
increase the risks they take to achieve them? Well, of the three "Ms" to trading success (Money management, Mind and Method) it is "mind" that is the
most important. It may sound flaky but it isn't. Ask professional traders and
they will tell you that psychology is more important than pouring over
charts or fiddling with company accounts (to unravel the fiddling the
company has already done).

Indeed Harvard, Yale, Stanford, they all run courses on "behavioral
finance" – where psychology meets money. Yours truly has even lectured
about it as a fellow at Oxford University. And three years ago the Nobel
Prize in Economics went for the first time to noneconomists – they were
psychologists – and their subject was – the psychology of the markets.
So there.

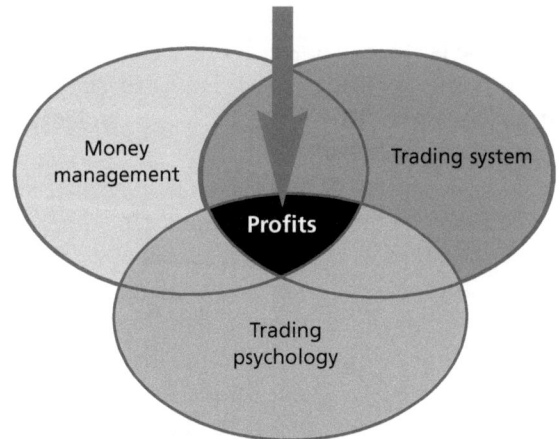

Figure 2.1 Three key areas of trading success
Source: © 2004 Trademind™ Ltd

So what are the key mental potholes on the superhighway to trading success? A report by the Centre for the Study of Financial Innovation (CSFI)[10] suggests overconfidence is merely one of many psychological "biases" afflicting traders' performance. What are the other causes of poor trader performance and what can they do about them?

Confirmation bias is the desire to seek confirmation and resist disconfirmation of one's beliefs. Trading experiments suggest maximum profits go to those few traders who resist confirmation bias by interpreting news dispassionately, without a tendency merely to confirm what they already believe. Instead they maintain more of an open mind to a contrary view than their colleagues.

With numerous sites offering stock stories, my advice to online traders is that if they are becoming elated at the slightest story which could be interpreted positively for a stock they are holding, they need to step back. Is the story or announcement objectively positive for your holding? The real issue is how will the market interpret it.

Another way to obtain more objective analysis is to focus on raw stock data. Examine the number of large block trades, market maker demand, and stock volume weighted average price, and compare those with other stocks to see if it is relatively positive.

Chat sites reveal the extent of online traders' confirmation bias. Stockholders often reply with abuse to bearish postings. Indeed one columnist Evil Kenevil who makes bearish stock comments receives abusive email from holders of those stocks.

Optimism bias is another problem online traders face. It is the tendency to believe that one is better than average. For instance, studies reveal 95% of drivers believe they are better than average. The CSFI study notes that overoptimistic traders underperform. This bias leads to overconfidence in predictions. Experts are particularly prone to this; expert predictions about financial markets, especially about interest and exchange rates, have been shown in experiments to be generally quite inaccurate and often less accurate than lay views. In one study dustmen were better predictors of inflation and GDP than finance ministers.[11] This also confirms many online traders' beliefs that they are the best managers of their investments and not "expert" fund managers.

As traders you must be willing to more readily accept that you may be wrong about a stock despite all your online research. Set price levels at which you will accept that you were wrong; let the price prove you right or wrong and then act on it.

Another lesson I take from this finding is that we ought to place less reliance on stock "experts" and their stock picks. I do not know what stocks are going to double next week, no one does. We can only guess probabilities. Experts' pedestals need lowering, they "know" far less than people think.

Risk aversion biases suggest that traders tend to be risk averse when facing a profit and risk loving when facing a loss. Consequently they let their losses run and take their profits prematurely.

I would advise traders with a losing position to consider if they would buy more stock at those price levels. If not, it may be time to sell. Also you if could reinvest the money in another stock for potentially better returns, do so, rather than falling into the common trap of hoping that losing stocks will rebound.

Similarly, when facing a profit, ignore how much you have made or how your other positions are faring. Many traders tend to go for higher risk trades after a string of losses in an attempt to eradicate their past losses, they then take a quick small profit to break their "losing streak." Instead, remember that your other past and present trades are irrelevant to when you should exit your current stock position.

Herding is yet another fascinating online trader problem. People tend to regret decisions that go wrong more if they were minority decisions. They tend therefore to seek other like-minded people to reinforce their views, perhaps in investment clubs and chat sites. The problem is that the quality of decision is not necessarily improved and on the contrary can lead to spurious trade selections, especially if those with contrary views are silenced because of confirmation bias. The key is to do your own research and be confident in it, and not simply because your own view is repeated by others.

Finally, a key skill that traders try to develop is to recognize these psychological pitfalls in the market and how they can profit from them. For instance, momentum strategies following price trends can be highly profitable and reliant on a herd mentality of others.

I think I had better book that psychiatrist appointment.

Common investor problems

"I have an investment problem ...". So starts another email in my inbox. The advantage of being a trader and involved in the financial media is that you are regularly sent emails about common problems. Consider me the Martha Stewart of trading (in the good, noninsider trading, allegedly of course, sense) or the Oprah Winfrey of markets!

Often these problems are easily resolved. But until then they are extremely costly for the millions of investors worldwide. Increasingly the questions have become more basic – doubtless because the next wave of traders enters the market.

What are these common problems and how much are they needlessly costing you?

> I am a private investor and have been downloading share prices from www.marketeye.com and then preparing my own charts. That site has now closed and the only other organization which would supply this information would charge me $10,000 for the privilege whereas marketeye was free!

So runs the most popular query of all. A slew of traders prefer to download stock prices into the spreadsheet program Excel so they can draw their own price charts. Without them they don't have buy and sell signals, and without those, they can't trade.

But why don't they just let specialist software do the work for them? I prefer using software such as Metastock (www.equis.com and www.paritech.co.uk), the costlier Tradestation (www.tradestation.com), and OmniTrader 2000 (www.nirv.com). All work with both U.S. and U.K. data.

Each generates trading signals based on tested criteria and scans stocks according to your own requirements. Whether you choose end of day data or the more expensive intraday real-time data for the above software depends on whether you are a short-term trader. There is no shortcut to visiting websites and trying the software demo disks.

Other popular well-regarded software includes Synergy (www.synsoft.co.uk), FairShares (www.updata.co.uk), Indexia (www.indexia.co.uk), and Sharescope (www.sharescope.co.uk).

Whether you only want share price data or need company data too depends on how you pick stocks; whether you examine just price charts or company valuations too. I prefer having both price and company data for the fullest stock picture.

An alternative to software for plotting prices are websites. Consider www.advfn.com which provide charts and plots company data in visual form for easier and quicker analysis.

For U.S. charts visit my favorites, the free, www.quote.com, and www. bigcharts.com.

Despite the choices for plotting price charts, if you still prefer data you can plot in a spreadsheet program, visit www.londonstockexchange.com, www.paritech.co.uk, www.finsight.co.uk, www.jf-systems.fsnet.co.uk, and www.liffedata.com.

Also email Trendline on trendl@compuserve.com for historic price and daily price data. For U.S. data visit www.reutersdatalink.com.

The novice will prefer starting with charting websites, which tend to be cheaper than software, then trying software demos and only finally investing in software.

Another question is: "Is it possible to get data, for example a table/spreadsheet on all companies including their essential fundamentals such as EPS, p/e ratio and profit?" This is a popular query as traders become increasingly weary about the time spent scouring for good stock picks. Imagine a market-beating annual 10% return with five hours research a week on a $50,000 portfolio. For a higher rate taxpayer, the return is a mere $11 per hour.

Of course the return beats the minimum wage. Our trader wants such data to both increase returns and reduce time spent producing those returns.

For U.K. fundamental data try www.sharescope.co.uk software and www.hemscott.net. Both are excellent sources of company data and save hours scouring for stocks. The U.S. web-based equivalents are the exceptional www.yahoo.com and www.multex.com.

More experienced traders often ask about trading psychology:

> At the beginning of this year I had a string of losses which knocked my confidence. Checking these trades I found I had allowed extraneous emotions to enter the equation resulting in overreacting, for example, to intraday data and getting out of the trade too early and often at a loss. Do you know of any reference material to help one deal more comfortably with trading stress.

A new site www.innerworth.com is dedicated to all trading psychology issues. Indeed trading psychology is so important that Bill Lipschutz, in *The Mind of a Trader,* explained it was "the most important factor in trading success." Other sites about preventing your emotions from sabotaging your trading include www.tradingontarget.com, www.tradeshare.com, and www.drrelax.com/traders.htm.

Finally, there is a whole category of questions which begin: "I bought [insert name of formerly popular technology stock] at [insert overinflated price] and now it trades at only [insert 0.1% of previous figure]. Is there any hope?"

Despite the dot-com collapse, innovation on investment websites has accelerated. New products to make all aspects of trading and investing simpler, more efficient, and hopefully more profitable are being launched at a faster pace than even in 1999. The problem is, without the huge marketing budgets of 1999–2000 behind the launches, you could easily have missed some of the latest online tools to make investing a whole lot easier.

The value of any tool should be measured by one criterion: does it solve a long-standing private investor problem. These next generation tools all do, moving well beyond providing just stock prices, news, simple charting, and company data.

Active trader tools

Active traders are best served by online investment innovation. Broker trading platforms often now resemble professional trading screens, making it easier to analyse stocks with a wealth of information like news, charts, prices, positions, analysis, all on one page.

For instance, IGIndex just launched a trading platform after two years of development. LIFFEinvestor.com released a trading simulator for universal stock futures (futures contracts on shares like Vodafone), and Deal4Free. com's revamped its "market maker" trading platform. GNI.co.uk continues to have one of the most professional-looking trading screens for clients.

But profits are not guaranteed of course. These are powerful tools, but skill takes experience. Novice traders chasing volatile share prices and losing money is common.

Value stock engines

Aside from active traders, what about long-term investors? We know value stocks are increasingly popular. Surely the 50% fall in the FTSE 100 since its peak created many good value stocks. Indeed, legendary value investor Warren Buffet's investment fund Berkshire Hathaway was up over 20% in 2002.

But even with ample company data, finding value stocks takes an understanding of accounting and days of detailed research of hundred of stocks.

Sites like valuengine.com are of a new generation. It does the hard analysis and tells you for instance that Microsoft trading at $25 is currently 30% undervalued. But, more importantly, based on thousands of calculations, it is only expected to appreciate 4% in 12 months. So don't rush in based on valuation alone.

Is it any good at finding value stocks? Its portfolio has returned on average just under 30% annually since 1999. Hedge funds and even the Bank of New York use the reports.

But what if U.S. stock picking is not for you? For U.K. investors Sharescope software (www.sharescope.co.uk) hunts for value stocks, or indeed any other, but based on criteria investors themselves must enter.

Similarly, Hemscott.net provides the raw data, but you must know what to look for. Thankfully, outstanding sites like www.quicken.com tell you what search criteria some of the best professional investors use.

Portfolio tools

Five years ago, we would have settled for a website simply telling us which stocks we own. However, do you know if you have the optimal mix of stocks, cash and other financial assets for your risk profile and financial goals? Could you significantly improve performance by simply switching one stock for another?

These are questions most private investors do not realize they should be asking, and probably too complex for most independent financial advisors to answer. Riskgrades.com continues to be the most innovative in this area for U.K. and U.S. investors, allowing them to use its site to answer all the above questions. But be warned. Such analysis takes concentrated effort and time.

Finding stock pickers

Sites such as www.validea.com, marketocracy.com, and Hulbert Financial (www.marketwatch.com) have all recently increased their services. Each solves the investor problem: "Who consistently is a good stock picker?"

After all, you're not working on the presumption that whoever is on financial TV is a good stock picker, are you? Who validated their records? At least with footballers or other performance-related professionals you have some idea of how good they are. Even those in the "performance industries" like pop stars have charts. But do you know if the fund manager performing a turn on CNBC is at number 1 or number 1001? Thankfully, now technology can help you.

Validea.com now tracks the records of 7000 experts and 75,000 of their stock picks from 30 media sources. Marketocracy.com now has hundreds of private investor track records and offers subscribers access to the stock picks of the consistently outstanding. A fund even tracks the best investors. And it outperformed the Dow in 2001.

Hulbert Financial Digest ranks and profiles more than 160 investment newsletters and the over 500 portfolios it recommends, telling you their performance on a risk-adjusted basis up to 20-year time-frames. That should avoid high, risk-taking, one-year wonders.

Although such sites stubbornly only track U.S. stock pickers, thankfully U.K. brokers offer U.S. investing cheaper than ever. U.K. stock picker Redskyresearch.com cleverly has a fund investing in its own small cap picks which has outperformed the FTSE Small Cap index.

Mechanical buy and sell signals

But what about computer-generated buy and sell signals? Surely, with computing power, we no longer need to rely on human stock picks? U.K. firm Quantigma tests trading systems based on mathematical equations to find stock market patterns to see which are the most profitable. It then generates buy and sell signals.

Its latest product is Tradequant, launched this year through financial portal ADVFN.com. "It has seen a sustained increase in the number of subscribers of up to 30% month on month," proclaims Quantigma CEO, William Akerman.

But you need nerves of steel with some of these automated systems. For instance, one system, Enigma, by Quantigma, generated 114% return since 1999 on a portfolio of 11 stocks beating a buy and hold strategy which only produced –38%. But the worst-point "drawdown" was 92% (fall in your trading capital).

"Signal Seeker" is a powerful and innovative tool launched by Recognia.com on Etrade.co.uk. It scans thousands of stocks to find price patterns which have historically preceded large price moves; a useful starting place for trading ideas. But it is easy to freeze from idea over-load too.

Why haven't we heard about them?
If these products are so good, how come you will have missed them? Because big marketing budgets no longer exist. Most brokers who can profit from providing you with such tools focus on promoting them to their existing customers. That is far cheaper than incurring the expense of trying to acquire new ones. Indeed, 80% of European executives from leading

financial institutions surveyed by researchers Forrester said that despite the
economic climate, they continue to innovate to retain existing customers.

So, you will only hear about many of these tools if you are an existing
broker client. The online investing revolution continues, but with far less
hype.

**I thought all this online trading lark was behind us. Are you
seriously telling me online investing is growing?**
Yes and no. You are right, the industry overpredicted online investing growth.
Back in 2000, JP Morgan, for instance, predicted there would be 17.1 million
European and 27 million U.S. online traders by 2003. Actually, there are now
around 5 million in Europe, according to Forrester. But on conservative estimates, it does expect that number to double to 10 million by 2007.

So how many online investors are in the U.K.?
According to industry research by APCIMS (the Association of Private
Client Investment Managers and Stockbrokers), there are around 400,000.

That doesn't seem a lot.
Well, they account for 32% of all retail stock trades, say Forrester. Share
ownership promotion group Proshare's research claims 6 million U.K.
investors are prepared to consider online investing.

But they don't trade online that much do they?
True, there were only an average 1.5 trades per internet investor in the last
quarter of 2002, according to APCIMS (there were over 16 at the internet
peak). And more account growth seems to continue: "Despite the dire
market conditions, we've typically attracted 250 or more new accounts per
week," says MD of Ample, Chris Bratchford.

**Okay, so online investing is slowly picking up, but it's nothing to get
excited about, is it?**
Actually, active online trading is booming after the crash of 2000–1, but not
in shares. For instance, in the last three months of 2002, Deal4Free.com
transacted 581,000 equity-based CFDs (contracts for differences which
mimic share price moves but have no stamp duty) and spread bet trades
online. That's almost the same as all the execution-only (which means without stock advice) trades transacted online by the London Stock Exchange's
26 member online stockbrokers.

"City Index has opened three times as many spread-betting accounts in
March 2003 than March 2002. Volumes of trades (unlike conventional

online stockbrokers) are at their highest levels (up over 100% from last year), and clients are generally trading bigger sizes", says City Index CEO Clive Cooke.

Even "mainstream" online stockbrokers like E*Trade offer CFD trading.

But it's not just online trading in these products. Euronext.liffe U.K.'s equity options volume in January 2003 was the second highest ever, even more than during the dot-com boom. And stock futures (futures on stocks like Vodafone and like CFDs without stamp duty) which it launched in January 2001 traded nearly 900,000 contracts in March 2003 – the best month ever. 2005 launches include www.worldspreads.com.

Next you will be telling me dot-coms are doing well.
Well, umm, I know it is not the done thing to talk about dot-coms, but the funny thing is that even an active trader financial portal like ADVFN.com plc is showing increasing revenues – it passed the £1m mark for the second half of 2002. It even has a competitor now in Moneyam.com.

Okay, so is this day trading all over again? And who is doing it? Don't tell me it is twenty-year-old layabouts with rich parents raised on a diet of computer games and without a job?
As David Buik of Cantor Index puts it:

> We are seeing loads of new clients, who are not toying at it. They don't have a bet at 9am, set off for the golf course and hope to have made a few quid by 2pm. Sadly many disenchanted spread betters from the old school have left the fray. They will return if and when the signs of a sustained bull market reappear.

These traders are making short-term bets on stock and index direction, up or down, based on price charts or news. For instance, a $100 per point up bet on Vodafone in the morning results in a $1000 profit if it is up 10 points by the afternoon.

But equally a $1000 loss if they get it wrong. So why don't they bet a smaller amount for a longer time?
Well, they want to make a lot of money quickly. They see holding for a long period risky; anything could happen overnight.

Ah, so these active trader products are the way to make money? Isn't that what everyone thought back in 1999 with online investing?
No, you're missing the point. These are all tools. They have advantages like being able to profit from a falling price. But you still need skill.

Okay, there are some big wins; David Buik of Cantor Index told me that one "intrepid punter" made $2.5m.

However, none of the brokers I spoke to would tell me how many of their clients were losing money. Deal4Free.com's CEO, Roger Hynes, did say that over the past 2–3 weeks, "the bears who were loath to release their short positions have taken substantial losses ... however the signal we are currently receiving from our clients is that this sharp rise is merely a blip on the overall downtrend of the markets."

Okay, anything else?
Well, don't read too much into this, but www.trade2win.co.uk even advertises forthcoming day-trading seminars. It's déjà vu all over again – as they say!

Other investing problems and solutions you will not find in the financial press

Sooner or later you will ask yourself whether you should add to a losing stock position. The reasoning will be tempting; "if it was good at $100, then it must be better at $80." Such lore is especially popular on online bulletin boards.

But stop. This and other trading myths are costly, yet pervasive – they burrow around in online portals disguised as "underground investment secrets" awaiting the unwitting. Read what the professional traders say first and it will save you money.

Take "buying more at a lower price," or another variation of this, "pyramiding." The idea is that by buying more stock as the price falls, you reduce your average purchase price and so lower your breakeven point.

For instance, if you bought $5000 of Microsoft stock at $100, then another $5000 worth when the stock halved in price to $50, the point at which you would break even moves from $100 to only $66. It is tempting.

Don't do it. Trading is not about "getting a win" on any one trade; it is about limiting your losses and maximizing your gains over all your trades. If you "average down," you're simply less diversified and own twice as much of a company whose price keeps falling. That's fine if you think it is the best place out of 3000 listed stocks for your money, bad if you just want to "get a win."

Moreover, novice investors often confuse price with value. I know my wife does when shopping. A falling price does not mean a cheaper stock. The value of a stock can be measured by earnings, assets it holds, and other ways. A falling price could simply reflect lower expectations of value.

The investor should instead consider: "In which stock can I best make a return?" It would be great coincidence if the answer is "the very same one which has been returning me a loss."

Another favorite among bulletin boardsters is "pound or dollar cost averaging." It is a sensible idea but overstated. For example, if you had $12,000 that you wanted to invest in a stock, they would tell you to invest $1000 per month over a year, rather than investing the whole amount immediately. The rationale is that you will automatically be purchasing more shares when the price is low, and fewer shares when the price is high.

However, since 1950, dollar cost averaging with the S&P 500 has actually failed to beat investing the lump sum at the start of the year in two years out of three. Of course, cost averaging will win if your start date falls right before a dramatic crash (like October 1987) or at the start of an overall 12-month slump (like most of 2000).

Since we are playing with numbers, it's worth remembering two further tricks that the markets play.

First is the "it's down 40%, so it only has to rise 40% to break even" mistake. If a stock moves down, say, 40%, then it has to rise more, a whopping 66%, before you are back to breakeven point. So think again, the next time someone on a bulletin board argues that the stock is "only down 40%."

Equally, if the stock moves up 40%, then it only has to move down just 28% for you to get all the way back down to the breakeven point. So a 40% rise does not afford you as much protection from a downturn as you might have thought.

I did a straw poll of 25 private investors, asking them the answer to the above "40% problems." Two got the right answers.

The best protection for investors from such myths is through greater financial education at school and on broker sites. A few websites, such as www.practicalmoneyskills.com and www.proshare.org rightly ensure a $5 mistake today does not become a $5000 mistake tomorrow.

Yet another trick the market plays with numbers is the "a stock that drops 90% can't go much lower" myth. If a stock drops 90%, you may well reason that it does not have much further to fall and is worth "a punt" or worth keeping hold of, or even buying more. Indeed, some investors only look for such stocks.

Well, if a stock is down 90%, you would probably concede that it could easily move down 95%. What is the change in value of your investment if that happens? No, not 5%, but 50%, because if a stock drops 90%, then halves, it is down 95%.

The problem is private investors often make investment decisions on where the price once was ($100), rather than where it is now ($10), which is why they reason, "surely being down 90%, it does not have much further to go."

Would you normally be willing to accept a 50% loss? Perversely, we are more willing to accept a relatively large loss (50%) if we have already suffered even larger losses (90%).

The professional investor does not think like that. The correct reasoning should be: "Where can I get the best return for the risk I am willing to take at this point; in this investment or some other?"

Sadly, private investors often have a fixation for making back their losses in the same stock in which they incurred them.

Mark Twain had the best advice for the investor who, loaded with market myths, becomes overly confident in his abilities: "April. This is one of the peculiarly dangerous months to speculate. The others are July, October, December, January, March, May …"

My sites: Investor education
www.moneychimp.com *****
www.practicalmoneyskills.com ***
www.proshare.org ****
www.investorwords.com ****
http://money.cnn.com/pf/101/ ***
http://www.investorsalley.com/money/education/ ****
http://news.bbc.co.uk/1/hi/business/business_basics/default.stm ****
www.moneyfacts.co.uk ****

Too many stocks

How many stocks does a financial TV channel mention in a day? Easily 100. With so much market information, how do you avoid stock ideas overload? Or perhaps you have the opposite problem – can't get enough good ideas? A new breed of web tools, "trade spotters," hunts for stock ideas promising outstanding returns. They do what no human can – scan millions of data points. Some even automatically execute trades for you. Scary? Or the answer for busy investors? It might mean you never need to look at a company annual report ever again.

Three types of websites spew forward computer-generated stock ideas; "momentum," "value," and "DIY". Before you think all such products are offering "snake-oil" – you should know that one is created by a professor of finance at Yale University.

"Value and growth" stock sites claim their computers do what professional stock analysts do, only better. They scan the financial minutiae of companies and then value stocks based on their expected future earnings and dividends and compare that with their existing prices. All this in milliseconds. That's more MBAs out of a job then.

Valuengine.com for instance calculated for me last January that Microsoft, then trading at $25, was 30% undervalued. The stock was up 25% nine months later.

Are these "engines" any good? Unfortunately, the "true" value and so "true" price of a stock may never be "discovered" by the market and so the stock price languishes for years.

Nevertheless, Valuengine.com says its portfolio has returned on average just under 30% annually since 1999. Hedge funds and even the Bank of New York use their reports.

DIY and automatic execution sites require traders to come up with their own ideas of what trading strategies might work, program them into a website and then the engine will scan thousands of stocks to generate buy and sell signals. Not surprisingly, such sites are for the hardcore trader. It's certainly not easy programming ideas, take it from me. The sites report on the profitability of your trading strategy on historical data and will also show the largest single losses, worst case scenarios and around 200 other evaluations of your system.

Some, like Tradestation.com will even automatically place trades through a broker – no human intervention required; just leave your money and come back later! Unbelievably, this is a popular service for U.S. stock investors.

Finally, "momentum" sites scan thousands of stocks to find price patterns which have historically preceded large price moves. A simple idea. If certain price patterns precede, say, a 10% rise in Microsoft, on 8 out of 10 past occasions, should we bet on whether 10% rise will follow the same price pattern in the future?

The mathematician will tell you that even if you throw eight consecutive "heads," it still means there is only a 50% chance of "heads" on the next coin toss. The systems trader, however, will tell you that stock price patterns reflect the sum of market psychology and sentiment which regularly repeats itself in price patterns.

But there is more to trading than getting buy and sell signals. Should you bin all your investment magazines and entrust your money to a website? First consider these pointers from an old hand.

Is it too good to be true, after all, many sites only charge subscribers $100 annually and even have a money-back guarantee? So test the signals on paper over the money-back period. What proportion of the signals worked? If three out of five worked – it is too few to tell.

More importantly, did you follow them? Many net traders lose money, not because of their stock picks, but because their lifestyles do not permit active monitoring. For them longer term investing, not these market-timing sites, is the only recourse.

The best system is not the most profitable one on back-testing, but the one you are most likely to follow. So consider the number of winning trades to losses, the number of consecutive losing trades, the largest single losing trade, the drop in trading capital from peak to trough. Are you really going to follow a system that promises 100% returns but along the way you face 10 consecutive losing trades and lose half your capital?

And before you get too excited about the spectacular historic returns, remember that many of these sites are coy about mentioning commission costs, "slippage" (the difference in share price between when you get the signal and the price you can actually trade in the market) – and the spread between the bid and the ask price as well as stamp duty.

If you had followed one site for Diageo and allowed for a realistic slippage of 2.5%, you end up with a loss of 9% after 25 trades. If you had wrongly ignored slippage, the site would have indicated an unrealistic unachievable gain of 50%. Experienced traders will tell you that the more trades that are needed for any given profit, the more important small differences in prices become.

The lesson is that if you want to avoid a lot of hard work in finding stock picks going forward, then you need to do some hard work now to test these systems.

My sites: Momentum
www.dow-trading-system.com **
www.dreamtai.com/index.htm ***
www.timingcube.com ***
www.iquant.com ****
www.recognia.com ****

Value systems
www.valuengine.com *****
www.quicken.com *****
www.stockworm.com ***
www.vectorvest.com ****

DIY/automatic execution
www.tradestation.com *****
www.equis.com ****
www.nirv.com ***

It's a business

Only by treating their trading like a business do private investor traders discover whether they should hang up their mouses. The harsh reality for many is they should. These are some of the likely costs:

■ Start-up costs are the first to consider, including computer costs. Let's assume you spent $1200 on hardware and assume that its lifetime is three years, the cost attributable for this year is $400.

■ Running costs need accounting too. Researching stock picks even on excellent free sites such as www.moneyguru.co.uk and www.european investor.com requires internet access. Flat rate internet access packages will typically cost $150 annually.

■ Software and datafeeds are another running cost. Assuming you use a popular software package, add around $1000 to your annual running cost.

■ If you subscribe to an online trading research or tip site, add another annual charge of $60.

■ You will also want some trading books (at discount through www. easyvalue.com or www.global-investor.co.uk) and probably take a couple of courses through, say, www.trainingforprofit.co.uk, www. investingbetter.com or www. success-events.co.uk. So add another $1000 annually.

■ Commissions are a major running cost of trading of course – even with discount online brokers. Assume a typical $15 per trade. Although, visit www.gomez.com to see cheaper online brokers. If you place three trades each week, add another $2340.

So before stamp duty and spreads (the difference between the bid and ask price representing the amount you would lose if you sold the stock an instant after buying), your total fixed costs (those that don't increase with the trade size) amount to $5000 annually.

Now, on a $20,000 portfolio that means you require an astounding 25% return annually just to beat those costs. And that's before capital gains tax too. Remember, Warren Buffett only achieves 24% annually on average – and that made him one of the world's richest men. If you're not Warren Buffett and expect a more typical 15% average annual return, then you would still need a £33,000 portfolio to beat these fixed costs. But with a $100,000 portfolio you need a more reasonable 5% increase to take care of the above fixed costs. How many online traders have such a large portfolio? Of course some investors use spreadbetting companies like worldspread. com to trade without so much capital. Clearly, too few online traders have the trading capital to overcome costs and consequently need improbable returns to make any profit.

Even if you could average a Buffet-like 24% annual return on your $20,000 portfolio, you're still not being well compensated. Imagine that you want to spend six hours a week researching and monitoring your positions. If you then eke an astounding $2000 profit after all costs, you are "being paid" $6 per hour for your time.

Instead, those with smaller sums of capital wishing to increase return on time should change how they trade and consider investing in funds. Even if a fund provides half the return you can yourself, it will sharply increase your return per hour.

If you want to be self-directed, the catch-22 is that with a large portfolio you could end up losing a lot more in absolute terms and if you are a novice you are more likely to lose. The solution? Paper trade and develop your skills first or trade with a small portfolio, but expect to treat it as a training activity and not a profitable one initially.

To increase my returns per hour, I looked for trading systems that produced larger returns from fewer trades. For instance, I reduced day trading on futures which involve many trades (and hence a lot of time and increased commissions) to holding positions that produced the same returns over a longer trading period (which require close monitoring only when the position is close to exit targets).

Also, like all good businesspeople, remember that cutting costs can be a false economy; throwing away those subscriptions and data sites will certainly hit your ability to make returns. Of course, you could always sell your PC to raise online trading capital!

And the prize for Best Fund Manager goes to ... you – the online investor. In second place is the professional full-time fund manager.

Can private investors do it?

Most definitely yes. The top 100 private investors on Marketocracy.com not only outperformed 99.8% of all U.S. professional fund managers during the second quarter of 2001, they also outperformed all the main market indices too.

And these extraordinary online investors are not simply outperforming the professionals by taking excessive risks. Marketocracy.com requires them to abide by strict rules that all online investors should consider.

Firstly, no position can exceed 25% of your total portfolio value. Secondly, half your portfolio must comprise positions under 5% each. Thirdly, you must classify whether your investment style is growth, value or a blend of the two. This last rule ensures an added professionalism and discipline.

So who are these online investors? Mike is a civil engineer at a water treatment plant. His return in the second quarter of 2001 was 65%. Michael, a postmaster, achieved 56% and Vladimir, a social scientist, 40%. The Dow rose a paltry 6% over the same period.

What are these exceptional online traders buying that is producing such outstanding results? Curiously, there are quite a few technology stocks including Foundary Networks, Advanced Micro Devices, EMC, Juniper Networks, Sun Microsystems, and Priceline.com. Visit www.marketocracy.com to see what else they hold.

Measuring your own portfolio performance isn't straightforward, however. Investors tend to overstate their performance because of mathematical or psychological errors. Mathematical errors include the (in)famous case of the Beardstown Ladies who included cash inflows as part of their returns.

Psychological errors involve revising history; "Oh, I had an off day when I picked those two stocks, I'll leave those out of my calculations."

The math is a little tricky. Imagine your $1000 investment grows to $1500 after three months (that is, R1 = a 50% gain). You then add another $1000. The $2500 then appreciates to $4000 over the next nine months (R2 = 60% gain). What is your total return?

Total Return = R1 + R2 + R1 × R2   *or* $0.5 + 0.6 + 0.5 \times 0.6 = 140\%$

The total return is not simply the profit/capital, that is, 2000/2000 (100%), because your profit was earned on different amounts of capital. For instance, if you produced a 100% return on $1000 and then introduced $10,000 into your account on the last day of the year, your return is still virtually 100%.

Having calculated your performance, how do you beat the fund managers? Exploit the advantages of being small, explains Peter Siris in *Guerilla Investing*. That often means small cap investments.

With billions to invest, many funds can't invest even 0.5% of their capital without owning the company outright. Yet it's small cap stocks that produce higher returns than large ones over a long time-frame, according to research by Nobel prizewinners Merton Miller and Myron Scholes. Moreover, Ben Warwick in *In Search of Alpha* confirms that with more money under management, pension funds confined to large caps find it increasingly difficult to generate alpha: market-beating returns.

As well as investing in small caps, how else can you beat the fund managers? By adjusting the number of stocks in your portfolio. Robert Hagstrom's *The Warren Buffett Portfolio* explains that a portfolio with 250 stocks is less likely to beat the market than one with 15 stocks. But the fewer the stocks, the more volatile the returns (the beta), that is, the greater chance you will trail the market too.

Hagstrom suggests that Buffett goes for the latter approach – "put all your eggs in one basket and watch the basket like a hawk."

If alpha and beta is all Greek to you, then of course consider investing through a fund manager, as should those who simply do not have the time or inclination to do their own stock picking. But don't be surprised if your civil engineer neighbor comes home from work in a Ferrari.

Trading around earnings: profits and protection

If you watch financial TV you'll know we're earnings junkies. Shareholders of Ashtead Group were presumably pleased in 2001 when they saw the company's share price rise 30% in a six-month period. Then disaster struck. The company's earnings were released, and the stock plunged to trade at levels seen years earlier. It's why I loathe trading around earnings announcements. For me it's where trading most closely resembles gambling.

Earnings are great news for financial TV because they occur quarterly in the U.S. Why is this good news? Because the "booker" whose job is to book guests has an easy time. Whatever makes life easier for the booker gets on TV.

Thankfully, all seasoned online traders know that there are ways to protect your stockholdings during such turbulent times – and maybe even profit from the volatility.

First consider a hedge. For instance, imagine you own 1000 shares in Barclays trading at 2200p. Fearing a drop post an earnings announcement, you can sell short (sell first with the intention of buying later) one Barclays universal stock future. Each stock future represents 1000 shares and traces the stock price movement. If Barclays does indeed drop to, say, 2100p, the loss you would have in the stock would be offset by the gain in the stock future. See www.liffe.com on stock futures.

Of course such hedging strategies can be used whenever you expect a short-term price decline and do not want to sell a long-term shareholding. If the decline becomes prolonged or permanent, then at least you've lost less than you otherwise would. And if the stock recovers, then you made additional profit during the falls.

How many Marconi shareholders wished they'd hedged their positions instead of helplessly watch them fall?

Even if hedging is not for you, there is still protection from falls. Consider a study[12] last year which suggests that large trades associated with price changes before an announcement produce greater permanent price effects ("send a stronger signal to other investors") than similar trades after the announcement.

For instance, Scottish Radio's precipitous fall in 2002 following its earnings announcement was preceded by some very heavy volume corresponding with price falls.

This suggests that clues to whether you should sell your holdings may come before the announcement and not necessarily from the announcement itself: sell if on heavy volume the stock price falls before the announcement. FTMarketWatch.com provides free price charts with volume and Citywire.co.uk provides good analysis of such activity.

Do you want to be a more aggressive trader around earnings announcements? Then try to profit from the volatility.

OCO (one cancels other) orders try to capture a gain whether a stock rises or falls. Take Logica in 2001 before its earnings announcement, when it was trading at 1600p. Assuming an OCO order on the day of the announcement to buy the stock if the price exceeded 1625p or sell if it dropped to 1575p.

The reasoning: if the market had liked the earnings figures, the price would probably have risen to 1625p and then continued upwards. But if the market found the figures disappointing, the price would probably fall to 1575p and then continue lower – at which cheaper price you could have bought the stock to close the trade at a profit.

And in the case of Logica you would have had a 20% return in two days as the stock rose.

Unfortunately, few online brokers offer this service, and those who do (www.deal4free.com, www.cantorindex.co.uk, www.gni.co.uk) tend to cater to the "sophisticated" investor.

So, with all these strategies, why do I still loathe earnings announcements? Because any existing trade will be rocked by such an upcoming report.

Employing any of the above strategies, rather like a captain having to divert from steering toward rough seas, expends time and effort.

Consequently, my preferred strategy at earnings time is to avoid placing short-term positions in a stock which has an announcement due in the subsequent two weeks. It's too much of a gamble on the outcome of the report. Consider it the equivalent of checking the weather forecast before sailing. Ft.com will tell you which companies are due to release earnings.

And what of the Ashtead shareholders who saw years of gains wiped out in minutes? One hopes they knew about hedging and OCOs – but suspect they too have grown to loathe earnings announcements.

Leading U.S. earnings sites include: www.whispernumber.com; www.earningswhispers.com; www.streetiq.com.

Is the rally for real?

We are kings of the short term on financial TV. It is disposable. We consume it and bin it. If you watch it often enough you may even think it is recycled. And sooner or later we mention a rally. The issue is can the rally be trusted?

The internet makes tracking earnings figures easier than ever – easier to get the information, easier to track trends, and quicker and easier to react to these signals. But, there's only one problem: none of it helps. Most of this information only tells you the quantity of earnings, not the quality. The investor's lesson of the twenty-first century is that the *quantity of earnings is as questionable as an Andersen audit.* Remember Enron, Tyco, Qwest, Global Crossing, Adelphia, WorldCom?

Even Disney confessed to overstating profits in 2002 (Mickey Mouse figures?). No, to find quality of earnings means being shrewd – and shrewd online. In looking for quality, these are the types of rising profits that I like – in order of preference:

1. Increased profits from increased revenue growth. If sales are growing and this is adding to profits, especially with wider profits margins, then that gets my vote. Just watch out for tricks like revenues showing an increase because of counting money that is expected but not in hand.

2. If profits stem from increased market share but this is achieved from a lower profit margin, then it suggests price-cutting to increase volume. That can be fine in the short term, but longer term I do not rate those earnings as necessarily high quality.

3. Profits from cost-cutting. I rate these even lower quality earnings improvement. Cost-cutting can be a short-term benefit before longer term profitability is hit. Imagine for instance companies cutting on

research and development. This year's earnings go up, but in five years you pay the real price for potentially underinvesting.

4. The lowest quality earnings in my view stem from one-off asset sales, that is, exceptional items in the accounts. Here, it is sometimes the most valuable assets being sold at a desperate discount.

And if, like Disney, you have to restate your earnings, you are out of my "stocks to consider" list. Research[13] published in October 2002 found that companies that had to restate their financial results tended to have "poor quality earnings." Restated financial results can be devastating for shareholders. The research also found that firms suffered stock price declines averaging 25% around the time the restatement was announced.

In short, I prefer cash to noncash, regularity to irregularity, and no restatements. Fall short of that, and I will move to the next stock thanks.

Lower quality earnings do not necessarily indicate poor financial reporting, but they often relate to transactions that are more subjective or have a higher degree of risk or uncertainty.

But good quality earnings do not necessarily mean a good value stock. Test the value using the sophisticated free online tools. For instance, the exceptional www.quicken.com/investments uses a "discounted earnings model" to calculate share values. It works by estimating future earnings based on analysts forecasts and recent results, and then discounts them (because a $10m profit today is worth more today than it would be worth in five years) to the present to arrive at a valuation for today. ValuePro.net uses a discounted cash flow model to calculate the stock's fair value.

All a lot of hard work? We private investors do have advantages. A study from Michigan University and Purdue University found private investor earnings estimates on the web were more accurate than analysts' estimates. Indeed, these earnings whispers also explain why stocks fall on "better-than-expected" earnings results; the results were better than analysts expected, but not better than the "earnings whisper" available from a select few private investor sites.

Heed the words of Arthur Levitt, the former head of the main U.S. markets regulator: "I fear we are witnessing an erosion in the quality of earnings … managing may be giving way to manipulation; integrity may be losing out to illusion." Next time you see a rally, ask about the quality of earnings of the stocks driving it.

My sites: Company accounts
www.carol.co.uk
www.corpreports.co.uk
www.edgar-online.com
www.wilink.com

Valuation models based on earnings
www.valuengine.com
www.valuepro.net
www.quicken.com/investments

Earnings data
www.whispernumber.com
www.firstcall.com
www.zacks.com

Quality of earnings information
http://aaahq.org/qoe/
www.fasb.org
www.hoylecpa.com/CPE/lesson002/Lesson.htm
www.investment.com/glossary/qdefs/qualityofearnings.html
www.sec.gov/news/speech/speecharchive/1999/spch276.htm
www.deloitte.com/dtt/cda/doc/content/DTQEfinal(1).pdf

We are always telling you to buy

Come rain or shine, 24/7, we on financial TV are always selling you the same old story – here are some stocks and here are some fund managers with their, usually, positive views. It's as if fund managers are on the investment equivalent of Viagra – they are always overexcited.

But as an investment strategy, is it better to buy in bear markets and sell in bull conditions ("hunt the bear") or buy during bull markets and hold cash in bear markets ("ride the bull")?

Research published in April 2003 by Guidolin and Timmermann revealed an unexpected answer for market beating returns.[14] But the researchers also say that to achieve the returns private investors will need professional advice. On this part they are wrong.

After all, in the web age there are ample tools to assist private investors without resorting to potentially costly professional advisors. Indeed, with many stock funds underperforming the market and product misselling scandals such as Equitable Life, professional advisors are not exactly the people investors trust. Most of these online tools are better than those that professionals use anyway.

Guidolin and Timmermann's research finds that an investor with a short horizon should buy stocks in bull markets, but should not do so in a bear market. No difficulty there. In contrast, an investor with a long horizon should hunt the bear and buy stocks in bear markets and reduce holdings in bull markets.

So what is so unexpected about the research? If we are near the bottom of a bear market, then a rebalancing from bonds and cash into equities for the longer term investor is due. Yet that is exactly the opposite of what many private and professional investors do. In 2002 $27 billion flowed from U.S. stock funds, and $140 billion moved into bond funds, according to the Investment Company Institute.

So what happens if you do the reverse of what the research suggests? Many investors buy stocks in a bull market. But profitable investors do not hold on to those stocks bought in the bull market for the long haul. How many saw Centrica, Shire, Amvescap all more than double in the bull run between 1999 to March 2001, then held on as they all gave up those gains subsequently.

The research also improves on the traditional view of constructing a portfolio. One method suggests that you subtract your age from 100. The resulting number is how much of your portfolio should be invested in stocks. For example, if you are 35 years old, 65% of your portfolio could be allocated in stocks and 25% to bonds and always a constant 10% to cash.

But the traditional view of holding more stocks the longer the horizon is incorrect, argue the researchers. Such a strategy only works in bear states.

The research suggests, based on 1970–2000 estimates, a risk-averse investor facing a bear market should have invested only 6% in the FTSE 100 index if the horizon was one month, 19% with a horizon of two years, and 32% with 10 years. The markets in 2001–02 would have handsomely rewarded the choice to stay 81% in cash or bonds.

As an active short-term trader, I have a longer term portfolio of value stocks. In the bull market ending in March 2000 finding value stocks was difficult.

So what does a long-term investor do in a bull market? Suffer, as they find it impossible to find value stocks for the long term; as Warren Buffett admitted in 2000 when his fund had one of its worst years.

But equally, in a bearish market it is easier to find longer term value stocks than short-term momentum ones; that's precisely why through bull and bear markets I like holding both short-term and long-term portfolios. Anyway, during the transition phase one simply does not know if the market is bullish or bearish, so one should hedge one's bets.

So how do we find longer term stocks during bear markets and momentum stocks in a bull market? Professional advisors have met their match: for the former there are ample sophisticated stock valuation online tools. For the latter, charting sites and stock signals tools spot rises.

Of course you should remember, there is an alternative viewpoint to all this portfolio pondering. It comes from a Nobel prizewinner, Paul Samuelson; "You shouldn't spend much time on your investments. That will tempt you to up the plants and see how the roots are doing and that's very bad for the roots."

My sites: Asset allocation tool
www.vanguard.com,
www.warburg.com/portfolio.cfm
www.fidelity.com.
www.asset-allocation.co.uk
www.tdwaterhouse.co.uk

Help finding long-term stocks in a bear market
www.quicken.com
www.hemscott.net
www.valueengine.com

Help finding short-term stocks in a bull market
www.bigcharts.com
www.wallstreetcity.com
signal seeker: www.etrade.co.uk

Notes

1   G. Soros (1998) *The Crisis of Global Capitalism*, Little Brown.
2   L.L. Lopes (1994) Psychology and Economics. *Annual Review of Psychology*, **45**: 197–227.
3   E. Stephen (1998) "Anchoring and Adjustment in Economic Forecasts". Conference on Judgemental Inputs, University College, London, November.
4   D. Hilton (1998) *Psychology and the City*, **38**, (www.csfi.fsnet.co.uk).
5   Dempster M.A.H. and Romahi, Y.S. "Intraday FX trading: An evolutionary reinforcement learning approach" Centre for Financial Research, Judge Institute of Management, University of Cambridge, Working Paper 3/2002. (www.jims. cam.ac.uk).
6   "Stock Returns Following Profit Warnings" by Professor George Buckley, Richard Harris and Renata Herrerias of University of Exeter presented at the Royal Economic Society's 2002 Annual Conference, March 26 2002.
7   Eugene Fama and Kenneth French 1996 "Multifactor Explanations of Asset Pricing Anomalies", *Journal of Finance*, **51**: 55–84.
8   Terence Odean 1998 "Are Investors Reluctant to Realise their Losses?", *Journal of Finance*, **53**: 1887–1934.
9   George Bulkley and Richard Harris "Irrational Analysts' Expectations as a Cause of Excess Volatility in Stock Prices", *Economic Journal* (March 1997); **107**:

359–71."Consistent Failure to Accurately Predict Mean Earnings: An Evaluation of U.S. Security Analysts Forecasts", Working Paper, November 2001 by Ahmed El-Galfy & William Forbes.

10 Denis Hilton (1999) *Psychology and the City,* Centre for the Study of Financial Innovation.

11 *The Economist*, April 1994, p. 86.

12 Markku Vieru "Essays on Investors' Trading Policy around Interim Earnings Announcements", August 2000, University of Oulu, Finland.

13 S. Richardson (Wharton), I.Tuna (Wharton), M.Wu (HK University) "Predicting Earnings Management", October 2002 http://accounting.wharton.upenn.edu/faculty/richardson/RTW-Restatements.pdf.

14 Massimo Guidolin and Allan Timmermann "Economic Implication of Bull and Bear Regimes in U.K. Stock Returns", presented at the Royal Economic Society', 2003 Annual Conference, 9th April 2003.

CHAPTER 3

Shhh … We produce programming and papers which get sponsors and advertisers – Oops!

What we are actually experiencing is not an information explosion. It is an explosion of data. Data provide neither enlightenment nor knowledge. What we are really experiencing may be access to excess. The mere fact that there is more data available does not mean that people either want it or can use it meaningfully. **Patricia Glass Schuman**

- Bad stock picks are like drugs
- How good financial products get no exposure
- Products you need to know
- Exchange traded funds (why they offer great advantages)
- Single stock futures (why the product is underutilized)
- What kind of a trader am I?

The media is stock crazy

Below are just some of the stock comments from one weekend of national newspapers. The combined readership would be in the millions. Millions of investors investing millions of pounds. Why do the papers take such a risk? After all they could lose readers if they get it wrong, and inevitably they will, no one is 100% correct. Sure, *no matter how much an investor loses from following newspaper tips he can still afford to buy the paper. (Maybe that's why newspapers are so cheap!)*

Papers take such risks for the same reason lottery tickets are bought each week by people who have lost for the past 600 weeks. We're hoping for a win. As long as investors' eyeballs hit those pages, advertisers will pay the paper. And that is key. *Newspapers with stock tips are like drug pushers* – if the demand is there, even if taking it is not good for you, they will supply and they will make money.

Below is just one day's comment. Beneath it I analyse if they are any good in their picks.

<u>SATURDAY PRESS COMMENT</u>

FT

THE LEX COLUMN comments on J SAINSBURY (conditions in the U.K. food market might tempt leveraged funds; but they would need an extraordinarily competent management team and a brilliant property strategy to justify the gearing required; maybe Brandes can spot this potential dream team; other investors, however, might find better everyday value shopping for TESCO shares), RANK, Advertising (with increasing signs of an economic slowdown, do not buy all the advertising spin), U.S. jobs (a clearer trend in data would be needed to change the Fed's plan for slowly weaning the economy off crisis level interest rates) – ALLIED DOMECQ (shares, on a forward p/e of 13 for this year and 12.4 for next, could be cause for more celebration for the canny investor) – SPECIALITY FINANCE: Decision time looming for Cazenove; as JP Morgan Chase and Lehman Brothers come courting, the 180-year-old City stalwart's days may be numbered – but its historical influence is guaranteed; Cazenove will consider approaches for its fund management division if a potential joint venture with JP Morgan Chase goes ahead (MONEY & BUSINESS p. 3) – Weekend share watch: ITV (investors are hoping that the recently announced autumn schedule will turn the tide before ITV starts negotiating rates with advertisers at the end of the year; the shares might also be lifted by the start of the group's program of disposing of noncore assets), GREGGS (providing the U.K. does not experience an Indian summer and cost pressures do not bite too hard, investors could continue to savour solid progress), DOMINO PRINTING (another good set of figures should propel the stock above the record level of 240 pence in 2000 that was nearly breached in June) – MARSHALLS (on a p/e multiple of 11.5 for 2004, the stock trades at a 15 pct discount to other large-cap material and builders' merchant businesses; that is good value given the attractive dividend yield of 4.7 pct) – GO-AHEAD (trades in line with a fully valued sector; winning the integrated Kent train franchise would provide further upside but a decision is not expected until the middle of next year) – JKX (investors should bear in mind that the higher the rating, the less forgiving the market) – London's casino jackpot is still up for grabs; LONDON CLUBS (offers highest potential returns on reform; the company may prove attractive to a foreign bidder keen to get into the deregulated U.K. casino market) – RANK (not as attractive to a foreign bid but offers security against possible delay to, or ill-considered reform of, the industry)

Guardian

ASTRAZENECA (a good chance Exanta will get regulatory approval in the U.S.) – CAPITA GROUP (spokesperson says an increase in the congestion charge in London would not affect the firm financially) – IP21PO (gossips speculate that next week's results will show that its investments have raised more money and therefore their valuations have increased) – BILLAM/RAB CAPITAL(companies expected to announce a 1.5 mln stg investment into green fuels business TMO Biotec, based in Guildford)

Mail

NORTHUMBRIAN WATER (rumours of an imminent 906 mln stg, or 175 pence-a-share, cash bid from KELDA) – SBS (talk of an imminent announcement) – GRIFFIN MINING (Tuesday's interim statement will be positive) – ULTRAFRAME (subsidiary Four Seasons on receiving end of an adverse jury verdict in the U.S. state of Ohio) – SOUTHAMPTON LEISURE (broker Charles Stanley is a fan) – INVESTMENT EXTRA: HAMWORTHY (worthwhile); with builders earning returns of 20 pct or better, more bids look likely; any mid-sized group, from BELLWAY to REDROW to CREST NICHOLSON, could be a target; WESTBURY at 435.5 pence sells at 5.5 times expected earnings, BEN BAILEY at 426.5 pence at only five times; very cheap; VIROTEC (should a group with 730,000 stg revenues hand out 3.2 mln stg of options?)

Independent

Private Investor: Sally White likes FRAMLINGTON U.K. SELECT OPPORTUNITIES, with its 18 pct in resources companies JPMP NATURAL RESOURCES and M&G GLOBAL BASICS; she says it is probably prudent to take a little profit in NATIONAL GRID TRANSCO and CENTRICA and might consider a little inspection company called SONDEX – Company Spotlight: SUTTON HARBOUR (a solid lock-away) – NORTHUMBRIAN WATER (KELDA bid speculation) – J SAINSBURY (market professionals talk of a move on Sainsbury's by the Reuben brothers) – UNITED BUSINESS MEDIA (analysts suggest that Lord Hollick's decision to step down as chief executive in May makes the media group vulnerable to a bid) – AMEC (finance director sells 96,000 shares at 317 pence) – HAMMERSON (finance director sells 49,000 shares after exercising various options) – THUS (new chairman buys 100,000 shares at 15.25 pence) – NCIPHER (traders bet its upcoming results will impress)

Times

Tempus: RANK (5 pct yield gives sufficient reason to hold on to the shares), GO-AHEAD (sell), MARSHALLS (buy) – BIG FOOD GROUP (rekindled bid rumours offset concerns of weak summer trading) – PD PORTS (talk of downturn in trading)

Telegraph

SBS GROUP (shares in the shell company run by Leo Knifton and Nigel Weller lifted by rumours of possible deals with Alltrue Investments and Oakgate, other shell companies under the same management) – QUESTOR COLUMN: HILTON GROUP (shares have had a good run, but still look a decent long-term bet), ROBERT WISEMAN DAIRIES (avoid), HOME ENTERTAINMENT (looks a promising small-cap pick)

Express

MFI (hopes revive that a long-awaited 1 bln stg management buy-out is about to mate-rialise; also rumours a private equity firm could be planning a deal to keep the key profit driver, the Howden joinery business, but sell the problem British operation to another retailer) – SENIOR (suggestions business is picking up as a result of a recovery in the aerospace sector) – INVOX (talk of a stock overhang) – WHO'S DEALING: THUS GROUP (new chairman buys 100,000 shares at 15.21 pence) – SHARE WHISPER: TELE-UNIT (suggestions that Monday's half-year results will not disappoint) – BROKER'S VIEW: SYNERGY HEALTHCARE (Investec positive)

SUNDAY PRESS COMMENT

The Business

MID-CAP INVESTOR: STANELCO (worth keeping an eye on, but it would be wise to wait the outcome of the BioProgress court case) – AIM INVESTOR: AERO INVENTORY (speculative buy) – BENCHMARK: Ian Watson comments on Royal Mail (the damage to businesses from late or lost mail is incalculable; one more performance like this and (Gordon) Brown should show them (Allan Leighton and Adam Crozier) the red card), Investment banks, France Telecom

Financial Mail on Sunday

STREAM (will make history on Thursday when it becomes the first British company to distribute its results by text message) – COMPANIES AND MARKETS: MORRISONS (company does not expect margins to recover fully for four years following its 3 bln stg takeover of Safeway – three years more than its original estimate), BIG FOOD GROUP (trying to negotiate a deal to open scores of Iceland concessions in Littlewoods stores in an attempt to boost its flagging sales), WPP (set to make a cash-and-shares offer for Grey Global); SECRET DEALINGS: BABCOCK INTERNATIONAL (New Star's AA-rated fund manager Stephen Whittaker bought shares for his U.K. Growth fund last week; he added 70,000 shares to the holding to take it to a little more than 2 mln, or 0.97 pct of the company; his equally rated rival Paul Mumford, has also bought recently, adding 20,000 shares to Cavendish Asset Management's stake in late July to take it to 965,000) – TAKING STOCK: Andrew Leach comments on J SAINSBURY (one name suggested as a suitor is Britain's second-largest retailer by market value, GUS), MATA-LAN, CAIRN ENERGY (appears odds-on that the oil company will join the blue-chip club) – MIDAS: BARCLAYS (buy); MIDAS UPDATE: PENDRAGON (remain worth buying), COSTAIN (keep buying), COUNTRYSIDE PROPERTIES (while an offer may not arrive from chairman Alan Cherry, we believe his interest might flush out a bid from a rival, so we would hold for now)

Sunday Telegraph

BLUE CHIP VALUES: ITV (buy), LONMIN (given the uncertainty, investors should sell the shares) – SMALL CAP COMMENT: MCCARTHY & STONE (buy), AMLIN (buy), COLLINS STEWART TULLETT (buy), HITACHI CAPITAL (worth tucking away) – TAKING STOCK: Edmond Jackson says trading in HONEYGROVE GROUP shares shows how RAB CAPI-TAL, the fund manager, influences the destiny of smaller companies

Sunday Times

JUDGMENT DAY: SHOULD YOU BUY SHARES IN EMAP? Andy Brough, fund manager at Schroders, says look to buy, while Tim Steer, fund manager at New Star, says buy – INSIDE THE CITY: Paul Durman comments on housebuilders (taking the long view, housebuilders are set fair because of the fundamental imbalance between the supply and demand of U.K. housing stock; the main risk is that a future government might sort out the planning problems; WILSON BOWDEN (looks a good bet that it will continue to prosper), SUPERSCAPE (it's high risk, but there will be winners in this sector); MARKET MOLE: COLLINS STEWART TULLETT (since August, Tony Willis, Lazard's star fund manager, has lifted the holding of his Lazard U.K. Alpha unit trust by 340,000 shares to 2.6 mln)

Observer

THROG STREET: Richard Wachman comments on HBOS (assuming HBOS actually fires off a bid (for ABBEY), and assuming it is let through by the regulatory authorities, the shares will eventually become a screaming 'buy' for every broker in the Square Mile), WOOLWORTHS/WH SMITH (at last, Trevor Bish-Jones is getting to grips with Wool-worths' problems; Kate Swann at WH Smith could do worse than take a leaf out of his book), SCOTTISH MEDIA GROUP (time to slim SMG)

Financial Sunday Express

David Parsley comments on VODAFONE (he got wind of the new marketing strategy by the world's biggest mobile phone group last week and the likes of O2, Orange, T-Mobile and 3 should be afraid – Vodafone is coming after the lot of you)

The media is stock crazy – but the journalists are just crazy!

I took one major national newspaper, the *Independent*, and examined the quality of its stock content. In its private investor column, on August 14 2004, Sally White made her "short-term summer punts." They were as follows:

CHACO RESOURCES, GAMING INSIGHT, AURUM MINING, CYBIT, DESIRE PETROLEUM, RAGUSA PETROLEUM, GALLAHER, STANDARD CHARTERED, LAND SECURITIES, GUS, BOC.

Now, I reckon by September 11 2004, summer is over. So how had the above punts done? After all, they were read by hundreds of thousands of readers. I picked some of them at random.

Chaco	This stock is priced at 1.8p (2.5 cents). It has a volatility greater than 93% of all other listed stocks in London. But it's excitement like that, that sells newspapers
Gaming Insight	One of the most illiquid, least traded stocks in the U.K.
Aurum Mining	Same price from pick to end of summer
Cybit	Another least traded, illiquid stock that hardly moves for you to end of summer
Desire Petroleum	Ooops, since the pick to end of summer you lose money
Ragusa	Ooops again, lower than when picked by the end of summer
Gallaher	Nope, another one lower than when picked by the end of summer
Standard Chartered	At last, one that is up … a tiny little bit, since it was picked

What kind of a trader am I?

I am a trend follower, aka a short-term momentum trader going long short. I do technical analysis more than fundamentals and my favorite indicators are the MACD (moving average convergence divergence) and stochastics. I strongly believe in money management and varying the number of long positions and short positions to overall reflect my view of the market. I usually keep positions open for a fortnight and look to have between three to five positions open at a time.

Your trading business plan

What might a trading business plan look like? Have a look at this below:

Assume 7 trades out of 10 are correct
Assume av. 20% return on correct trades: Only enter a trade if you expect 30% return
Assume max. 25% loss on incorrect trades, that is, 0.7 x 20>>0.3 x 25
Assume total original capital of $60,000

Value at risk (VAR)

Assume $12,000 per trade
Therefore risk per trade = 0.25 x $12,000 = $3000, that is, 5% of original capital
If max. 4 open positions at one time then max. VAR = 4 x $3000 = $12,000, that is, 20% of capital
If av. 3 open positions then av. VAR = 3 x $3000 = $9000, that is, 15% of original capital

Annual profit forecast
Expected profit per trade (0.7 x 0.20 x $12,000 = $1680) – (0.3 x 0.25 x $12,000 = $900) = $780 net
Therefore net profit margin = 6.5%
And net annual profit = $780 x 30 trades = *$23,400*
that is, *39% p.a net return on original capital*

Profit optimization variables:

# of trades per annum	(assume constant)
probability of successful trade	(assume constant)
percentage return for a correct trade	(assume constant)
personal ability to stop-losses	(assume constant)
return per trade	(dependant on total capital)

The willingness to hold funds uninvested awaiting real opportunities is a key to success. If you're wrong the opportunity will return later. Cash can be held comfortably for long periods.

Reactive not predictive

As a trend follower, I react and do not try to predict the market. This is an important mindset difference. But the real key is money management which is dealt with later. We await the price to move in the right direction and be in a trend before we get in.

Look at Figure 3.1. A trend follower says he will react to the price rising above the down trend line (diagonal line) by entering at "1". But that he will know there is no trend and exit on the basis he is wrong by getting out at "2". That stop-loss being quite close to the entry means we do not need to lose, or risk a lot, before we know we are wrong.

As you can see from Figure 3.2, the stock does indeed rise and we are happy. If it did not and we were wrong, then our stop-loss was narrow. There is much, much more to trading than the above – the indicators I use, the money management rules, basically all the things the financial media are completely ignorant about because it would be too much like hard work.

Trading plan – what you never learn on TV or in the press

- A trading plan is probably the most important part of any trade. It is also the most neglected

- We examine your trading strategy in brief and what planning a trade ought to involve

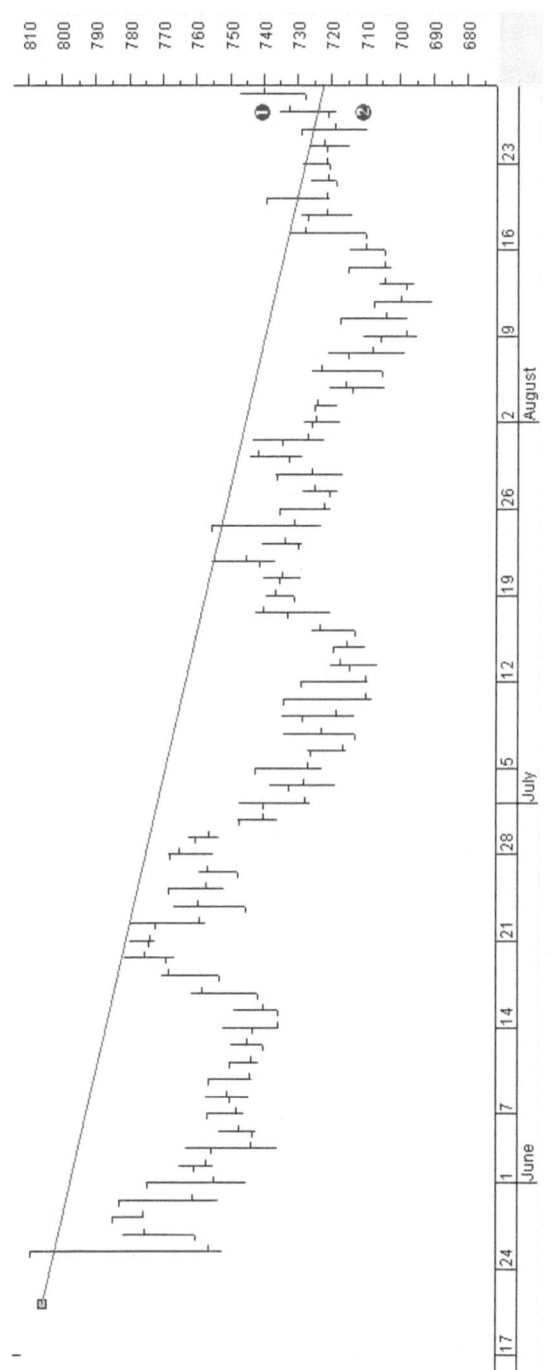

Figure 3.1 Waiting to react

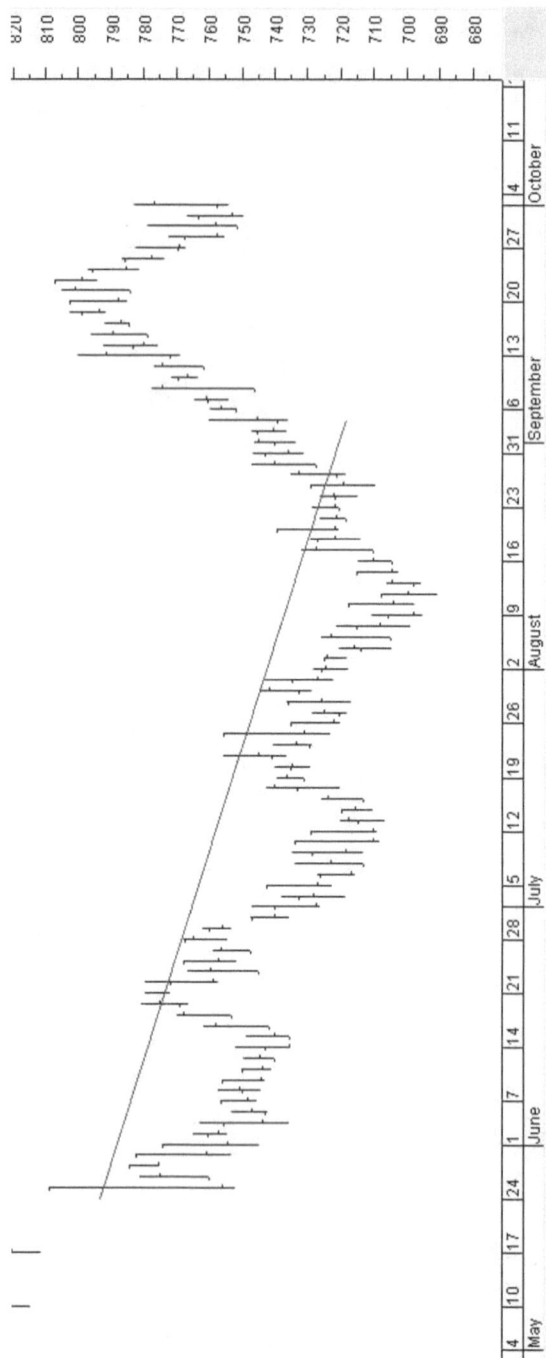

Figure 3.2 Moving forward

- Then you will be able to use this in an actual trade and produce an actual trading tactic

- To avoid the many pitfalls of trading, we also examine keeping a journal, diversification, your tolerance to risk and risk management and the types of traders who fail.

With a decent trading plan you can:

- Learn to produce and use a trading strategy and trading tactics as part of a trading plan

- See how to keep a journal as part of profitable trading

- Examine the types of traders who fail

- Find yourself (that is, risk tolerance)

- Manage risk, understand proper diversification (risk tolerance questionnaire)

- Share analysis template and transaction template (photocopy and fill out for record keeping and assessment purposes).

DIY trading strategy

So where do we go from here?

A trading strategy is a set of rules which must be met before you enter a trade, as opposed to trading tactics, which are the actual specific plans for what to do once you enter a trade.

> **HOT TIP**
>
> Every individual's trading strategy will vary and likely be unique, based on their own perspectives.
>
> This is a very simple guide to building a trading strategy to give you some idea of how it ought to be done. As you actually do it you will begin to realize the complexities and your plan will doubtless become more sophisticated.

Hypothesize!

Choose some rules you consider worth testing, bearing in mind the period of time you want to be in and out of the market for each trade. Choose a target price for exit, a stop-loss figure and other circumstances for exit.

Example
A fundamental analyst of company stocks may choose to buy a stock only if
the following rules are met:

- p/e ratio less than 8

- analyst recommendations all being buy or higher

- profit margin of 10% or higher

- dividend yield of 13% or higher

- target price: rise of 15%

- stop-loss: drop of 10% or below the nine-week low

- exit if one of these fundamental factors changes adversely.

A technical analyst may choose stock purchase rules based on:

- MACD crossover

- stochastic crossover

- rising parabolic SAR (Stop and reverse)

- a bounce off a trendline

- target price: rise of 15%

- stop-loss: drop of 10%

- exit if one of the above technical factors changes adversely.

Important
Overfitting. There is a tendency when testing trading rules to "overfit" the
rules (that is, amend them) to the data at hand so the results are good for
those data only. To avoid this, do some "out-of-sample testing," that is, test
the same rules on a completely different set of data. But beware: It may be
that your trading rules do genuinely only work with that one company, both
historically and in the future, and you may be throwing away a good system
by out-of-sample testing. To avoid this, do some paper trades on the same
stock as well.

Test
Now test the rules. Select some stocks and obtain their historical price
charts (see skeleton plans for sites). Next see what would have happened

had you used your trading strategy. What would a notional $20,000 have been at the end of one year, after dealing costs? Is the return better than bank rates of return? Did you beat the Dow or a typical mutual fund?

The preponderance of evidence rule

When testing and developing look for a balance of probability. Examine many different indicators, for example news stories on your product, analysts' views, market momentum. When there is a preponderance of evidence suggesting price movement, make a paper trade.

Keep doing this until you are comfortable that what you are doing works. If it does not, find out what aspects do not work, for example the technical indicators are always wrong, and either amend or ditch that particular indicator – be ruthless.

Always paper trade with different methods of selecting trades. For instance, you may try to combine stock filters with technical indicators and plot the results together with other systems, and go for what appears to make sense and is profitable.

When you find a trading strategy you are fairly happy with, you are then ready to trade.

HOT
TIP

How to back-test well

1. I tend to test one indicator at a time and add more and more and see how that affects results.
2. Look at a chart and identify areas in which your indicators should produce signals and then find indicators that tend to.
3. Are the results very volatile, for example large losses and profits (even though overall profitable)? Can you handle such losses along the way?
4. Do not just test bull markets, test bear and sideways or find a different set of indicators for each type of market.

Set an upside target. What do you expect the price to reach and in what time-frame? You may want to attach a rough probability of this occurring. Set a stop-loss – a point at which you will exit the trade: either a specific price level or a percentage. Set a point at which you will sell irrespective of the stop-loss, that is, you may get negative news on the company and decide to sell even though the stop-loss has not been reached.

Part of a simple trading tactic

Pros	*Cons*
MACD crossover occurred	Sector undergone long bull run
Stochastic crossover	
SAR upward	
Trendline bounce	
All analysts buy or strong buy	
Sector strong	

> *HOT*
> *TIP*
>
> **The mind of a trader**
>
> Stick to your plan. Do not start hoping for price moves, or denying losses. Try to stay objective. Do not get attached to a position: each day is a clean slate. To learn more about trading plans and trading like a professional you might consider reading *The Mind of a Trader.*[1]

Journal keeping

I am regularly asked by traders what they can do to improve their trading. One of the easiest and simplest steps that can be undertaken is to keep a journal. Imagine all that information and experience you collect as you trade:

- Without a journal you are throwing so much of it away

- Without a journal you are in serious danger of repeating your mistakes

- Keeping a journal is a money and risk management technique. By identifying possible trading problems, you can start to resolve them. So, make journal keeping a goal.

What to record

1. You will want to have a **copy of your goals**, and note your progress in achieving them.

2. The **anatomy of every trade.** Write down, from the moment you started analyzing a stock to the moment after you sold it, how you felt at each key moment about every activity you undertook. For example, how did you feel as you approached your stop-loss?

3. **Write down what feels good and what feels uncomfortable** about what you are doing.

Remember to keep your notes clear and well presented. You will have to return to them at a later date.

Seven traders

There are many types of trader. An awareness of the varieties when looking at your trading plan allows you to avoid the pitfalls.

- *Disciplined* – This is the ideal type of trader. You take losses and profits with ease. You focus on your system and follow it with discipline. Trading is usually a relaxed activity. You appreciate that a loss does not make for a loser.

- *Doubter* – You find it difficult to execute at signals. You doubt your own abilities. You need to develop self-confidence. Perhaps you should paper trade.

- *Blamer* – All losses are someone else's fault. You blame bad fills, your broker for picking the phone up too slowly, your system for not being perfect. You need to regain your objectivity and self-responsibility.

- *Victim* – Here you blame yourself. You feel the market is out to get you. You start becoming superstitious in your trading.

- *Optimist* – You start thinking, "It's only money, I'll make it back later." You think all losses will bounce back to a profit, or that you will start trading properly tomorrow.

- *Gambler* – You are in it for the thrill. Money is a side issue. Risk and reward analysis hardly figures in your trades; you want to be a player: you want the buzz and excitement.

- *Timid* – You enter a trade, but panic at the sight of a profit and take it far too soon. Fear rules your trading.

How much risk can you tolerate?

You might need to pursue an aggressive investment strategy but you might also have a conservative stomach. Greater volatility is double-edged; the potential upside is bigger, but the potential downside is bigger. The issue is where do your preferences lie?

Conservative risk takers are likely to define risk as a potential loss of their principal. Concerned more about safety than anything else, they're more willing to accept a lower rate of return in exchange for a lower degree of risk. This may mean that they choose fixed income investment tools like bonds and even a higher percentage of money in their portfolio.

More aggressive risk takers are less willing to tie up too much money over long periods in low-yielding fixed investments, preferring the bigger potential returns that the riskier stock market may offer.

Of course, your degree of risk tolerance can change over time as you approach certain goals. For example, investors tend to hold on too long to falling stock (risk loving on downturn) and can sell too quickly on the upside.

A questionnaire on risk tolerance

An investor's risk tolerance in making investment decisions can depend on investment goals as well as the investor's personality. The following question-naire will measure your reaction to market risk, weight the relative importance of your goals and uncover your personal investment preferences.

Give yourself the points in the brackets for your answer

Points

1. How much volatility are you willing to accept?
   A Slight. I do not want to lose money, even if it means my returns are small. (1) ☐
   B Some. I am willing to accept the occasional loss as long as my money is in sound, high-quality investments that can be expected to grow over time. (3) ☐
   C Considerable. I am willing to take substantial risk in pursuit of significantly higher returns. (5) ☐

2. Suppose your investment portfolio contains a significant portion of large company stocks in addition to several other assets. Large company stocks have averaged a compound annual return of 11% over the past 72 years. However, if large company stocks had lost 18% of their value in the past year, what would you do?
   A Sell the large company stock portion of my investment portfolio and realize the loss. (1) ☐
   B Sell some, but not all, of the large company stock portion (2) ☐
   C Continue to hold the large company stock portion of my investment portfolio, following a consistent long-term strategy. (3) ☐
   D Buy more large company stocks. (4) ☐

Points

3. Please provide your response to the following statement.

    Given my investment time horizon, I am willing to accept
    significant fluctuations in the value of my investments to achieve
    potentially higher long-term returns.

    A Strongly disagree   (0)
    B Disagree   (1)
    C Agree   (2)
    D Strongly agree   (5)

4. Which of the following statements is most true about your risk
    tolerance and the way you wish to invest to achieve your
    goal(s)? My investment should …
    A be completely safe; I do not wish to run the risk of
       losing any principal at any time.   (1)
    B generate regular income that I can spend.   (2)
    C generate some current income and also grow in value
       over time.   (3)
    D grow over time, but I would also like to generate some
       current income.   (4)
    E grow substantially in value over time. I do not need
       to generate current income.   (5)

5. An investor must be prepared to expose his/her investments to
    increased chances for loss in attempting to achieve higher expected
    returns. The following statements represent possible outcomes for
    three hypothetical portfolios at the end of one year. Which
    investment portfolio would you be most comfortable holding?
    A Portfolio A has a likely return of 6%, and there is a
       10% chance for loss at the end of the year.   (2)
    B Portfolio B has a likely return of 10%, and there is an
       18% chance for loss at the end of the year.   (3)
    C Portfolio C has a likely return of 14%, and there is a
       25% chance for loss at the end of the year.   (4)

6. I understand the value of my portfolio will fluctuate over time.
    However, the maximum loss in any one-year period that I am
    prepared to accept is:
    A 0%   (1)
    B −5%   (2)
    C −10%   (3)
    D −20%   (4)
    E −30%+   (5)

Points

7. Investments in which the principal is "100% safe" sometimes earn less than the inflation rate. This means that, while no money is lost, there is a loss of purchasing power. With respect to your goal(s), which of the following is most true?

   A My money should be "100% safe," even if it means my returns do not keep up with inflation.   (0)

   B It is important that the value of my investments keeps pace with inflation. I am willing to risk an occasional loss in principal so that my investments may grow at about the same rate as inflation over time.   (3)

   C It is important that my investments grow faster than inflation. I am willing to accept a fair amount of risk to try to achieve this.   (5)

8. Which statement best describes your main concern when selecting an investment?

   A The potential for loss.   (1)

   B Mostly the potential for loss, but also the potential for gain.   (2)

   C Mostly the potential for gain, but I am still concerned about the potential for loss.   (3)

   D The potential for gain.   (4)

9. Consider the following two investments, A and B. Investment A provides an average annual return of 7% with minimal risk of loss of principal. Investment B provides an average annual return of 10% but carries a potential loss of principal of 20% or more in any one year. If I could choose between Investment A and Investment B to meet my goal(s), I would invest my money:

   A 100% in A and 0% in B   (1)

   B 75% in A and 25% in B   (2)

   C 50% in A and 50% in B   (3)

   D 25% in A and 75% in B   (4)

   E 0% in A and 100% in B   (5)

Add up your scores; the lower the score, the lower your risk tolerance. So, if you scored:

8–20   you tend to be particularly risk averse

21–35   you tend to be neutral towards risk and volatility

36–42   you like market volatility – regarding it as the best opportunity to make money.

TYPES OF RISK

Does investing online lessen the risk of losing money?

Investing online can lessen risk but only to the extent that it puts all the tools and resources in your hands to conveniently make your own investing decisions. When you're online, you can easily scan the market indicators, and track price movements. This will reduce risk of error in judgment.

Interest rate risk

When the cost of borrowing money goes up, it erodes the value of certain investments since it reduces the relative return on the investments. This is especially vigorous for long-term fixed securities like bonds. For example, if you bought a bond with the "fantastic" rate of 8%, and five years later interest rates move above 8%, you will have a lower relative return compared to, say, savings accounts.

Investor psychology

Overreaction to fluctuating interest rates and inflation fears by panicky investors prompts a market sell-off that affects the value of investments, even among those who kept their heads. Herding behavior can create exceptionally volatile markets.

Market conditions

Stock prices can soar to such highs per dollar invested that the market and your individual investments become more vulnerable in the event of a decline. This is also referred to as 'market indices'.

Liquidity

A liquidity risk is the inability to convert, when needed, an investment quickly and easily to cash, which is purely liquid, without incurring a significant loss in the value of the investment.

How to manage risk

There are some simple yet wily strategies that can help to mitigate the effects of most risk. Here are some.

Asset allocation

- Spreading your investment among different investment products – stocks, bonds, mutual funds, and risk-free cash equivalents – lessens the chance of a poor showing by one.

- Choosing stocks that are not perfectly correlated will give similar results. For example, stocks from different sectors will move imperfectly, that is, they will not drop together but neither will they rise perfectly together. The weight you give to each sector should be re-evaluated and shifted on a regular basis depending on how your perceptions of your aversion to risk change.

- Although no strategy can guarantee success, history has shown that a balanced portfolio is less vulnerable to economic shocks.

Dollar cost averaging

Dollar cost averaging is a very effective investment tool. Say you have $20,000 to invest. If a security you're interested in is trading at $2 a share in January your $20,000 will buy you 10,000 shares. But with a dollar cost averaging strategy, you instead buy $1000 worth every month for 10 months.

Using dollar cost averaging you do not expose your whole $20,000 in one go, but rather stagger the investment along the fluctuating cycle of the share price.

How good financial products get no exposure

The picture opposite shows how the system works in TV.

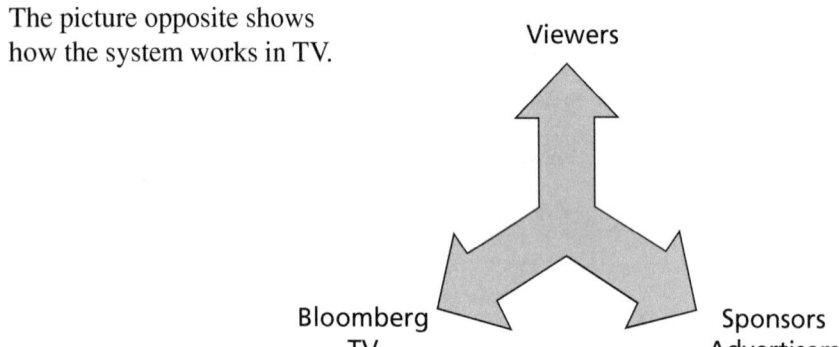

Viewers

Bloomberg
TV

Sponsors
Advertisers

You get viewers if the content is good, if you get viewers you get sponsors. Then, sooner or later someone realizes, that if the content was influenced by the sponsors, we would be even more likely to get sponsors and advertisers. Normally that is forbidden. The person in sales never knows what the person in editorial is planning. But isn't it funny how often an advertiser of say, spread betting, appears as a guest on the show.

So the advertiser's product is being plugged. This is why spread betting and CFDs (contracts for difference) are pushed heavily on channels like CNBC and Bloomberg, but stock futures are not.

I was asked at Bloomberg to create a program proposal for stock futures and options. Now options are a complicated subject to convey on TV, whereas if you can explain spread bets, you can explain stock futures. We even did a pilot of the program. Unfortunately the sponsor never showed up.

The television authorities have strict rules about who can sponsor what. For instance, the news cannot be sponsored but features can. But the bottom line is that stock futures get no coverage. You may argue, what's wrong with that? Well, the result is that second-rate products get better coverage, so let me try in some small way to reverse this injustice by covering stock futures and exchange traded funds – two of my favorite trading products.

Stock futures

A stock future is a relatively new invention in the U.S. and U.K. which allows you to trade on the movements of major companies' stock prices. They mimic the price of the stock. So if Microsoft rises 10c, so will the stock future. As you will see below, there are many reasons for trading the stock future rather than the stock.

You can hold the stock future until settlement or buy and sell and close the trade earlier.

Although terms like settlement and the definition of stock futures might seem complicated, all you need to remember is you are trying to buy low and sell high and that the price depends on the price of the stock – so you have to take a view on the stock.

Definition

A stock future is, quite simply, an agreement between a buyer and seller to exchange cash or stock at a fixed future date (the settlement date). All stock futures are either cash settled or physically settled (that is, stocks changing hands). For instance, those traded on the OneChicago exchange are physically settled and you receive shares at the settlement date.

- Each futures contract or lot represents a certain number of shares depending on the stock.

- Futures contracts are listed with up to six months' life. There is only one contract per stock expiring in a specific calendar month. At the end of the life of the contract, you could sell it and "roll over" to a further out stock future, or take cash settlement or physical delivery. Of course you do not need to hold the stock future to expiry, you can close the trade sooner.

■ Trading is done electronically through brokers.

These futures contracts on the shares of some of the world's largest companies are traded in major currencies: euros, pounds sterling, Swiss francs, Swedish kronor, and U.S. dollars. The key attractions are:

■ *Capital efficiency:* you are not buying the stocks upfront, only paying margin which acts as deposit. For instance, one stock future in Microsoft represents 100 shares or $25 x 100 = $2500. But the margin on that would be around 20% or $500 to control $2500.

■ *Investment efficiency:* the cash-settled aspect of stock futures means that all the background costs involved of settlement and stock transfers make cost savings for the trader. Commissions are consequently cheaper.

■ *Ease:* there is one account from which you can access some of the world's largest most popular stocks. There is no need for multiple accounts with multiple brokers and the resulting complications and inconvenience. Diversification is therefore easier too.

■ *Profit from falls:* you can short stock futures, that is, sell them in anticipation of buying them back more cheaply in a falling market.

Buying a stock future is similar to agreeing to buy shares at a future date, but agreeing the price at the time of trade. The key difference is that where stock futures are cash settled, no shares change hands. Conversely, selling a stock future is similar to agreeing to sell shares at a future date (although the seller does not need to own shares to enter into this agreement).

Price

Both the buyer and the seller face the risk that the share price will change between the date the future is traded and the end of the future's life. To cover this risk,

TABLE 3.1 A typical price chart for a stock future

	Bid	Offer
Stock	50.00	50.05
January future	50.19	50.25
February future	49.99	50.05
March future	50.19	50.26
June future	50.80	50.87

the seller of the future could buy shares and hold them until the future's last trading day.

The price of the future should be equal to the cost of buying the shares and holding them until the expiry of the futures contract – any more and a trader buying stock and selling futures would make a guaranteed positive return – any less and a trader selling stock and buying futures would make a guaranteed positive return. If the price of the future were to move away from the correct theoretical price, the process of buying/selling stock and selling/buying futures – usually referred as "arbitrage" – would bring the price back in line.

Assessing the total cost of buying stock and holding it until the expiry of the future may seem difficult to anticipate but it is really made up of three main elements:

1. The price of the underlying stock

2. Any interest income foregone by holding shares rather than cash

3. Any dividends paid to the holder of the stock before the expiry of the future.

There is, theoretically, a formula for testing the fairness of a futures price:

Fair futures price = today's share price + interest costs – dividends received

However, the normal forces of supply and demand operate just as much on stock futures as in any other market and prices are subject to fluctuation. Equally important, each investor will have his or her own set of priorities leading to an individual set of expectations as to what constitutes a fair price for a future.

The price of the stock future will typically follow the price of the underlying stock until the contract expires.

Bid/ask spread

The bid/ask spread is a major concern for traders in stock futures because their fear is that if the product does not have a big take-up, so that the volume and liquidity are low, then the bid/ask spreads will be wide and so a hidden cost of trading.

The exchanges through which stock futures are traded – LIFFE, NQLX, OneChicago – are all aware of this and have made efforts to reduce spreads:

- First, there is an obligation on market makers (the firms who are obliged to quote bid/ask prices so people can get in and out) as to how wide spreads can be. Second, to the extent that this leveraged product is a substitute for other leveraged products like options, traders are not as dispersed because for each security there are not multiple strike prices as there are in options.

- Third, the exchanges have been keen to ensure that they list stock futures on the most liquid stocks, such as Microsoft.

A quote from a trader:

X's early impressions of the market are positive "So far, so good," he says. "From a trading standpoint, there a couple of reasons I am optimistic about this new market. First I give NQLX a thumbs-up on their platform. Looking at pure performance and reliability, I'm very impressed and I've found it very usable."

Additionally, Mr. X's comments mirror others we've heard about the tightness of the markets. "There is a lot more liquidity than meets the eye. The bid/ask on Microsoft is usually 2–5 cents, at times maybe even a penny. Then every two pennies up and two pennies down, there might be another bid or offer. The size might be showing only 20 on the screen. If I want to sell 1000, there is a market maker willing to pay 2 for 1000, but he doesn't show it all at once. You can't judge the market just by looking at the book, he adds. "A few months down the road, I wouldn't be surprised if I were trading 2000 to 3000 SSFs a day." (*Stock Futures and Options Magazine*, February 2003)

Dividends

Holders of stock futures do not receive dividends. Stockholders do. The difference is reflected in the price of the stock future. So the more valuable the dividend to be paid, the lower the price of the future. The buyer is paying less for the future and so is compensated for the dividend he misses. The seller of futures is happy to sell at the lower price because he or she does not have to pay a dividend to the buyer.

Margin

Most readers will be familiar with the margin. In case you are not, it is like a deposit, rather than the full potential cost of the trade. The initial margin is set by the exchange. The variation margin is the change in this daily amount based on market movements.

Example:

Let us say you have $16,000 you want to trade with in a stock future trade in Vodafone. That equates to £10,000. The stock is trading at 100p. So you sell 10 Vodafone stock futures.

The margin required by the broker will only be around £1500. So the remaining £8500 can be kept in a bank account earning interest. As the price of the stock falls, so does the stock future. If you then buy back the stock future to close the trade when the stock future is at 90p, since one stock future on a U.K. stock represents 1000 shares, that is a £100 profit (1000 × 10p × 1 contract). Across 10 contracts it is a £1000 or $1600 profit.

Euro, Swiss franc, U.S. dollar, and Swedish krona stock future contracts represent 100 shares, while Italian shares like Telecom Italia are 1000 shares per stock future.

Comparison to other financial products

Of course we want to know why we should pick a stock future to capture a share price move and not, say, an option. Well, first let us look at the comparison with spread bets and contracts for differences (Table 3.2). Now these two financial products are generally not available to U.S. citizens so it applies to those in Europe or Asia.

You can find out more in my book *Alpesh Patel on Stock Futures*.

Exchange traded funds

It's the most liquid security in the world, meaning its daily traded value is more than any other. Yet the chances are you've never heard of it, despite being able to profit as easily from its rises as its falls. It's better than a stock, because it's more diversified, and can outperform most fund managers trying to mimic its risk – reward profile because of its lower charges.

No, it's not Microsoft or IBM. It's the QQQ and it represents the Nasdaq 100. Moreover, it's especially beneficial if you are not a U.S. investor. The QQQ is an exchange traded fund (ETF) which trades just like a single stock but tracks the whole index. Other ETFs track regions, sectors and other indices – but none are as popular as the QQQ.

TABLE 3.2 Comparison between stock futures, spread bets and contracts for differences			
	Universal stock future	Equity spread bet	Equity contract for difference
Description	Contract where participant gains/loses difference between the opening traded price and the final closing price set on a predetermined date	Bet where participant "wins" or "loses" change in value of shares at a predefined future date	Contract where participant gains/loses difference in equity value between opening and closing the contract
Price determination	Standard futures pricing model operated by each market participant – best prices	Standard futures pricing model used to determine value, but not price competition, to determine best market price	Traded price equal to prevailing share price. An additional financing cost is imposed on CFD positions
Liquidity	Competing quotes supported by market makers	Volume is "guaranteed" by spread bet firm, exit price is an uncertainty	Access to market is "guaranteed" by counterparty
Expiry date	Yes	Yes	No
Settlement style	Cash settled	Cash settled	Cash settled
Final closing price	Determined by the exchange based on underlying share price	Determined as per terms of the agreement	No automatic closure – closing price established as prevailing share price at closing trade

Only ETFs combine diversification (the ETF represents a basket of stocks) with the fact that they can be bought and sold like a stock through most online brokers without entry or exit charges, and avoid stamp duty.

Net traders usually overlook their ability to mimic institutional money management techniques. The "core/satellite" strategy is becoming the "bedrock for institutional managed money," according to Dresdner Kleinwort Wasserstein. There is no reason why net traders can't follow suit.

Under this strategy, pension funds, for instance, hold a passive index-tracking core (maybe 55%) and an active satellite (45%) equally divided between value, growth and alternative investments such as hedge funds or specific sector ETFs.

The passive element provides low-cost diversification and the knowledge that index tracking is particularly successful over long periods, whilst the active element allows the online trader to use other stock-picking skills to outperform the index.

For instance, if you feel that Cisco's results herald a turnaround in technology stocks, you can buy the QQQ as your 'core' holding. You add to this GlaxoSmithKline, Marks & Spencer and Barclays because you feel retail, pharmaceuticals and banking stocks will outperform.

With just these four stocks you have a diversified portfolio. Equally the satellite elements can short particular sectors and regions. For many portfolio managers, the ETF tool is what a scalpel is for surgeons.

A core/satellite strategy likely to benefit is on overweight in cyclical stocks (which do well when climbing out of recession) and underweight on defensives such as tobacco, utilities, pharmaceuticals.

But surely, you ask, there is no place for trading the Nasdaq? What are the chances of a good return? After all, the TMT (technology, media, telecoms) boom is over and the Nasdaq 100 underperformed the Dow Jones 100, the S&P 100, the FTSE 100 and indeed Microsoft in 2000.

How does a 50% return in 12 months sound? There is a 50% chance of a 50% return in a year on the QQQ, according to Riskgrades.com, based on its historic volatility and returns.

For more exotic returns try the iShares MSCI South Korea ETF, up 50% in 2000 – it outperformed 98% of FTSE 100 stocks.

Of course if you are not convinced the QQQ is going to rise, the advantage of the QQQ is you can short it (sell it in anticipation of a fall then buy it back more cheaply to close the trade at a profit).

So why don't U.K. investors use it? It can't be the fear of high cost, because online brokers charge the same commissions on these stocks as any other – some such as comdirect.co.uk offer free trading.

Neither can it be that ETFs do not suit online traders' trading style. For the day trader, the ETFs trade like stocks anyway. For the long-term investor, they can be held in perpetuity. For the value investor, there are "value"-based ETFs such as the "iShares Small Cap 600/BARRA value index fund" which returned over 30% in 2000.

Could it be a lack of online tools? Because it is the most popular security in the world, there is no shortage of sites offering trading strategies and commentary on the QQQ and indeed other ETFs.

No, there is no good reason why ETFs are not more popular; our ignorance of them is the barrier to superior trading strategies as well as the relatively better performance of index tracking and benefits diversification that ETFs offer to our portfolios. The QQQ is the most liquid security in the world, thanks to informed institutions not private investors for whom the cost of ignorance remains high.

My sites: Exchange traded funds

QQQ Strategy and commentary sites
http://www.mrswing.com/QQQ/
http://www.marketvolume.com
http://www.timingmutualfunds.com/
http://www.qqq-marketmaker.com/

Search for ETFs
http://quotes.nasdaq.com/asp/ETFsScreen.asp

ETF information
www.londonstockexchange.com/extraMARK
www.indexfunds.com
www.amex.com
www.ishares.com
www.frescoshares.com
www.vit-x.com

Note

1   Alpesh Patel (1997) *The Mind of a Trader* FT Pitman.

CHAPTER 4

What does not sell advertising so you will not see it: money management

In statistical terms, I figure I have traded about 2 million contracts ... with an average profit of $70 per contract. This average profit is approximately 700 standard deviations away from randomness, a departure that would occur by chance alone about as frequently as the spare parts in an automotive salvage lot might spontaneously assemble themselves into a McDonald's restaurant. **Hedge fund trader, Victor Niederhoffer**

On Wednesday Niederhoffer told investors in three hedge funds he runs that their stakes had been "wiped out" on Monday by losses that culminated from three days of falling stock prices and big hits earlier this year in Thailand. **David Henry *USA Today* (October 30, 1997)**

- ■ Risk and money management (what risk really means and how professionals reduce it)
- ■ How much money should you place on any trade?

Risk and money management (what risk really means and how professionals reduce it)

Risk in financial journalism and on TV is covered in the most superficial way imaginable, if it is covered at all! We are reward junkies. The typical question asked of analysts and stock predictors is "what price target?" It is never "when do you know you're wrong? Are you riding this to $0?"

The analyst is safe in the knowledge that no matter what target he sets, no one will remember a few months down the line. Except the poor viewer who acted on the tip.

The presenter is safe in the knowledge that he has ticked off the question he had down to ask, did not miss the autocue and can return to thinking about the drinks party the analyst's bank has invited him to that night.

The TV station is safe in the knowledge that the viewers got the stock equivalent of a sugar-rush; that stock tip felt like added value, it sounded good, heck it even felt good. But in investment terms it has the nutritional value of a meal at McDonald's. And like McDonald's, no one mentions risk.

Money management is like sex: Everyone does it, one way or another, but not many like to talk about it and some do it better than others. But there's a big difference: Sex sites on the Web proliferate, while sites devoted to the art and science of money management are somewhat difficult to find. **Gibbons Burke**

Why manage risks

RiskMetrics, in trying to explain risk to investors, interviewed the fictional Wanda Lottery, recent winner of the cash sweepstakes:

Wanda Lottery: Why should I care about risk management? In the long run, equities go up.

RiskMetrics: Although the U.S. equities markets' rally has been quite impressive during the '90s, a glance at market history illustrates the need for careful risk management.

Imagine it's January 2, 1929 and you have $10,000 in the local bank. Considering the recent strength of the stock market and the fact that your friends are making a killing in the stocks, you decide to invest your cash in a Dow tracking fund rather than a new car. After all, with all the money you'll be making, you can buy two new cars in a few months. On September 3, 1929 your little nest egg has grown to $12,417. Only a few more months and you can reap the benefits of your investment. October brings what will be known as Black Thursday, and the nest egg shrinks to $7495. As you close the newspaper's business section, you sigh and exclaim "The market will come back. I didn't really need a new car. I should be investing for my retirement anyway." But on your way home from work on a hot July summer day in 1932, your car breaks down and cannot be

Date	Investment	Gain/Loss
02–Jan–29	$10,000	
03–Sep–29	$12,417	$2,417
29–Oct–29	$7,495	$–2,505
08–Jul–32	$1,342	$–8,658

repaired. No need to worry, you can cash in your investment and buy that car.

Think again. Your investment is now worth $1342. In three and a half years, your $10,000 has dwindled $8658 down to a total of $1342, a loss of more than 86%.

At this point you come to two conclusions: 1) I have no choice but to leave the money invested for the long term, to try to recoup my losses, and 2) I will be commuting to work on the bus. Sadly enough, markets don't always go up.

Wanda Lottery: But I heard on TV if I'm willing to wait 10 to 20 years I will make at least 10% on average by investing in stocks.

RiskMetrics: You may be capable of generating returns of 10% or more by investing wisely over the long term. However, applying a long-term average to a specific time period can be deceiving. Recall in the previous example, the investment of $10,000 had shrunk to $1342 in an amazing three and a half years. How long would you guess it took to grow back to the original $10,000?

Wanda Lottery: This must be a trick question. If it took three and a half years to go down, I'll bet it took twice that to come back – say seven years.

RiskMetrics: Would you believe it took a little more than twenty-five years for that nest egg to grow to the original $10,000 amount? For the investment to grow to $12,417, which you had briefly earned in September of 1929, you would need an additional year, making your investment horizon twenty-six years. Your average return over this period was less than 1%.

So, had you been 30 years old when you first invested your money, you would be none the richer at age 55.

Wanda Lottery: That was the Great Depression. Things have changed. Wake up. We're in the dot.com era. Something like that could never happen again.

RiskMetrics: The Great Depression era is an extreme example. However, protracted market retracements or downturns do occur. If you took that same $10,000 dollars and invested it in January of 1973, you would have suffered a loss of $4401 by December of 1974. Ten years later, in 1983, you would eventually break even. Considering your track record and being a little bit gun shy, you take your $10,000 and put it in a safe place – under your mattress.

In 1988 you decide it's time to invest once again. By now you have had enough of the U.S. markets and decide to invest overseas. Asia looks good. After extensive research you invest in the Japanese stock market. Your research pays off as your original $10,000 soars to $18,342, almost doubling by December of 1989. You decide to take the advice of experts and let your profits run by leaving the money invested in Japanese stocks.

Unfortunately, what goes up fast can come back down faster and by July of 1992, four years later, again you are in negative territory and have suffered losses. The original $10,000 dollars is worth only $6708. Interestingly enough, twelve years later, you are still waiting to break even.

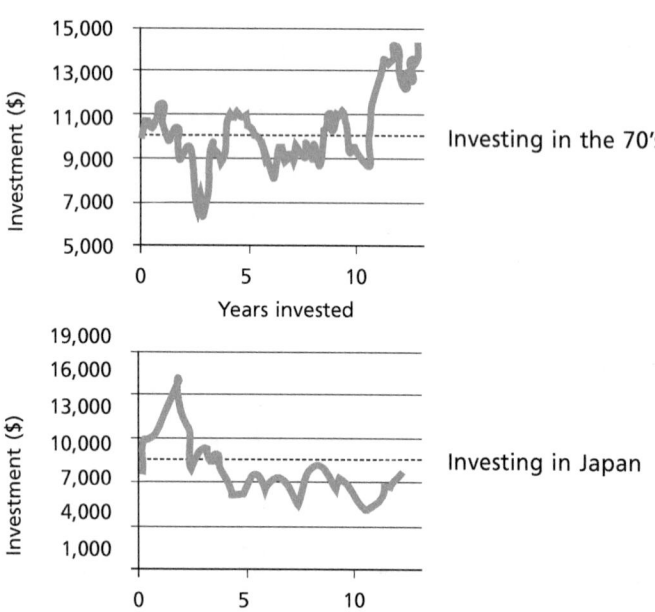

Wanda Lottery: Well you've certainly scared me. Maybe I'll just stick my money in the bank.

RiskMetrics: You shouldn't be scared about investing. You need to be aware that the decisions you make, while having potential returns, also have risks. Once you understand the risks, you can judge if the expected returns are worthwhile.

Definition of risk

Risk is uncertainty. Risk is often measured in terms of *volatility* (or variability) of returns. For example, as measured by RiskMetrics in 1999, the daily variability of returns for the S&P 500 and Yahoo! were 1.1% and 5.6 % respectively, so that Yahoo! was a much riskier investment than the S&P 500 index.

In fact, Yahoo!'s returns were about five times (or precisely 5.6/1.1) as volatile as the returns of the S&P 500. But if Yahoo! was five times riskier, why did it outperform the S&P by 229%? That's because risk works both ways. Investing in Yahoo! stock means that you are more likely to experience sudden large drops in value, but you also stand a chance to make a higher return.

Now, compare Yahoo!'s biggest daily drop and return (−23.5% and +13.5%) against the S&P 500 (−3.5% and +2.8%) in Table 4.1 below from RiskMetrics. Higher volatility means the possibility of larger losses AND larger gains.

If no one ever took risks, Michelangelo would have painted the Sistine floor.
Neil Simon

TABLE 4.1 Comparison of risk and return for three popular investments				
Investment	1999 daily volatility, %	1999 return, %	Biggest 1999 daily drop, %	Biggest 1999 daily return, %
S&P 500 index	1.1	19.6%	−3.5	2.8
Yahoo! stock	5.6	248.9%	−23.9	13.5
GE stock	1.8	55.8%	−4.4	5.8

Risk and time

When you consider the complications of risk to attaining a return, you quickly appreciate how financial journalists have completely derogated their duties to explain these basics to their readers. The next time you read about a financial scandal and a reporter crows about how appallingly the investors who have lost money must feel, consider this:

- If the journalist had explained risk and reward in the first place, might investors not have fallen foul of the potential scandal?
- If in politics we can have investigative journalism, then why not in financial journalism?

> *If financial journalists were in the army, how many would be court-martialed for gross dereliction of duty?*

'I don't know your needs, so let me tell you what you should do anyway'

That certainly seems to be the attitude of many financial presenters and writers. As RiskMetrics put it: "Risk is different for every person." First, different people have different investment time horizons.

The first question to ask when making an investment is: "When do I need the money?" A good investment for an 18-year-old is probably not a good investment for an 81-year-old. If you're likely to need your money within five years, you should not invest your entire wealth in high-risk assets. On the other hand, if your investment horizon is long (20–30 years), you should be more willing to accept the short-term fluctuations of risky securities in exchange for long-term growth prospects. In general, you can accept more risk the longer you can put off touching your money, because you have more time to recoup potential losses along the way.

All too often, people set one objective (that is, "I'll buy this stock for a quick trade") and when the markets do not move as expected, they change that objective ("I'll make it part of my long-term portfolio").

What is money management?

Some of the vital issues covered in money management which are second nature to any professional investor include:

- Handling volatility
- Adjusting your trade/bet size to allow for profits
- If you are 'short' as well as 'long', can you have more positions?
- What do you do if you have a losing streak; how do you change position size?

- When do you take a loss?

- How much money do you place in each trade?

But all the above are news to financial journalists. Don't get me wrong, go on any trading floor and they will have Bloomberg TV and CNBC playing. But then, you will notice two things.

One, the volume is off. Two, they all have their backs to the TV anyway. When I was at Bloomberg TV and we would be preparing for the show in the evening, every desk had a TV on it. Now, few if any employers would provide every member of their workforce with a TV and it didn't take much to work out the TV was not there so we could tune in to the latest daytime soaps thanks to our benevolent employer. And no one who wanted to keep their jobs would switch onto a soap, except perhaps fleetingly as they looked for the output from Bloomberg.

But, we would occasionally switch onto CNBC, just to keep an eye on what stories they felt were important. Interestingly, one day, some dignitaries were visiting and a note went round saying that it does not exactly look well if we are seen to have CNBC playing on our desks whilst producing a show. Well I can assure any dignitary, VIP, viewer that if Bloomberg took ideas from CNBC, then I didn't notice it.

And here is another secret. It looks comforting for the client to think that these guys, and it is mainly guys, are so well informed they don't watch anything except financial channels. Well, I have news for the naive client being shown around a trading room. If you want to know what the dealers and traders are really watching, don't look at the TV screens, take a look at their computer screens. Sure, they will have a Bloomberg screen up and be monitoring their positions, but they all have more than one screen and at least one of their eight screens will be logged on to www.porsche.com.

I don't want to maximize my returns from trading online. If I had invested, say, $10,000 equally at the start of the tech boom in 1999 between the best five performing TMTs, I would probably have well over $30,000. But I am not losing sleep over having missed them.

FinPortfolio.com's definition of "risk-adjusted return":

The return on an asset or a portfolio adjusted for volatility; typically represented by the Sharpe Ratio. Risk-adjusted return is a very important performance measure because it tells us how much "bang for the buck" we are getting. Since we pay for returns by taking on risk, achieving a high return while taking on little risk is a real accomplishment!

"Sharpe Ratio"

A ratio of return to volatility; useful in comparing two portfolios in terms of risk-adjusted return. This ratio was developed by Nobel laureate William Sharpe. The higher the Sharpe Ratio, the better – a high Sharpe ratio implies the portfolio or stock is achieving good returns for each unit of risk. Because we earn returns by accepting risk, it is great when we get more return for less risk.

The Sharpe Ratio or the risk-adjusted return score allows us to compare different assets or different portfolios. It is calculated by first subtracting the risk-free rate from the return of the portfolio, and then dividing by the standard deviation of the portfolio.

At the end of this chapter, I explain more about the above concepts if you are not familiar with them. If however you are, then read on.

I don't want too great a reward: why?

I want to maximize my reward to risk ratio and buying those stocks would not have done that.

How can I measure the risk I am exposed to?

Even those who have some idea about risk, use outdated, unsophisticated or discredited measures. Beta is a popular yet incomplete measure of risk. Beta measures how much an individual stock is likely to move with the general market. A beta of 1 means that a stock will tend to move lockstep with the general market, while a beta of 2 means that the stock will rise 2% for any 1% rise in the stock market, and fall 2% with any 1% fall in the stock market, on average.

What is wrong with beta?

But beta can be misleading, for instance, because two stocks with the same beta generally have a different level of risk. Standard deviation is another common measure of risk and it too has deficiencies. For example, it fails to weight historical share prices to give more significance to the most recent prices.

What other tools of risk management are there then?

Newer online tools remove traditional problems with risk measurement. This will potentially result in greater online trading returns. JP Morgan have taken their internationally and institutionally acclaimed RiskMetrics risk calculations and converted them for the private investor through RiskGrades (www.riskgrades.com).

This is a very powerful tool. It would reveal for instance that two stocks can be equally risky (in simple terms they have been equally volatile in the past six months), yet the one year returns can be very different.

What else can RiskGrades do?
RiskGrades also suggests that online traders have riskier stock portfolios than they realize. Consequently their returns are often lower than they expect – losses greater than anticipated or profits lower than they should be. The problem is so great that even model portfolios on reputable websites misjudge the level of risk they advocate.

Inconsistencies can exist in many portfolios, even brokers' model portfolios. The fault is not theirs. It is due to a general lack of understanding of the nature of risk and an unnecessarily intuitive not quantative approach to risk.

If inconsistencies can arise in my portfolio on how I handle risk, what should I do to correct them?
I suggest that serious private investors should know the following about their stock portfolios:

- which stocks contribute the greatest risk to their portfolio

- how well diversified their portfolio is

- what you should expect to see as an average worst-case one day trading loss

- whether replacing any stocks reduces risk without impacting return, or even improving it

- Use RiskGrades to evaluate the above for your portfolio.

Since risk and diversification go hand in hand, how many stocks should a well-diversified portfolio contain?
As few as a dozen stocks can yield good diversification. A diversified portfolio is one where the negative impact on a portfolio of an event due solely to a specific stock is minimized.

What about the type of stocks I choose?
All important in diversification are the stocks you select. Again, too many private investors have stocks closely correlated to each other. Simply buying a stock from different sectors is not the answer, for sectors can be linked in their movements too. RiskGrades allows a quick assessment of how diversified your portfolio is.

So, if not maximizing my returns per se, what am I maximizing?
The trick with a portfolio is to maximize the reward for any level of risk through asset allocation. According to RiskGrades, an aggressive portfolio can produce an expected annual return of 30%, but only if the assets are allocated to minimize risk.

I would rather underperform and have a better risk to reward ratio than be a star performer taking great risks. Trading is not a one-shot game and in the long term I would be the outperformer.

But what if I am tempted by those risky tech stocks?
Unfortunately many traders first select risky "growth" internet stocks, reasoning that if they are risky then growth will follow. Such fallacious reasoning is equivalent to saying "if producing high-grade steel results in pollution, then if I pollute, I will produce high-grade steel." Consequently they have all the risk, but little of the return because of the assets selected. Once again the online tools of RiskGrade assist in resolving that problem.

The bottom line?
Too few private investor websites understand online trading. If they did they would provide as many statistics about risk as they do about P/E ratios. Doubtless brokers will provide such information with the motive of encouraging greater trades as investors rejig their portfolios in pursuit of the ideal portfolio. *E-traders need to beware there is the risk of overtrading* and incurring commission costs for themselves from doing so that is not measured by RiskGrades.

How much risk can I take?
Know thyself. It is essential that as an investor you know how much risk you can tolerate. If you are quite conservative, you may be quite adverse to the probability that the market may fall 5%. An aggressive investor may take a 5% drop with a pinch of salt since he thinks there is a good probability of a 5 or 10% rise.

The risk tolerance test later in the chapter will help you know yourself.

Why financial journalism is a weapon of mass portfolio destruction
Okay, so when was the last time a financial TV presenter recommended a stock and analysed how it impacts your existing portfolio? He doesn't, does he? He can't, because there are thousands of viewers watching (or millions watching if you are a TV presenter reading this and have a high estimation of yourself).

Consequently, if you get your stock ideas from watching TV or reading stock magazines, the chances are you collect stocks like you do socks – a real hotchpotch accumulation over time.

Within your portfolio, do you know how many shares you need to reduce risk or what is risk, how it is measured, and how much you are taking in any investment? Most private investors would be clueless. Why is our knowledge of risk so poor when online sites offer free answers for any U.K., U.S. stock or bond? Indeed, when it's not even that complicated, and a few uncontroversial rules can save thousands?

So, what if you want to construct a FTSE 100- or Dow-Jones-beating portfolio? Alternatively you may want a portfolio with, say, a 90% success rate of reaching $500,000 in five years, from your starting point of $100,000. A risk-aware investor should use three steps to construct a portfolio with tools used by the professionals from firms like JP Morgan.

First, there is *selection*. Using sites like FinPortfolio.com and RiskGrades.com you can screen for stocks that have a higher risk-adjusted average return than, say, the Dow. Focusing on return without risk is the same as agreeing to buy a car without asking the price.

Risk is the uncertainty of a return. If two stocks both have an average annual return of 30%, but one has a volatility, or risk, of 10% (that is, according to statistical tables, two times out of three its return will be between 20% and 40%, that is, 30% +/– 10%) and the other of 50% (two times out of three its return will be between –20% and +80%), then the former has a better risk-adjusted return. Again, the websites listed below provide such data and stock names.

Second comes *correlation*. Of the stocks thrown up, the sites tell you how correlated (moving in lockstep) the stocks are to each other. Adding volatile stocks to a portfolio actually decreases the portfolio's overall volatility if the stocks are not highly correlated: so you increase returns for the same level of risk. Don't worry about how and why – someone got a Nobel prize for working that out.

For instance, take a dummy portfolio with £5000 of Granada, Whitbread and BP stock. Online tools tell me that if I replace Whitbread with Sainsbury's, my expected return increases from 8% to 12% (a 50% improvement) without increasing my risk. I just used a website, I didn't ask a stock picker or read an annual report.

Thirdly, move to *optimization*. Through hundreds of calculations, the sites tell you how much of each stock and which combination of stocks you should purchase to ensure the highest possible rate of return for your target level of risk. The result is what the professionals call an "optimally asset allocated portfolio on the efficient frontier", also known as a "darn good portfolio" to you and me.

For example, if you hold £5000 of Granada and Whitbread, you may think the worst-case loss would be roughly the same for each stock – they are FTSE 100 stocks and you hold the same amount of each. Wrong. On a bad day (one of their worst performing 20 days in a year), you're likely to lose double (around £200) with Granada. I bet a fund manager couldn't tell you that in 0.01 seconds.

These tools also allow you to play around with issues like: "If I want more/less returns in a shorter/longer time, want to take more/less risk – tell me what stocks or funds I should own."

The sites apply the work of Nobel laureates, are designed to be used by private individuals, but boast about the number of institutions employing them. So you can be your own broker or independent financial advisor (IFA). With no IFA to be irked by a barrage of questions from you – the website answers them all automatically – you can also even play around with forecasts at 4am, or simply change your mind – now that's liberating. Or you could always keep your IFA and outsmart him!

Risk is a difficult concept to master for other reasons beyond the maths. "Ride your losses until they become profits" is one of the key beliefs of trading legend John Meriwether, according to a book about him.[1] Many private investors will be pleased they share the same trading philosophy as the man who ran a $100 billion fund. That fund, using that philosophy, also lost billions as it self-destructed.

Risk is as much about the mind as it is about numbers. For instance, imagine you are asked to make a range prediction such that you are 90% sure that the price of, say, Vodafone will be within that range in 12 months. The chances are you will be wrong and the price will be outside your range. We know traders would get it wrong because 2003 research shows that over 80% of traders, even professionals like Meriwether, wrongly forecast the price range of equities 12 months hence, even when asked for a range which was so wide they felt 90% sure the price would fall within it.[2]

We're psychologically overoptimistic on risk. It is why I rely on the grey computer under my desk as much as the grey matter between my ears.

> **My sites: Portfolio sites**
> www.finPortfolio.com *****
> www.riskmetrics.com/wealthbench.html ****
> www.quicken.com *****
> www.invest1to1.com ****

How much should I place on any one trade?

It is the knowledge of how to calculate the answer to this question that makes the main bedrock of a successful trading record. So should I have buried it in one part of one chapter of the book or should I have emblazoned it on the title to the whole book?

The problem with calling this book "how much should I place on any one trade" is the same problem the financial media face: how can we attract viewers? The difference with me is, I will give you your medicine, too often they only give you the sweet sugary title, the fluff.

If you risk too little on each trade, the returns will be too low to overcome transaction costs, small losses, and overheads (quote fees, electricity, rent, costs of books such as this, and so on).

Risk more and the returns will increase, but one bad trade and you are wiped out and have to explain to the spouse how you have had to cancel the annual vacation and pawn the mother-in-law.

Traders use different formulae to work out how much money they should put on any trade. Gibbons Burke, in an outstanding article in the excellent *Active Trader* magazine,[3] provides one such useful formula. You can use this formula to determine how many shares of stock to buy (actually, the formula should have been the title of the book, but for some reason the publishers thought it might not make the *New York Times* bestseller list if I did that):

$$s = \frac{e \times r}{p - x}$$

where

s = size of the trade
e = portfolio equity (cash and holdings)
r = maximum risk percentage per trade
p = entry price on the trade
x = predetermined stop-loss or exit price

Gibbons Burke gives the following example:

Belinda has a trading account with a total value (cash and holdings) of $100,000 and is willing to risk 2 percent of that capital on any one trade. Her trading system gives her a signal to buy DTCM stock trading at $100 per share and the system says that the reversal point on that trade is $95. Plugging this into the formula tells Belinda that she can buy 400 shares of DTCM. The cost of this investment is $40,000, but she is only risking 2 percent of her capital, or $2000, on the idea.

Belinda then gets a tip from her brother-in-law that KRMA is about to take a nose dive from its lofty perch at $40 because he heard from his barber that KRMA's earnings will be well below expectations. She's willing to go short another $10,000 of her stake on this idea. She studies a KRMA chart and can't see any logical technical points that would be a good place to put in a stop, so she uses the money management method to determine the stop according to this formula:

$$x = \frac{p(i - e \times r)}{i}$$

where

x = predetermined stop-loss or exit price
p = entry price on the trade
i = investment amount
e = portfolio equity (cash and holdings)
r = maximum risk percentage per trade

Since she's shorting KRMA, the value for i, $10,000, should be negative. Placing these figures into the formula tells Belinda that her stop price on the short sale of KRMA should be 48. If she didn't want to assign a high confidence on this trade, she could reduce the max. risk to 1% ($r = 0.01$), which would bring the stop down to 44.

How much money to place on any one trade II

Another variation is to use legendary trader Ed Seykota's "core equity" for e in the formula rather than the total value of all holdings in the portfolio. Core equity is what you have left when you subtract the total value at risk in all open positions from the total equity; value at risk in each trade is calculated by multiplying the number of shares in the position by the difference between the current price and the stop price on that trade.

It is important to watch your positions as they progress and adjust your stop prices as the market moves in your direction.

In the first example, if DTCM moves from $100 to $120 and the stop is left at $95, what started as $2000 or 2% at risk is now $10,000 (9% of the total equity) at risk.

Moving your stop-loss up with the price on a winning trade has several key advantages:

1. It locks in your profits and if you are using core equity to size new positions, it will allow you to take more risk on new trades.

2. Never move a stop backwards from its initial price – stops should always be moved to reduce, never increase, the amount of risk on a trade. Past the initial risk you are willing to take, stops should be a one-way valve for the flow of money. You should not let money go from your account to the market, it should be coming from the market to your account.

Kelly's formula for bet size

John Kelly, who worked for AT&T's Bell Laboratory, originally developed the Kelly criterion to assist AT&T with its long distance telephone signal noise issues. But investors and betters have since realized that importance also lies in bet size!

There are two basic components to the Kelly criterion:

1. Win probability – The probability that any given trade you make will return a positive amount.

2. Win/loss ratio – The total positive trade amounts divided by the total negative trade amounts.

These two factors are then put into Kelly's equation:

Kelly $\% = W - (1 - W) / R$
where:
W = Winning probability
R = Win/loss ratio
The output is the Kelly percentage.

Kelly's system can be put to use by following these simple steps:

1. Examine your last 50 trades. The Kelly criterion assumes, however, that you trade the same way you traded in the past.

2. Calculate "W," the winning probability. To do this, divide the number of trades that returned a positive amount by your total amount of trades (positive and negative). This number is better as it gets closer to 1. Any number above 0.50 is good.

3. Calculate "R," the win/loss ratio. Do this by dividing your total number of positive trades by the total number of negative trades. You should have a number greater than 1 if you have more wins than losses, and less than 1 if you have more losses than wins.

4. Input these numbers into Kelly's equation: $K\% = W - (1 - W) / R$.

5. Record the Kelly percentage that the equation returns.

Interpreting the results

The percentage (a number less than 1) that the equation outputs represents the size of the positions you should be taking. For example, if the Kelly percentage is 0.05, then you should take a 5% position in each of the equities in your portfolio. This system, in essence, lets you know how much you should diversify.

The system does require some common sense, however. One rule to keep in mind, regardless of what the Kelly percentage may tell you, is never commit more than 20–25% of your capital to *one equity*. An allocation higher than this is far more risk than most people should be taking.

Using the Kelly Simulator at www.hquotes.com/tradehard/simulator. html, we can see how hypothetical portfolios might perform. In Figure 4.1 you can see the activity in 75 simulated trading accounts by means of an equity curve.

We assumed for each account, the average amount won is the same as the average amount lost; however, the people are able to win 60% of the time. The Kelly criterion then told them to allocate 19% of their capital to each equity. The result is a positive return in the long run for all traders (notice some short-term downside, however). The highest return was 140% (started at 100, went to 235) over 453 bars. Bars represent the time between trades, which may be daily, depending on the system our hypothetical traders use.

Let's look at another one (Figure 4.2). If your trading system means that you win as much money when you win as lose when you lose, but you win 55% of the time, then the simulated results appear below. Basically, according to the Kelly formula, you should put 10% of your portfolio in each equity. But note that you may end up on some occasions not doing too well.

But note Figure 4.3. Even where you have more losing trades than winning ones (in the example below you win 45% of the time), but win more on your winning trades (in the example below you win £1.5 in every winning trade for every £1 lost on a losing trade), then you can still have outstanding portfolio results. This reinforces the importance of cutting losses over the number of wins. (The Kelly formula says you should only put 8% of your portfolio in any one position, that is, own 12 stocks.)

If you extend the logic, it also means that which stocks you pick is less important than whether you cut your losses. But, when was the last time a stock picker said: "I don't have a stock for you, that is irrelevant. Instead, cut your losses by strict money management. And you don't need me here next week." That would not be good TV. That's why such genuine knowledge only appears in books and not on TV. Ask an analyst if he's heard of the Kelly formula for position sizing. I'll bet he hasn't!

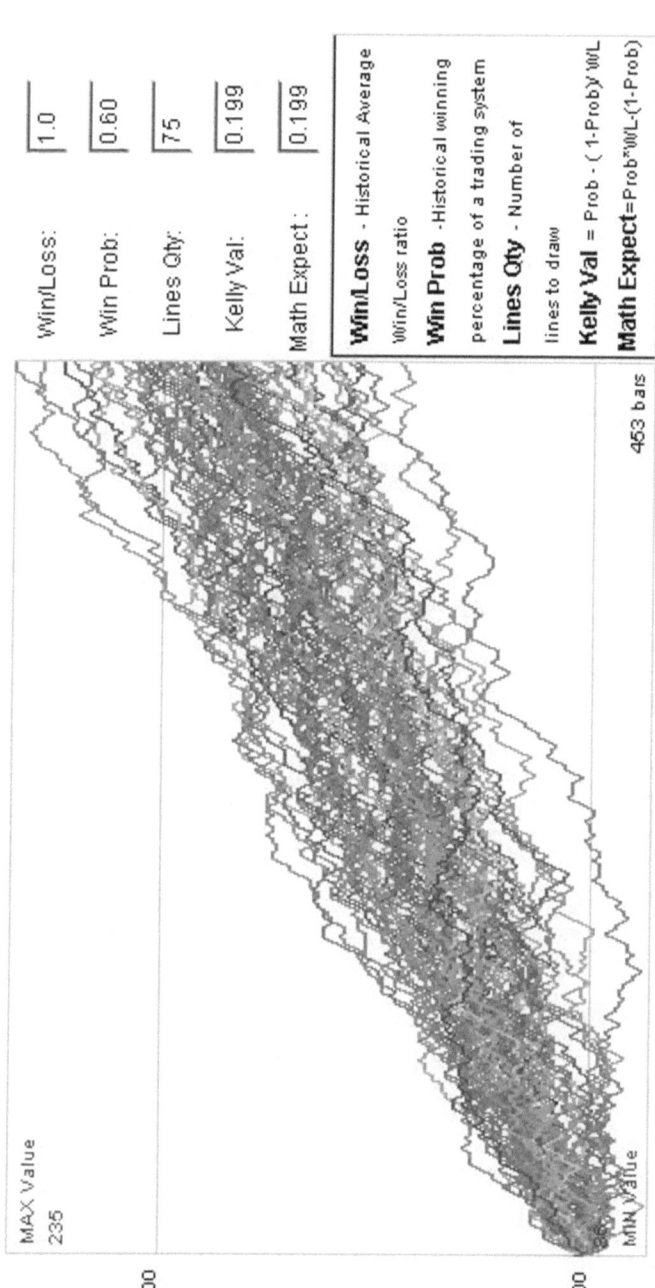

Win/Loss: 1.0

Win Prob: 0.60

Lines Qty: 75

Kelly Val: 0.199

Math Expect: 0.199

Win/Loss - Historical Average

Win/Loss ratio

Win Prob - Historical winning

percentage of a trading system

Lines Qty - Number of

lines to draw

Kelly Val = Prob - (1-Prob)/ W/L

Math Expect=Prob*W/L-(1-Prob)

MAX Value
235

200

100

MIN Value

453 bars

Figure 4.1 Simulated portfolios

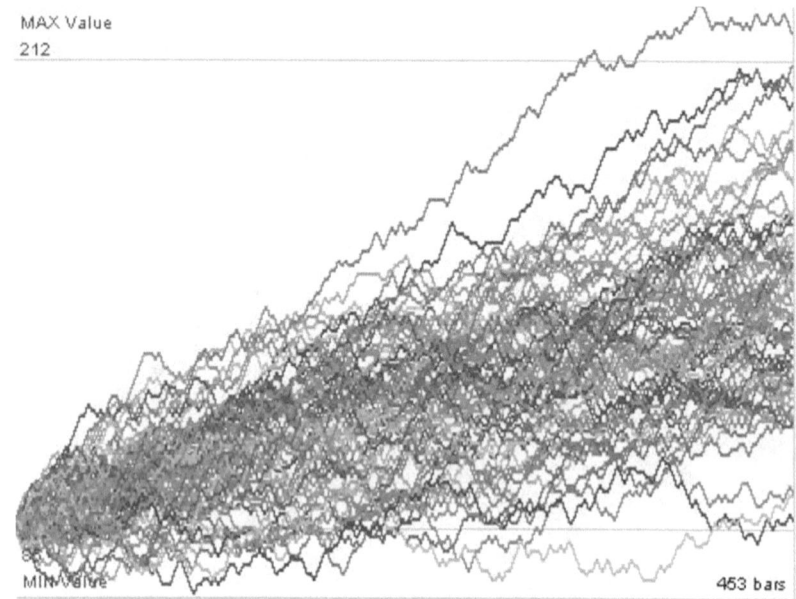

MAX Value
212

MIN Value
453 bars

Figure 4.2 More Kelly simulations

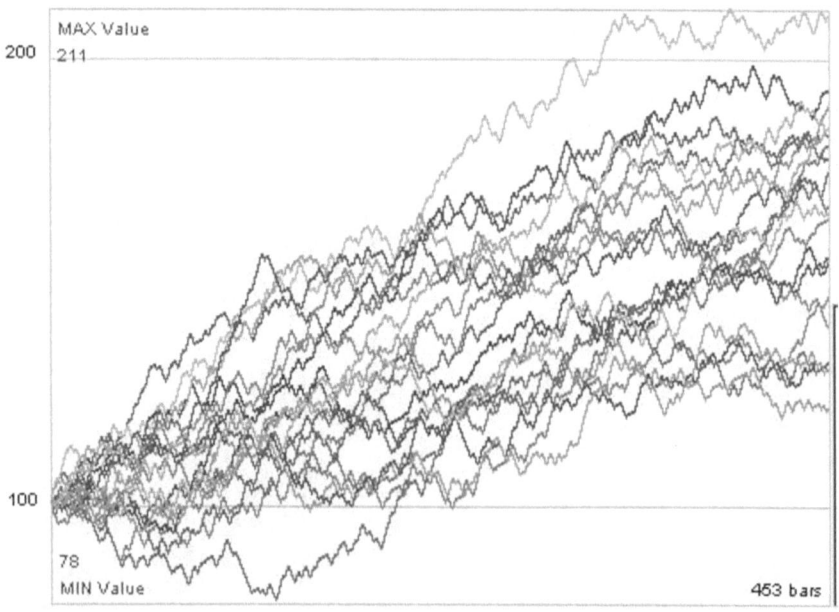

MAX Value
200 211

100

78
MIN Value
453 bars

Figure 4.3 Cutting your losses is more
important than the stocks you pick

In Figure 4.3, note that in the short-term, the simulated portfolio may be under water for some of the time.

How money management subtleties get lost on TV

You may think there are two types of analysts on financial TV – the one who always says "buy" to everything and the other who talks like a lawyer: "On the one hand I like this because of this, that and the other, and on the other hand it has these downsides." The former finds himself in jail thanks to the New York attorney general, the latter is also in the painful position of sitting on a fence and the pain that causes to one's behind.

Actually there is of course a third type of commentator – the one who knows what he is doing and his answers reveal that, but the time on screen only permits viewer misperception.

Let me explain. Credit Suisse First Boston's Michael Mauboussin and Kristen Bartholdson describe it well: *The frequency of correctness does not matter; it is the magnitude of correctness that matters.* Say that you own four stocks, and three of the stocks go down a bit but the fourth rises substantially. The portfolio will perform well even as the majority of the stocks decline:

> Building a portfolio that can deliver superior performance requires that you eval-
> uate each investment using expected value analysis. What is striking is that the
> leading thinkers across varied fields – including horse betting, casino gambling,
> and investing – all emphasize the same point. We call it the Babe Ruth effect:
> even though Ruth struck out a lot, he was one of baseball's greatest hitters.[4]

In 1979, Daniel Kahneman and Amos Tversky[5] outlined prospect theory, which identifies economic behaviors that are inconsistent with rational decision making. One insight is that people exhibit significant aversion to losses when making choices between risky outcomes, no matter how small the stakes. In fact, Kahneman and Tversky found that a loss has about *two and a half times* the impact of a gain of the same size. In other words, people feel a lot worse about losses of a given size than they feel good about a gain of a similar magnitude.

This behavioral fact means that people are a lot happier when they are right frequently. People look for the number of winners, not the magnitude of wins. The *percentage* of stocks that go up in a portfolio does not deter-mine its performance, it is the dollar change in the portfolio. A few stocks going up or down dramatically will often have a much greater impact on portfolio performance than the batting average.

In the book *Fooled by Randomness*, Nassim Taleb[6] relates an anecdote that beautifully drives home the expected value message. A colleague asked Taleb about his view of the market. He said that he thought there was a high probability that the market would go up slightly over the next week. Pressed further, he assigned a 70% probability to the up move.

Someone in the meeting then noted that Taleb was short a large quantity of S&P 500 futures – a bet that the market would go down. Taleb then explained his position in expected value terms. He clarified his thought process with the following table:

Event	Probability	Outcome	Expected
Market goes up	70%	+1 %	+0.7%
Market goes down	30%	−10%	−3.0%
Total	100%		−2.3%

In this case, the most *probable* outcome is that the market goes up. But the expected value is negative, because the outcomes are asymmetric.

Now think about this for a television interview. How many of you, hearing a commentator say he expects a high probability of a price rise, would think that is a signal to buy?

Now consider the downtrodden stock. The majority of the time it disappoints, nudging the stock somewhat lower. But a positive result leads to a sharp upside move. Here, the probability favors a poor result, but the expected value is favorable.

As the CSFB authors explain:

Investors must constantly look past frequencies and consider expected value. As it turns out, this is how the best performers think in all probabilistic fields. Yet in many ways it is unnatural: investors want their stocks to go up, not down. Indeed, the main practical result of prospect theory is that investors tend to sell their winners too early (satisfying the desire to be right) and hold their losers too long (in the hope that they don't have to take a loss).[4]

To Buffett

Warren Buffett says: "A lot of people start out with a 400-horsepower motor but only get 100 horsepower of output, it's way better to have a 200-horsepower motor and get it all into output." (Quoted on IFA.tv).

And one of the keys is to consider all investment opportunities in terms of expected value. As Buffett's partner Charlie Munger notes: "One of the advantages of a fellow like Buffett is that he automatically thinks in terms of decision trees."

Says Buffett: *"Take the probability of loss times the amount of possible loss from the probability of gain times the amount of possible gain. That is what we're trying to do. It's imperfect, but that's what it's all about."*

The discipline of the process compels an investor to think through how various changes in expectations for value triggers – sales, costs, and investments – affect shareholder value, as well as the likelihood of various outcomes. Such an exercise also helps overcome the risk-aversion pitfall.

As the CSFB analysts explain: "The expected value mindset is by no means limited to investing". Steven Crist's *Bet with the Best*[7] offers various strategies for pari-mutuel betters. Crist, CEO, editor and publisher of *Daily Racing Form*, shows the return on investment, including the track's take, of a hypothetical race with four horses. To summarize the lesson, he writes: "The point of this exercise is to illustrate that even a horse with a very high likelihood of winning can be either a very good or a very bad bet, and that the difference between the two is determined by only one thing: the odds." So a horse with a 50% probability of winning can be either a good or bad bet based on the payoff, and the same holds true of a 10–1 shot. He is saying, in plain words: *It is not the frequency of winning that matters, but the frequency times the magnitude of the payoff.*

"Yet another domain where expected value thinking is pertinent is blackjack, as Edward Thorp's bestselling book, *Beat the Dealer*,[8] shows. In blackjack, the payoffs are set, and the player's principal task is to assess the probability of drawing a favorable hand. Thorp showed how to count cards in order to identify when the probabilities of a winning hand tilt in the player's favor. When the odds favor the player, the ideal strategy is to increase the bet (effectively increasing the payout). Thorp notes that even under ideal circumstances, favorable situations only arise 9.8% of the time; the house has the advantage the other 90.2%.

So we see that the leading thinkers in these three domains – all probabilistic exercises – converge on the same approach. We also know that in these activities, the vast majority of the participants don't think through expected value as explicitly as they should. That we are risk averse and avoid losses compounds the challenge for stock investors, because we shun situations where the probability of upside may be low but the expected value is attractive." (www.IFA.tv).

A useful analogy

Long-term success in any of these probabilistic exercises require certain "know-hows:"

- **Focus**. Professional gamblers do not play a multitude of games – they don't stroll into a casino and play a little blackjack, a little craps, and spend a little time on the slot machine. They focus on a specific game and learn the ins and outs. Similarly, most investors must define a circle of competence – areas of relative expertise. Seeking a competitive edge across a spectrum of industries and companies is a challenge, to say the least. Most great investors stick to their circle of competence.

- **Lots of situations**. Players of probabilistic games must examine lots of situations, because the "market" price is usually pretty accurate. Investors, too, must evaluate lots of situations and gather lots of information. For example, the very successful president and CEO of Geico's capital operations, Lou Simpson, tries to read for five to eight hours a day, and trades very infrequently.

- **Limited opportunities**. As Thorp notes in *Beat the Dealer*, even when you know what you're doing and play under ideal circumstances, the odds still favor you less than 10% of the time. And rarely does anyone play under ideal circumstances. The message for investors is even when you are competent, favorable situations – where you have a clear-cut variant perception vis-à-vis the market – don't appear very often.

- **Ante**. In the casino, you must bet every time to play. Ideally, you can bet a small amount when the odds are poor and a large sum when the odds are favorable, but you must ante to play the game. In investing, on the other hand, you need not participate when you perceive the expected value as unattractive, and you can bet aggressively when a situation appears attractive (within the constraints of an investment policy, naturally). In this way, investing is much more favorable than other games of probability.

Beating the fear to trade

But there is another aspect of risk and trading. Despite the best efforts of financial TV and media, millions prefer to watch Letterman instead of catching up on the latest from CNBC Japan – "go figure".

They, alongside offline private investors, are being excessively and irrationally risk averse and missing opportunities to maximize their stock returns, according to one study, "Why Stocks may Disappoint", from Columbia University.[2] Why are we missing out on readily obtainable gains? Especially when a visit to any bookstore reveals the deluge of magazines promising huge returns?

Private investors are tending to misallocate their resources. They would rather have a high probability of a small loss, as in a lottery, than a small chance of a bigger loss by trading equities, even though equities provide better returns. The study labels this "disappointment aversion." The effect is fewer people hold stocks than should, given their personal circumstances and the potential equity returns. Even those who hold stocks are irrationally risk averse and conservative in their trading. They put a small slice of their wealth into equities even though equities are expected to outperform other asset classes.

A 2001 McKinsey report, *Beyond Day Trading*, confirms that while the number of people trading online increases, the amount of their assets allocated to this new form of investment remains stubbornly low.

It is investors' attitude to risk that leads to poor asset allocation and therefore poor returns on their resources. Age, wealth, and living expenses do not predict the proportion of investments held in stocks, while attitudes to risk aversion do, according to a study by Kahneman:[9] thus risk-taking investors (who tend to hold more stocks) regret avoiding risk, unlike most investors who fear taking risk and losing. Given that over the long term stocks tend to outperform less risky investments, this suggests that personality is a predictor of superior investment performance.

If you are in the category of people who, despite the ever seductive pied-piper lure of financial TV, do not act upon all those stock ideas, what should you do to overcome your fears? Two simple solutions. One, use the same tools detailed in this chapter that the overexcitable financial TV junkie uses and, two, take the risk tolerance test later in this chapter.

Risk measurement tools

Don't even expect someone on financial TV to mention these important concepts

As I have mentioned, reward without risk is worthless. But most people do not know what risk means. It is the volatility (or probability) of different returns. The Sharpe Ratio allows you to factor in the potential impact of return volatility on expected return, and objectively compare assets or portfolios that vary in returns.

A PRACTICAL EXAMPLE

Consider Assets A, B, and C in the chart below.

	Avg. annual return	Return volatility	Sharpe Ratio
Asset A	54.52%	177.20%	0.279
Asset B	36.91%	68.20%	0.468
Asset C	25.64%	22.69%	0.910

If we compare these assets on average annual return alone, Asset A appears to be the clearly superior investment, and even Asset B appears to be a better bet than Asset C. However, if we factor in return volatility, Asset C emerges as the superior investment in terms of risk-adjusted returns.

VaR (value at risk) is another important risk measurement tool used by major financial institutions that presents risk in terms of potential financial loss on your portfolio. VaR expresses portfolio volatility into an actual value, which represents (with 95% confidence) the most money your portfolio is likely to lose within a given time-frame in the future.

Of course, since VaR is presented "with 95% confidence," this implies that you can pessimistically anticipate maximum future losses exceeding a VaR amount 5% of the time within a given time-frame.

Note: In general, a portfolio with low return volatility and low correlation between individual assets will have a low VaR.

A PRACTICAL EXAMPLE

In the chart below, an example from FinPortfolio, we have a user portfolio and the S&P 500 portfolio. While both portfolios have equal market values, the user portfolio's higher VaR numbers indicate that it carries significantly more risk than the S&P 500 portfolio.

For example, we can say with 95% confidence that on any given day in the future, the currently held user portfolio could lose up to $1159, and the S&P 500, up to $776. Since the user portfolio's daily VaR is presented "with 95% confidence," our user must understand that on any given day in the future there is a 5% probability of maximum financial loss exceeding $1159.

	User portfolio	S&P 500 portfolio
Market value of portfolio (as of latest market closing)	$95,910	$95,910
Daily VaR	$1159	$776
Monthly VaR	$5311	$3557
Annual VaR	$18,399	$12,322

Now explain what use it is having a stock pick such as "buy Google." It is meaningless. How does the stock picker on television know whether you are willing to be exposed to the value at risk that Google ownership entails. It is downright negligent not to mention it.

What financial journalists should do

I hated giving stock picks on Bloomberg TV. Each week my job was to give a buy and a sell. The price would then be noted alongside the price and in six months' time my pick would be reviewed, live on air. Don't get me wrong, I didn't hate it because I was bad at it, or because of the ribbing and teasing I would get before each show if the returns were not there. I did not hate it for fear of viewers emailing me, or for fear of the damage to my reputation on online bulletin boards.

None of these things worried me. I knew I was, and still am, good. Sure, you may say that's arrogant, but when you are one of the best, I don't think that's arrogant. Anyway, one year, an intern was told to go through all my picks over a 6-month period – my "buys" and my "sells" – and compare them to all other stock pickers on Bloomberg TV. My performance beat all the other gurus, analysts, and fund managers.

No, I hated it because I simply did not know the risk profile of any viewer who might act on my picks. Sure it is great when I meet a viewer for whom I have made money and he offers to buy me a drink (they never offer a profit share!).

What I used to do on Bloomberg TV, whenever I had the time or opportunity, was to say alongside any pick how risky it was, the time-frame for a price target and the price at which I would know I was wrong and so investors should cut their losses. It's the bare minimum, even in a time-constrained environment, that any financial commentator should do. But they don't teach you that anywhere in financial journalism or stock-picking school. No, only professional traders understand that.

More definitions – it's all Greek to the financial journalists

Alpha   As traders we are trying to "capture alpha," The higher your alpha, the better your portfolio has done in achieving "excess" returns. It is generally considered that the higher the alpha, the higher the "value added" to the portfolio by the portfolio manager. (*Note:* The market portfolio alpha is always 0.0.)

Beta   Measures the portfolio's sensitivity to movements in the market portfolio, or benchmark index (for example S&P 500 always has a beta of 1.0). A beta > 1.0 means that the asset or portfolio is more volatile (risky) than the benchmark index, and a beta < 1.0 means the asset or portfolio is less volatile.

R2   Indicates the percentage of a portfolio's movement that is explained by the movement in the market portfolio or benchmark index. R2 ranges from 0 to 100%, with a score of 100 indicating that all movements of the portfolio are completely explained by the market portfolio or benchmark index. In general, the higher the R2, the more reliable a portfolio's alpha and beta measurements will be.

A portfolio's beta is calculated by comparing a portfolio's volatility to the market's volatility over time. The more sensitive a portfolio's returns are to movements in the market, the higher the portfolio's beta will be. Higher betas therefore imply higher risk.

R2 helps us to understand how useful the beta and alpha numbers are for any given portfolio. The closer to 100%, the more meaningful our beta and alpha measurements are.

A PRACTICAL EXAMPLE

The chart below illustrates the user portfolio's exposure to market risk.

Market exposure measurement	User portfolio	S&P 500 portfolio
Beta	1.4	1.0
Alpha	7.2	0
R2	77%	100%

A beta of 1.4 suggests that the user's portfolio is more volatile than the S&P 500. An alpha of 7.2 tells us that the portfolio exceeded its expected return, given the portfolio's beta. Finally, the user portfolio's R2 measurement suggests that 77% of its volatility can be explained by volatility in the market. The user portfolio's high R2 lends credibility to its alpha and beta measurements.

"I don't know what else you own, but buy this anyway"

There are certain key things it is useful to know about your portfolio. Anyone, including you, who does not know them, might as well make their "investments" in Las Vegas. If you ever meet a financial writer, ask them if they know what the "diversification benefits" or "risk impact" are. I'll give you better odds than Vegas that they do not know what they mean or why they are important.

1. Diversification benefits – why you can't just add any old stock to your portfolio

Should you add that hot stock tip mentioned in the newspaper to your portfolio? Well, the stock-picking analyst never discusses your existing portfolio, he doesn't know or care about it. But you should. Here is why.

If we use the example of a portfolio of four stocks – IBM, General Electric, General Motors, and AT&T – we get a RiskGrade of 145 for the portfolio.

Stock	RiskGrade
IBM	214
General Electric	193
General Motors	202
AT&T	278
Portfolio	145

A RiskGrade of 145 is less than the RiskGrade of each of these individual stocks. We also calculate a diversification measure in RiskGrade terms, which for this portfolio is 77. In essence diversification is making your portfolio 34% less risky. Hence, in a portfolio, the sum of the individual stocks' RiskGrades do not equal the whole.

So how can someone tell you to buy a stock without considering the portfolio you already own and the impact on it?

2. Risk impact

Another reason why that magazine article headed "10 stocks you must own now" is the intellectual equivalent of a *National Enquirer* headline "President is an Alien, details inside."

RiskMetrics research has identified historical stress scenarios that have resulted in the largest losses for a diversified global portfolio consisting of 60% equities and 40% fixed income. The following historical scenarios resulted in the largest one- and five-day portfolio losses:

Crisis	Date	1-day loss	5-day loss
Black Monday	19 Oct 87	–2.2%	–5.9%
Gulf War	3 Aug 90	–0.9%	–3.8%
Mex Peso Fallout	23 Jan 95	–1.0%	–2.7%
Asian Crisis	27 Oct 97	–1.9%	–3.6%
Russia Devaluation	27 Aug 98	–3.8%	–2.6%

Many investors, including professional money managers, lost much more money during these days because their portfolios were not as well diversified. For example, the LTCM hedge fund lost over 80% of its value during the 1998 Russian devaluation, because of excessive leverage and overconcentration.

It's not funny how many bad "once-in-a-lifetime" market drops happen in a single lifetime.

3. Journalists studied English not math at university

Math may not be a strong suit of business TV presenters, hence no one ever mentions, along with their trading stock picks, how quickly things can go wrong and how long it takes to recover from losses.

Look at the table below. If your portfolio loses 20%, then you need to achieve a 25% gain to break even, which is more than even Warren Buffett's long-term average. The point is, make sure that you do not even make a paltry 20% loss. It is easily lost. So look at the figures. Print them out. It is why the world's best traders cut their losses short and quickly. Phone any TV program and ask any stock-picking analyst who appears on TV: 'If my portfolio drops 30% as a result of your stock pick, how much does it need to rise to break even?' I guarantee they will not know.

Loss of capital (%)	Gain to recover (%)
5	5.3
10	11.1
15	17.6
20	25.0
25	33.3
30	42.9
35	53.8
40	66.7
45	81.8
50	100.0
55	122.0
60	150.0

Look at Figure 4.4. Notice how the percentage to recover increases exponentially as the loss increases.

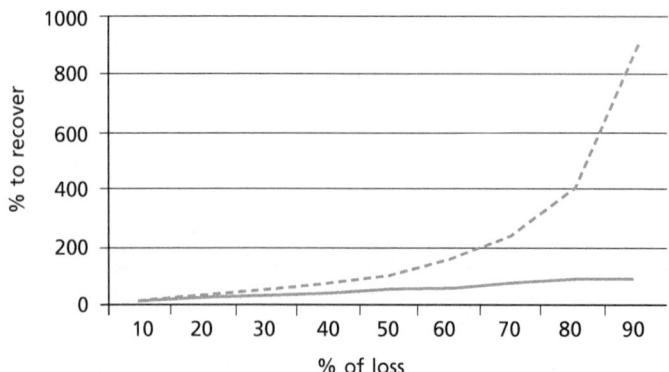

Figure 4.4 Deep under water

4. Smart, on TV, picking stocks and without a clue

You may think the above title is harsh. Especially because all those banking analysts are surely very clever people – maybe with PhDs. An experiment was conducted involving forty people with doctors' degrees, who were asked to trade on a computer. They started with $10,000 and were given 100 trials playing a game in which they would win 60% of the time. When they won, they won the amount of money they risked in that trial. When they lost, they lost the amount of money they risked in that trial.

How many PhDs made money at the end of the experiment? Two. The other 38 lost money – 95% of these very academically smart people lost money playing a game in which the odds of winning were better than any odds in Las Vegas. Why did they lose?

They lost because of poor money management. For instance, if you start out risking $1000 and lose four times in a row, you are now down to $6000. You might be thinking: "I am due for a win now." But that's nonsense. Your chances of winning are and always will be 60%!

Even though your chances of winning are still 60%, let's say you decide to double your bet size since you believe you are due for a win now. You lose again and you're down 60% now.

Just a few trades and you're out. The lessons are:

1. Money management not stock picking is key and vital

2. Don't increase bet sizes because you lost money, do the opposite – reduce bet size.

3. When a fund manager on TV says a stock has fallen and so he is buying more – don't fall for it. Either he is buying more of something the market is willing to sell ever more cheaply, or he is sweating and trying to drum up business and save his neck or his ego is making promises he wants you to pay for by buying the stock. On Bloomberg TV, I would give fund managers who told investors to buy more of a falling stock an especially hard time. On behalf of the viewer, I saved my venom for them.

Risk tolerance test

Here is one test from RiskMetrics. So what's the right amount of risk to take? First, consider your risk preference. After all, what good is a profitable investment if it costs a heart attack along the way? One person may be inherently comfortable with risks that make another's stomach churn. How would you feel if your portfolio lost 10% or even 21% in a single day (that's how much the Nasdaq fell by on April 14, 2000 and the S&P 500 fell by on Black Monday in October 1987)? You can take some tests to discover your risk preference.

Two questions to test your risk preference might be:

1. Given the following selection of envelopes, which would you choose?

    A Envelope with a 50% chance of containing $1000 (or nothing)

    B Envelope with 5% chance of containing $10,000 (or nothing)

    C Envelope with 0.1% chance of containing $400,000 (or nothing)

2. It's January 3, 2000 and having missed out completely on the U.S. bull market, you decide to enter the millennium with a plan to invest in stocks. You start with an investment in Amazon.com and Lucent Technologies. Of course that's right before the technology sector tanks, with both investments plummeting by 28% before the week is over. What do you do?

    A Sell these scary stocks and move back into safe money market haven

    B Hold on and ride it out

    C Hold on and continue with your plan of making other equity investments

    D Buy more and take advantage of the discounted price

You're an **Aggressive Risk Investor** if you answered C and D, respectively (too aggressive, in fact, considering that in question 1 the expected return of option C is lower than for alternatives A and B).

You're a **Medium Risk Investor** if you answered B, and B or C, respectively, which means that you are willing to take some risks to earn your return, but shy away from making big bets. For question 2, answer C is what investment gurus would advise – the most proven way to make money in the market over the long run is to steadily invest, and avoid trying to time the market.

You're a **Low Risk Investor** if you answered A both times. You are someone who values predictability of returns above all and may be prone to mattress stuffing when left unsupervised.

People will always have different preferences for risk taking. Some claim that we are born with an innate risk tolerance level, although our appetite for risk tends to diminish as we grow older. In general it makes sense for a young person to take more risk. Conversely, an 81-year-old has little incentive to risk his or her retirement

Risk in life and risk in trading are two different things. Whilst this book is not about life skills, but trading skills, let me leave you with an outstanding speech on risk by a man who understands business and market risks as well as risk taking in life, Charles Sanford, chairman of Bankers Trust:[10]

> From an early age, we are all conditioned by our families, our schools, and virtually every other shaping force in our society to avoid risk. To take risks is inadvisable; to play it safe is the counsel we are accustomed both to receiving and to passing on. In the conventional wisdom, risk is asymmetrical: It has only one side, the bad side. In my experience – and all I presume to offer you today is the observations drawn on my own experience, which is hardly the wisdom of the ages – in my experience, this conventional view of risk is shortsighted and often simply mistaken.
>
> My first observation is that successful people understand that risk, properly conceived, is often highly productive rather than something to avoid. They appreciate that risk is an advantage to be used rather than a pitfall to be skirted. Such people understand that taking calculated risks is quite different from being rash.
>
> This view of risk is not only unorthodox, it is paradoxical – the first of several paradoxes that I'm going to present to you today. This one might be encapsulated as follows: Playing it safe is dangerous. Far more often than you would realize, the real risk in life turns out to be the refusal to take a risk. In other words, the truly most threatening dangers usually arise when you shrink from confronting what only appear to be the most threatening dangers. What is widely regarded as playing it safe turns out not to be safe at all.
>
> What I'm offering here is not a surefire, guaranteed formula for success. No such formula exists. It never will. If anyone ever tries to sell you one, keep your money in your pocket. For life, above all else, is a risk. I'm not trying to dispel that risk with a bottle of Charlie Sanford's Magic Elixir. I can only arm you with a little food for thought. I do have a few suggestions. You may not wish to follow them. But if you'll think about them, I'll consider our time together most productively spent.
>
> We all know that modern civilization owes much to the ancient Greeks. As the 20th century draws to a close, it's difficult to single out a Greek thinker who speaks more directly to us than Heraclitus. All is flux, nothing stays still, said Heraclitus some 2500 years ago. Nothing endures but change.
>
> Most of us have come to believe that nothing endures but change, but its consequences still deserve some reflection. Obviously, if change is the fundamental rule of life, then resistance to change is folly – doomed to defeat. Just as obvi-

ously, if change is our constant, then uncertainty is an inescapable part of our lives. Uncertainty is unavoidable. Life is unpredictable. The very essence of life is the unexpected and the unintended, the unanticipated turns that we may metaphorically ascribe to Fate or Destiny or Providence.

Therefore, unless we wish to be tossed about like so much flotsam on the waves of inescapable change, we must place ourselves squarely in the midst of change. We must learn to ride the current of change rather than to swim against it – although people who haven't taken the trouble to learn how the world really works will think we're doing exactly the opposite.

In other words, risk is commonly thought of as going against the current, taking the hard way against high odds. In a world of constant change, however, a world where Heraclitus said we can never step into the same river twice, taking risks is accepting the flow of change and aligning ourselves with it. Remember the first paradox: Risk only looks like reckless endangerment. For those who understand reality, risk is actually the safest way to cope with a changing, uncertain world.

To take a risk is indeed to plunge into circumstances we cannot absolutely control. But the fact is that the only circumstances in this life that we can absolutely control are so relatively few and so utterly trivial as hardly to be worth the effort. Besides, the absence of absolute control – which is impossible in any case – does not entail the absence of any control, or even significant control.

There, again, is the paradox: In a world of constant change, risk is actually a form of safety, because it accepts that world for what it is. Conventional safety is where the danger really lies, because it denies and resists the world.

I trust you understand that when I say risk is actually safety, I'm talking about a certain sort of risk. I'm not advising that you leap off tall buildings in the hope that the operation of constant change will reverse the law of gravity in mid-flight. I'm speaking rather of a sort of risk that actually aligns you with the direction of change.

To be more specific, I believe firmly that the sort of risks that put one in a position to control one's lot in a world of incessant change are the risks that attempt to add something of value to that world. To create value, to focus one's efforts on increasing the fund of that which is worthwhile, involves (as we shall see) a sort of risk. And yet, paradoxically, it provides you with the greatest control over a changing world and maximizes your chances to achieve a truly meaningful personal satisfaction.

Advice from leading traders

> EXPERT
> *advice*
>
> **Bernard Oppetit,** *global head of equity derivatives, Paribas*
>
> You have to have good money management. You have to ensure you are not going to be hopelessly underwater. You can have rules like maximum drawdown, or value at risk, or limits. You can also have your own internal rules like "this is too much money to lose." You must have that in your mind and that you are not going to risk more than that at any one time. You have to make sure you are left in the game. That is very important. Once this is clearly established, you need fear, you need to feel that things can very quickly go wrong.

From a trader on the *Silicon Investor* website:

> The figure of merit is how much of your equity is at risk for each consecutive trade. The book suggests that 1 percent is a reasonable figure. This applies to the amount at risk, not the gross amount of the trade. For instance, if you could relatively expect to scalp a reasonably liquid stock without ever having a loss worse than $3/4 per share, then in order to trade 1000 shares, you would need to have $0.75 × 1000/0.01 = $75,000 in your account.

What if you limit the most equity you are willing to lose on a trade from 5% to 3%?

> In this case you would reduce your overall risk to 3 percent, but you also reduce the number of contracts you would be trading, so if the trade were profitable your rewards would be reduced. By reducing your risk, you protect your downside more.

Example: It is not necessarily a risky business

Imagine that you risk 2% of your equity in any one trade. Allowing for the fact that your account size drops on each occasion, your initial equity would be down 50% after 34 consecutive losses. What are the chances of 34 consecutive losses? Well, if there is a 50–50 chance of profit on any one trade, the chances of 34 consecutive losses would be 0.5 (3/4) or one in 17 billion. Makes you want to trade, doesn't it?

What if I am willing to accept a 1:1 reward to risk ratio?
The upside would be that you would give the price more room for maneu-

ver, that is, allow the trade more space to prove itself; the price could drop further before you had to exit. But the downside is that if the price just kept falling you would suffer a bigger loss when you exited. Another risk is that you are not playing the odds and if you got a string of losers you could be wiped out.

EXPERT advice

Bill Lipschutz, *former global head of foreign exchange, Salomon Brothers (in conversation with author)*

With a trade you always look at a multiple upside to downside. But how much greater? A good rule of thumb for a short-term trade – 48 hours or less – is a ratio of three to one. For longer term trades, especially when multiple leg option structures are involved and some capital may have to be employed, I look for a profit to loss ratio of at least five to one.

The loser's spiral – the dark side of trading

From a trader on *Silicon Investor:*

All of us, as traders, normally sense that trading can become "dangerous," if you let it get out of control when it's not going well. It can indeed be a rather dangerous (risky) endeavor, financially speaking. A friend of mine, after trading marginally successfully for a few months, said to me "Man, I sense this is really dangerous – I could get into a lot of trouble here." He was right. There is one basic process that destroys almost everyone that "blows out" of trading; I call it "the loser's spiral." I know all about it, as I went through it myself several times, in the process of really learning how to trade more consistently.

Only extreme interest in trading, and perseverance through travails got me through this one! I've never met a good trader who hasn't been through grappling with this, either. As they say, "You must learn how to lose before you can win." It is "the filter" which keeps most away from full-time, long-term trading success.

It goes something like this (simplified for brevity). Trader makes a bit of money. Skills develop. Trader makes a lot of money. Trader takes bigger risks. Things going well. Then … Wham! Big loss. Wham! Bigger loss. Trader tries to "make back" loss by taking bigger risks … and so on. The spiral is self-perpetuating.

Think that won't happen to you? Well, it happens to 80 percent of beginning traders within six to nine months (mileage varies depending upon prevailing market conditions). It happens to a lot of intermediate traders, and experienced traders. It happens to world class traders who run huge hedge funds, and it happens to people that have written scholarly books (Victor N.) and who are geniuses. So don't think it can't happen to you – it will, unless you study the mathematics of money management, and carefully calculate how much you can risk, versus your total tradeable capital.

The statistics are overwhelmingly against you, if you violate the cardinal rules (generally, if you are risking more than 1–5 percent per trade, depending on your trading style). For those with higher net worth, more tolerance for risk, or a longer time frame (usually a combination of these factors), the parameters are different. But the basic idea is, if you are trading too "large" (of risk on each trade), sooner or later it will destroy you and blow you out of the game – probably sooner rather than later.

EXPERT advice

Bill Lipschutz, *former global head of foreign exchange, Salomon Brothers (in conversation with author)*

With a trade you always look at a multiple upside to downside. You can look at the percentage probability of a rise or a fall. The problem with that is that you may have many trades that are 50–50. So you are trying to set something up which may have a 8:1 payoff. The fact of the matter is that if you put a lot of 14:1 structural ratio spreads, you are going to make money, because you have to be wrong 14 times in a row to lose, for every once you are right.

I think risk is asymmetrical. To achieve successful longevity, you have to focus on your losses, or drawdowns, or whatever you call them. It's very simple. Just know what you are prepared to lose. It doesn't matter how big, little, right or wrong your position is. You have to know what you are prepared to lose, I don't mean mentally prepared, I mean mathematically what can be lost when you enter a trade. You must not put yourself out of business. You have to be back. You have to be there tomorrow, the next day and the day after. If you manage the downside, the upside will look after itself.

Of course, when you first put on a trade you do have target levels, levels at which you think you are wrong. The price levels of those targets should be determined as a result of your absolute dollar loss constraints. For example, let's assume that the current price level of dollar to yen is 125 yen per dollar. Let's

EXPERT advice cont'd

further assume that your analysis of the latest round of trade negotiations between Japan and the United States leads you to believe that the yen may weaken to 130, but due to technical considerations should not strengthen beyond 122.50.

Further analysis of the pricing of yen options leads you to determine that the optimal trade structure will be to simply sell the yen against the dollar in the spot market. How large should the position be? The answer lies in the asset size of the account you are doing the trade for and its loss limit. If you are only prepared to take a three percent loss on a ten million dollar account, then it follows that you should buy $15,000,000 against the yen. If you are wrong on the trade, your loss will be $300,000 and if your analysis was correct and you sell the position at 130, your profit will be $500,000.

PROBABILITIES

Strictly speaking you should calculate your reward to risk ratio based not just on absolute figures but expected profit and expected loss. What does that mean? Well, let me give you some (painless) probability theory first.

Your expected gain is the probability of the gain occurring multiplied by the value of the gain. Trust me, this is relevant to trading. So, imagine there is a die. If it shows 1–5 I will lose $5, but if it shows 6, I will win $30. Should I take the bet? Trading the markets is a little like this.

In this example, my expected gain is $1/6 \times \$30$, that is, £5 (that is, the probability of a 6 on a die is 1/6). My expected loss is $5/6 \times \$5$, that is $4.17. So, since my expected reward is greater than my expected loss, I should take the bet.

Of course, I will lose more times than I win, but when I win, I should wipe out my accumulated losses. You could have a trading system that produces $30 profits one-sixth of the time and $5 profits five-sixths of the time. But note that your reward:risk ratio would not be 30:5. This is very important. If you forget the probabilities of your system, then you will think you are placing more favorable a trade than you actually are.

So how do you calculate the probability? You could use sophisticated computers, or back-test your system and estimate. Remember, even in a game of dice, there are no guarantees, only theory and reality, and they seldom converge. Large price moves have a lower probability of occurring than smaller ones. My suggestion is not necessarily to be hyper-scientific, but to take probabilities into your calculations.

When should I quit?

From a trader on *Silicon Investor:*

Successful trading is very difficult. The vast majority of those who try day trading end up losing money. However, the few successful day traders make huge sums of money – once they gain the knowledge and experience to be successful.

During the inevitable "learning curve" virtually all traders lose money. The tough decision is when to "pull the plug" and give up day trading if you are not successful. The following ideas may be worth considering:

- Are you financially secure enough to trade without the anxiety of needing a "paycheck" at the end of every day?
- Does day trading still interest you? Do you look forward to the opening of the market every day? In short, do you enjoy trading? If not, you're likely not committed to the extent that is required. Most people cannot excel at something they don't enjoy. The most successful people are virtually immersed in their fields.
- Is your trading improving? If you have made several hundred trades, you should be seeing some improvement in your trading results. Keep detailed records of your trades in a spreadsheet. This will give you irrefutable data that show your results in black and white. Don't argue with the facts.
- In addition to the statistical data, do you feel you are avoiding many of the dumb mistakes that you made when you first began trading?
- Are you trying to trade with some kind of plan, or are you just trading from the seat of your pants? Hopefully, after several weeks or months of trading, you are beginning to formulate some ideas on personal trading strategy to guide your trading. Even if not successful with a particular strategy, you will

gain knowledge by *learning* that the strategy was not successful. Then you can modify or refine your system to improve performance. If you trade by the seat of your pants, you have no reference point to *what* you were doing that was unsuccessful.

The decision to quit trading is a very difficult one. Over 90 percent of day traders wish they had made this decision sooner. Do not let your ego prevent you from giving up trading. The odds are stacked extremely heavily against success. People who lose money are in very good company. Not being a successful day trader should be nothing to cause embarrassment or to be ashamed of.

In the end, it is a personal decision of when to stop day trading if you cannot find success. I think an individual needs to very honestly review their situation and make their best decision.

Note: Don't decide during market hours!

> **EXPERT advice**
>
> **Jon Najarian,** *CEO, Mercury Trading*
>
> I believe discipline could be a learned response. You could teach somebody to do it, but you really have to hammer it into them too if they have got a problem – you cannot let them ride it at all. You have to be very, very honest with yourself. The single biggest thing is that they need to have a goal for every trade that they make. So if I do a trade and, say, I am buying a stock at $30 because I think it is going to $35, then I know what my downside limit is; it is $25, because if I am going to make $5, if I am right, then I do not want to have to lose more than $5 if I am wrong. So if I have goal which I think the stock is going to reach, then as a minimum I set my loss at where I think the gain could be if I am right.

How much money to start with?

A very popular question raised by many new traders is how much money they should start trading with. Well, the answer is not as simple as giving a figure. You didn't think it would be, did you? Consider the rich trader and the poor trader.

Rich trader
This trader has oodles of cash, let's say $1,000,000 for argument's sake. His problem is not whether he has the minimum needed to trade, but rather: "What is the minimum he should trade with?"

Just because you have a small fortune does not mean you should look to use it all in your trading. It is advisable to paper trade first, then trade small, and gradually build your way up as your confidence rises. The issue of how much the rich trader should start trading with depends on his answers to the following:

- How confident do you feel?

- How much trading experience do you have?

- Have you traded this product or time-frame before?

- How profitable have you been so far with the system you plan to use?

The other problem the rich trader has is one of opportunity cost. Does he really want to use all $1million trading a system producing 20% return a year? He may be better placing some money into other ventures.

Poor trader
This trader is more like the most of us. He does not have a silver spoon in his mouth, consequently he is wondering whether he has enough money to trade with at all. The first thing to bear in mind is that if you trade with money that is needed for other more pressing things, such as school fees, mortgage, clothing, food, then pretty soon you will lose it. You would simply be putting too great a strain on yourself to "perform" to succeed. You should be trading with "uncommitted" funds.

The minimum needed to trade with depends on the following factors:

- Those listed in the "rich trader" section above

- Broker account minimums: These are so low nowadays they are not too large a hurdle

- The volume of trading you are intending to do: If you are planning to day trade, that means you will be expecting to make a lot of small profits daily. So you will be trading high volume each day, and incurring commission for each trade.

Of course, the optimist will argue that he will reinvest all the profits he intends making back into his trading account. In which case, he may calculate a shorter time-frame than a year as a benchmark for profits.

The key point is that the lower the volume of trading, the less trading capital you need.

Two further points to remember:

- Profits to make the endeavor worthwhile: If your system was likely to produce 100% a year return before commissions, then in the first month you may expect 9% return before commissions.

- To improve your profit, you can either: increase your trading capital, or your system's return, or reduce commission costs by trading less while maintaining returns.

Example

If you trade 10 times a day, and pay $8 to open and $8 to close a position and trade 250 days a year, then you will pay $40,000 in commissions.

Example

If you had trading capital of $50,000, at the end of the first month you would have 2.3% return for the first month after commissions (using our previous example of 10 trades daily at $8 to open and to close). That would equate to 28% annualized *after* commissions *without* reinvestments of profits, or $14,000 in profit for the year (before tax). That is not much of a return for a lot of hard work, and that was with a system producing 100% a year.

Minimum trading money for day trading

From a Palo Alto trader on *Silicon Investor:*

> I would say $50,000 is rock bottom to have decent odds. $75k is OK, $100K is a good number, not too big, not too small. I've day traded and swing traded $25k and $50k accounts at times in the past myself.

> Below $25k, I'd recommend instead of trying to day trade, swing trading positions to build up the account. It can be done! You just have to be really cautious, since there is less margin for error.

Notes

1 Roger Lowenstein 2001 *When Genius Failed.* Fourth Estate.
2 Andrew Ang, Geert Bekaert and Jun Liu "Why Stocks may Disappoint", www-1.gsb.columbia.edu/faculty/aang/papers/DA.pdf.
3 Gibbons Burke article in *Active Trader.* July 2000, p. 68.
4 Mauboussin, Michael and Bartholdson, Kristen "The Consilient Observer", *Credit Suisse First Boston* (June 2002) 1(11): 2.
5 Kahneman, Daniel and Tversky, Amos (1979) "Prospect theory: an analysis of decision under risk", *Econometrica*, Econometric Society, **47**(2): 263–91.
6 Nassim Taleb (2004) *Fooled by Randomness.* Texere Publishing.
7 Steve Crist (2001) *Bet with the Best.* Daily Racing Form Press.
8 Edward Thorp (1966) *Beat the Dealer.* Random House USA Inc.
9 D.E. Kahneman "Psychological biases and risk taking in financial decisions".
10 Charles Sanford quoted on Turtle Trader website – turtletrader.com.

CHAPTER 5

How to interpret CEOs' and analysts' comments on financial TV

Why pay people to gamble with your money? **William F. Sharpe**, *Nobel Laureate in Economics, 1990*

Only two things are infinite, the universe and human stupidity, and I'm not sure about the former. **Albert Einstein**

- How 300 CEO and analysts' interviews later I can speak their language and here's the translation
- How news gets reinterpreted: do we report the news or make it
- "Blah, blah blah … and my forecast for next year"

How 300 CEO and analysts' interviews later I can speak their language and here's the translation

Every Wednesday on Bloomberg TV I would cross-examine the CEO of a company which had had its results that day. Most of these interviews were pre-Enron, when it was novel for financial TV journalists to probe the quality of earnings.

You may think CEOs speak English. It may sound like the language you use to communicate. But it is not. It is "CEOese." Here are some translations.

CEO: Profits are up
Translation: Profit is opinion, but cash is fact. Our profits are up even though we have less cash in the bank because:

1. We sold some of our "crown jewel" assets as a one-off. So the profit rise is a one-off exceptional item not the start of a trend. And those assets we sold, we'll need those in the future.

2. Actually, when we said we sold those assets, it wasn't for cash. It was a barter arrangement and ummm … so our cash balance isn't improved

… but hey, we can still call it profit because we put a "notional value" in the accounts.

CEO: Prospects are good

Translation: We are not telling you about the contingent liabilities; the lawsuits and the pension provisions. We can lean on the accountant to say it is not too bad and so our figures don't look too bad, until the proverbial hits the fan, that is. But hey, I'll have left by then.

CEO: I have every confidence in the company

Translation: That damn headhunter still hasn't agreed my golden hand-shake at the next job.

CEO: We have increased profits from increased revenue growth

Translation: You might think sales are growing and this is adding to profits, especially with wider profits margins. That would get your vote. But I am afraid I am tricking you. We are counting money that is expected but not in hand. That allows us to show greater revenues and profits. Guess what? Sometimes we think there is little chance of getting that money. Bristol-Myers Squibb overstated $2.5 billion in revenues and $900 million in earnings between 1999 and 2001 by giving incentives to move products before the end of its quarters.

CEO: We have increased market share

Translation: Sounds good doesn't it. Actually this is achieved from a lower profit margin and that means cutting prices to increase volume. That can be fine in the short term, but longer term I do not rate those earnings as necessarily high quality.

CEO: Our cost-cutting program means our profits are up

Translation: Cost cutting can be a short-term benefit before longer term profitability is hit. Imagine, for instance, companies cutting on research and development. This year's earnings go up, but in five years you pay the real price for potentially underinvesting.

CEO: People selling our stock are misguided

Translation: Actually they're assholes! In April 2000, the Enron CEO called hedge fund manager Richard Grubman an asshole during a conference call with analysts and investors. Less than eight months later, the company was filing for bankruptcy, costing investors billions.

CEO: Don't worry about the footnotes
Translation: Heck that's where I have hidden everything.

CEO: If you ignore the one-offs, it looks very healthy
Translation: Yeah, these one-off expenses come in every year, they're not so one-off. Cendant, Kodak, Edison International, HCA, Weyerhauser. Each of these companies took a special charge/gain in each of the 20 quarters between 1998 and 2002.

CEO: We're sorry to lose him as a director, but he'll still be a consultant
Translation: Yes, a very lucrative consulting contract indeed and I hope to get one when I leave … we're trying to make it a tradition in the boardroom.

CEO: The director did well and so we feel the perks are sound practice
Translation: Damn you're good, no one hardly ever notices the noncash perks such as flights on the corporate jet. Of course that doesn't mean we run the company like a personal bank account … much.

CEO: Yes, we have increased the amount in nonaudit fees we pay the accounting firm
Translation: Damn again, you really know your stuff. Okay Enron also paid a lot more to its auditors, who just happened to look the other way, but we're not playing that game. Honest.

Little wonder that one PR agent who arrived with a CEO called me "Satan." I took it as a compliment. I had just grilled the CEO on figures he obviously did not understand. I am sure his excuse would have been that he was not a "details" man, he was more big picture! Well, guess what, when his shareholders lose money – that is detail.

How news gets reinterpreted: do we report the news or make it?

I am sorry if you are about to be shocked by the following, but financial columnists often explain things ex post facto. They change their explanation to fit the facts and as the facts change with the passage of time, their explanation changes. In other words, their explanations are meaningless. They are the equivalent of "the Dow was up because it was up."

Let me give you some examples. Below are some *Wall Street Journal* market summaries. Note that the experienced trader DOES NOT read them as an explanation of what is happening, but how others may read it in light of the journalist's spin.

So, for instance, if the journalist puts on a positive spin, chances are that many will read it as such and one should be bullish the next day – not because the journalist is a genius, or because of what is "really" happening, but because market reality is shaped by how many people perceive reality to be and that is shaped by the messenger.

September 19, 2002: U.S. stocks slid Thursday as investors were bombarded by **bad news** from EDS, Morgan Stanley and Merrill Lynch. **Few analysts saw the EDS news coming.** The Dow Jones Industrial Average fell below 8000, dropping 230.06, or 2.8%, to 7942.39, while the Nasdaq Composite Index sank 35.70 or 2.9%, to 1216.43.

Sept. 25, 2002: U.S. stocks bounced back Wednesday from a four-week sell off as earnings news helped sway sentiment. The Nasdaq Composite Index surged 40.12, or 3.4%, to finish at 1222.29, while the Dow Jones Industrial Average gained 158.69, or 2.1%, to 7841.82.

Sept. 27, 2002: U.S. stocks moved lower Friday, weighed down by concerns about corporate profits and **somber economic news**. In late-afternoon trading, the Dow Jones Industrial Average **fell 250 points**, or 3.1%, to 7745, while the Nasdaq Composite Index slipped 13 to 1208.

Nov. 27, 2002: U.S. **stocks rebounded** Wednesday, with an abundance of upbeat economic data helping push the Dow Jones Industrial Average **up 255.26, or nearly 3%,** to end at 8931.68. The Nasdaq Composite Index jumped 43.51, or 3.1%, to 1487.94.

March 10, 2003: U.S. **stocks sank** as geopolitical tensions heightened, and investors steered clear of the market ahead of possible action in Iraq. The Dow Jones Industrial Average **lost 171.85 points**, or 2.2%, to 7568.18, the lowest since last October, while the Nasdaq Composite Index gave up 26.92, or 2.1%, to 1278.37.

March 13, 2003: Major U.S. stock indexes logged their **biggest gains of the year** on hopes for a delay in a possible war with Iraq. The Dow Jones Industrial Average **surged** 269.68, or 3.6%, to 7821.75 in heavy trading, while the Nasdaq Composite Index had jumped 61.54, or 4.8%, to 1340.78.

March 17, 2003: U.S. **stocks surged** Monday on signs the U.S. will go to war with Iraq, a move some say will remove a level of uncertainty in the market. The Dow Jones Industrial Average was **up about 239 points** in late-afternoon trading, while the Nasdaq Composite Index was ahead roughly 3.2%. The dollar rallied, while bond and oil prices sank.

March 24, 2003: The Dow Industrials **tumbled 307.29 points**, or 3.6%, to 8214.68 Monday as investors began to worry that the war in Iraq could drag out longer than anticipated. The Nasdaq Composite lost 52.06, or 3.7%, to 1369.78.

July 7, 2003: U.S. **stocks surged** Monday, with the S&P 500-stock index rising above 1000 as investors pinned hopes on a strong second-quarter earnings season. By midmorning, the Dow Jones Industrial Average was up 179 points, or 2%, to 9251. The Nasdaq Composite Index jumped 45 points, or 2.7%, to 1708.20, and **the S&P 500 rose 18.20**, or 1.9%, to 1003.90.

May 25, 2004: Major stock indexes regained their footing Tuesday as oil prices fell. The Dow Jones Industrial Average finished up 159.19 points, or 1.6%, at 10117.62, while the Nasdaq Composite Index jumped 41.67, or 2.2%, to 1964.65. The **S&P 500-stock index gained 17.67, or 1.6%,** to 1113.08. Crude fell to $41.14 a barrel.

August 6, 2004: Stocks sank to their lowest level of 2004 as Wall Street expressed **disappointment over weak payroll data**. The Dow Jones Industrial Average fell 147.70, or 1.5%, to 9815.33, the Nasdaq Composite Index dropped 44.74, or 2.5% to 1776.89, and the **Standard & Poor's 500 Index shed 16.73, or 1.6%, to 1063.97.**

Aug. 10, 2004: Stocks climbed Tuesday after the Fed raised rates and said the economic soft patch was temporary, caused by high energy prices. The **Dow Industrials climbed 130.01, or 1.3%,** to 9944.67, while the Nasdaq Composite grew 34.06, or 1.9%, to 1808.70.

Blah, blah, blah

So what do you think the market will do next year? Me, I don't know. I don't need to know. I react to its move and change my mind accordingly.

But occasionally I am asked to make a forecast. Here is what the *Financial Times* had to say about my forecasting abilities and those of my competitors:

The winner of our competition to forecast the level of the FTSE 100 over a full year is Alpesh B. Patel, an online investor and FT Money and Business contributor, whose prediction of 4500 was just 23.1 points above the close of 4476.9 on Wednesday, the last trading day of the year.

Patel, who wins a bottle of champagne for his efforts, finished just a whisker ahead of Mike Warburton, a partner in Grant Thornton, the accountancy firm, whose prediction of 4400 was a mere 76.9 points too bearish.

Patel and Warburton head the results table because they got the direction of the market and the pace of the improvement broadly right. But both admitted that luck had played a part in their success.

"I would be being far too presumptuous if I said it was just judgment," says Patel. "Even in my normal trading – week in, week out – I am expecting to be right only six or seven times out of 10. No trader can be right every time. I took a calculated bet based on experience, but there has to be an element of luck in it."

Warburton, who would have won if the competition had ended a few days earlier, says his forecast was based largely on his view that the world economy would improve over the year, helping to lift markets.

"What I said last year was that there was some uncertainty about Iraq and that there would be some difficulties, but once that was resolved I expected the market to lift," he recalls. "These things always have a bit of luck in them, but I just did not believe we would have four bad years in a row."

Two of our other top five finishers were also more bullish than the market: stock market historian David Schwartz's forecast of 4600 was 123.1 points above the FTSE's closing level, and CSFB European equity strategist Kevin Gardiner was 223.1 points out on 4700.

Only one other competitor was too bullish – small cap specialist and FT columnist John Lee. His forecast of 5000 was 523.1 points too high and leaves him languishing in 11th place. Still, since Lee has just accumulated more than £1m in personal equity plans and individual savings accounts, he will not be losing too much sleep about his overly-bullish estimate in this competition.

All our other competitors turn out to have been too bearish, which probably reflects the gloomy state of the markets when the competition was launched in December 2002. Back then a year-end close of 4476.9 looked almost impossibly optimistic.

Perhaps because of their daily exposure to the gloom merchants, all of the FT's own expert commentators were too bearish, although Philip Coggan, our Investment Editor, got close to the outcome with his prediction of 4180.

That turned out to be 296.9 points too low, putting him in 5th place.

Nick Louth and Peter Temple, both My Portfolio columnists for FT Money and Business, were only slightly more bearish on 4,150.

They finish in joint 6th place, 326.9 points below the close.

Deborah Hargreaves, our Markets Editor, ended up in 16th place, 776.9 points away from the outcome. But it could have been much worse.

In December 2002 she thought her forecast of 3700 was "optimistic", and noted that "a case can be made for a much more bearish outcome".

Vince Heaney, then our Onlooker columnist and now a writer on the Lex column, was even farther out. His forecast of 3300 was 1176.9 points too low, mainly because he failed to foresee the "Baghdad bounce" in equities once the Iraq war had begun.

Heaney did much better when we reviewed the competition at the nine-month stage and allowed him to make a supplementary forecast. He said then: "When the markets bottomed in March within a few points of my forecast I felt I had to revisit the timing. I'm now looking at something like 4466 for the end of the year, which is the high from last August, but I have reservations about whether that is sustainable."

John Walter, another of our My Portfolio columnists, also forecast 3300, and shares bottom place.

Happily for the rest of us, his prediction of falling house prices and higher unemployment failed to materialise.

Sadly for those of us who love a good story, our two random forecasters failed to beat the experts.

Jasper the cat, who made his prediction of 3723 by eating from labelled bowls, was 753.9 points too low and ends the competition in 15th place.

Elizabeth Brown, then just four, now five and mistress of most of the alphabet, made her forecast of 4012 by choosing numbers written on pieces of card laid on the floor.

Earlier this year, Elizabeth looked a good bet for a top five position, but the gradual improvement in the market has left her in 9th place, 464.9 points below the close.

Nevertheless, Elizabeth's random choice did manage to beat a top economist, an academic, a millionaire investor, a top fund manager and a brace of FT columnists.

The performance of outside commentators has varied just as much as that of FT writers. Apart from Schwartz, Warburton and Gardiner, the highest finisher is Paul Marsh, the Esmé Fairbairn professor of finance at the London Business School, who ended in 8th place on 4030.

Bookmaker Mark Davies, of Betfair, finished in 10th place on 3990, just ahead of John Lee on 5000 and Bridget Rosewell, the well-known economist, on 3800. Invesco Perpetual's star fund manager Neil Woodford's forecast of 3750 leaves him well off the pace in 13th position.

We are grateful to all of our competitors for taking part. As most have pointed out, forecasting the level of the FTSE 100 over a full year of trading is a mug's game, made more difficult in this competition by huge uncertainties.

These included the Iraq war: it was not clear late last year that there would be a conflict, and it could not be taken for granted that the coalition forces would win as quickly as they did.

The forecasters were also influenced by the gloom triggered by three consecutive years of market declines.

From a high of nearly 7000 at the end of 1999, the FTSE 100 fell steadily to just 3940 on December 31 2002.

No fewer than seven of our forecasters thought the market would fall for a fourth straight year. Many also pointed out that markets are naturally volatile, which means that forecasting for a specific date is virtually impossible.

As if to bear out this argument, the FTSE hit a low of just 3277 on March 12, and then soared to 4329 on September 17 before drifting up gradually to its current level.

Taken together, our forecasters got the direction of the market movement broadly right, but the extent badly wrong. The mean prediction was 4150, a rise of 5.3 percent. At 4476.9 on Wednesday, the FTSE was up 13.6 percent.[1]

What is worrying about the above is how badly wrong experts get their forecasts. Take another example. In 2003 the markets rallied. But for you to have captured that you would have had to ignore a lot of experts. So how did I forecast the FTSE 100 to within 0.5%? Happily I ignored what the "experts" were saying:

It's going to be a difficult environment for stock investors. Don't count on the market to move up. To make money, you've got to select the right names. (Attributed to David J. Winters in Franklin Mutual Advisers LLC, "Brainwork from the Experts," *Business Week,* December 30, 2002: 102)

What the market will probably do is end up in a big trading range next year … a very good year for active managers and stock pickers. (Attributed to Brian Belski of U.S. Bancorp in Jaffrey Piper, "The Way to Play This Market," *Business Week,* December 30, 2002: 67)

I suspect that 2003 will end up being the fourth consecutive down year for the first time since 1932. (Attributed to Jeremy Grantham of Grantham, Mayo, Van Otterloo & Co in "Is The Bear Market Over?", *Smart Money,* January 2003: 71)

Many investors have become skeptics, inclined to sell and take profits when stocks rise, rather than buy in hopes of more gains. (E.S. Browning, "Euphoric Burst, Then It's Back to Usual Blahs," *Wall Street Journal*, January 6, 2003, p. C1)

War worries also are driving money back into Treasury bonds and even into the money market, despite the fact that both of those investments feature some of the lowest interest rates in years. (E.S. Browning, "Stocks Drop, Wiping Out January's Gains," *Wall Street Journal*, January 23, 2003, p. C1)

I do not believe a long-term investor will make money in this market because it is a secular bear market. (Attributed to Felix Zuelauf of Zuelauf Asset Management in "On the Money – Roundtable Part II," Barron's, January 27, 2003)

The fear is that it could be a long war and we could have a sustained sell-off because of it." (Attributed to Tim Heekin of Thomas Weisel Partners in "Fears of War with Iraq Send Blue Chips Below 8000," *Wall Street Journal*, January 28, 2003, p. C1)

Heating oil prices jumped nearly 20% last week as Venezuela's oil strike continues to roil energy markets and freezing temperatures grip the Northeast. (Thaddeus Herrick, "Heating Oil Cost Could Rise 52% From a Year Ago," *Wall Street Journal*, February 10, 2003, p. C1)

According to a monthly survey by Merrill Lynch, global money managers are more risk-averse than at any time since the days following the terrorist attacks of September 2001. (E. S. Browning, "Investment Pros Want No Part of Current Risk," *Wall Street Journal*, February 24, 2003, p. C1)

Soaring energy costs, the threat of terrorism, and a stagnant job market have sent consumers' spirits plunging to levels normally seen only in recessions. The Conference Board's index of consumer confidence fell to 64 in February, the lowest since 1993. (Greg Ip, "Consumer Spirits Decline to Levels last Seen in 93," *Wall Street Journal*, February 26, 2003, p. A3)

Mr. Grantham's study of bubbles suggests that it takes them about as long to deflate as it did to inflate … He says the Standard & Poor's 500-stock index could fall more than an additional 20% from its current level. (Attributed to Jeremy Grantham of Grantham, Mayo, Van Otterloo & Co, in E.S. Browning, "A Party So Wild, the Cleanup Goes On," *Wall Street Journal*, March 3, 2003, p. C1)

Richard D. Hastings, chief economist at Cyber Business Credit, says that consumers have already begun curtailing their spending, and that he expects them to keep cutting back in the coming months … Since mid-2000, consumer spending has been bolstered by mortgage refinancing, home equity loans, and falling retail prices. None of those sources can be relied upon much longer. (Gretchen Morgensen, Money & Business, "Economy Can No Longer Count On Consumer," *New York Times*, March 9, 2003, p. 1)

U.S. moves toward war against Iraq sent nervous Asian stock markets to lows not seen in years, even decades, threatening an already shaky regional economy. (Martin Fackler, "Nikkei Declines to Lowest Level in Two Decades," *Wall Street Journal*, March 10, 2003, p. C14)

Investors continue to sour on stocks. So far this year, investors have made net withdrawals of $11.3 billion from their stock mutual funds, including a hefty $3.7 billion just last week – according to AMG Data Services. (Gregory Zuckerman, "Investors Rush to Buy Bonds, Fleeing Stocks," *Wall Street Journal*, March 11, 2003, p. C1)

No rally may be enough to entice some investors back. "I don't trust it anymore," says Polly Sveda of the market, "I never should have trusted it" … There is plenty of evidence that a growing number of individual investors are shunning stocks. (Tom Petruno, "After the Fall," *Los Angeles Times*, March 16, 2003, p. C1)

This quarter is shaping up to have the worst ratio of negative warnings to positive outlooks since the third quarter of 2001. (Jesse Eisinger, "Ahead of the Tape," *Wall Street Journal*, March 31, 2003, p. C1)

Just as in the U.S., once investors in Europe turn their attention back to the economic and corporate picture, they will wince. It's not pretty at all. Germany is still in the doldrums, and now the economies in France and Spain are starting to slow. (Attributed to Markus Hansen of SG Cowen in Jesse Eisinger, "Ahead of the Tape," *Wall Street Journal*, April 7, 2003, p. C1)

If we see 8% this year, that will be good. (Attributed to Edgar Peters of PanAgora Asset Management in E.S. Browning, "Trading Ranges Keep the Bulls In," *Wall Street Journal*, April 21, 2003)

These stocks still are way ahead of themselves. I am not at all sure we have seen the bottom; I think we could see new, lower lows. (Attributed to John Rutledge of Evergreen Investments in E.S. Browning, "Experts Duel Over Fate of Bellwether Rally," *Wall Street Journal*, June 16, 2003, p. C1)

Several important signals suggest that prices at best have topped out for the time being, and at worst are primed to move back down. Such signals "are classic signs of a market top". (Charles Biderman, president of market research firm Trimtabs.com in Jeff Opdyke, "Four Signs Stocks May Be Near a Peak," *Wall Street Journal*, June 26, 2003, p. D1)

In our view, the quality of earnings of the S&P 500 from an accounting standpoint is the worst it has been in more than a decade. (Attributed to David Bianco of UBS Financial Services in Henny Sender, "At Earnings Halftime, Stocks Hear Mixed Messages," *Wall Street Journal*, July 28, 2003, p. C1)

Even some bears now acknowledge that, when they warned people to stay away from stocks one year ago they were wrong. But they insist that now, after the market's big gains, it is too late to buy. (E.S. Browning, "Stocks Are Defying the Critics," *Wall Street Journal*, October 13, 2003, p. C1)

After all the above, the Dow rose 23% in 2003.

Note

1   *Financial Times*, January 1, 2004.

CHAPTER 6

Never having to be confused by financial news again

In 2000 there were 28,000 recommendations by brokerage-house analysts. As of the start of October, 99.1% of those recommendations on U.S. companies were either strong buy, buy, or hold. Just 0.9% of the time, analysts said sell. **First Call**

- Analyst double-talk and gobbledygook
- No EBITDA is not "earnings before I tricked damn auditor"
- What all those charts mean
- Our secret cheat sheets – exclusively for you

Analyst double-talk and gobbledygook

Analysts are simple creatures to understand on television … until they open their mouths. From my years on Bloomberg TV, on the BBC or interviews on Sky TV, I cannot recall a single analyst who did not like the stock he was talking about. Worse still, when I interviewed them about this common theme, no matter how you couched it, it always seemed to be that in the long term they were positive and in the short term "they saw market volatility."

What they meant was "in the short term it will go up and down and not the direction I am saying, so I don't want to be embarrassed if you call me back in six months because I may still be in this job at this bank. In the long term, heck all stocks go up don't they? And anyway, who's going to remember in the long term anything I say?"

I am not simply saying this without ample evidence. Since the prosecutions by the New York attorney general even more evidence is available.

Roni Michaely and Kent Womack state:[1]

Brokerage analysts frequently comment on and sometimes recommend companies that their firms have recently taken public. We show that stocks that under-writer analysts recommend perform more poorly than "buy" recommendations by unaffiliated brokers prior to, at the time of, and subsequent to the recommendation date. We conclude that the recommendations by underwriter analysts show significant evidence of bias. We show also that the market does not recognize the full extent of this bias. The results suggest a potential conflict of interest inherent in the different functions that investment bankers perform.

Journalists cutting corners

Journalists of course hate figures. They read English not math at university. If they were good with figures they would be making real money. Besides, earnings figures always come after 4pm and by then the bar is too crowded for a drink. And all companies report around the same time all together, so it is very easy to get bored.

Let me show you an example of how companies manipulate their earnings so that financial journalists get taken in, then report the spin to you the investor. Below is an AOL press release.

AOL, Inc. FY2000 Second Quarter Income, Fully Taxed and Excluding One-Time Items, Rises 160 percent to $224 Million, or $0.09 Per Share

EBITDA Increases 108 percent to $453 Million:

DULLES, VA, January 19, 2000 – America Online, Inc. (NYSE : AOL) today announced results for the second quarter of fiscal 2000 ended December 31, 1999 – setting new records for consolidated revenues, advertising and commerce revenues, operating income, and quarterly membership growth.

The Company's fully taxed net income totalled $224 million, or $0.09 per diluted share, excluding one-time items, up from $86 million, or $0.04 per diluted share, on the same basis in fiscal 1999's second quarter. Operating income for the quarter, excluding one-time items, climbed more than 155% over the year-ago quarter to $319 million.

Second quarter revenues rose to $1.6 billion, or 41% over last year's second quarter, and advertising, commerce and other revenues reached $437 million, 79% over fiscal 1999's December quarter.

Reported earnings per share, including one-time items, increased to $0.10 per diluted share on $271 million of net income, up from $0.05 per share on $115 million of net income in last year's second quarter.

Here is what some financial journalists consequently reported:

- *WSJ:* America Online net more than doubled – Fiscal second quarter profit jumped to $271 million on subscription growth.

- *USA Today:* Leap in users helps lift AOL profit 160%. Report expected to quash fears about Time Warner deal.

- *NYT:* AOL posts gain in second quarter income

The true picture could be found in the SEC filings. In May 2000 AOL settled with the SEC $3.5m over its aggressive accounting policies. The press release above failed to mention how liberally the company accounts for revenue or the cost of options. So why did financial journalists not read the SEC filings?

They are long, boring and only sometimes in English. And journalists are fundamentally lazy. www.sec.gov – you'll just have to do it yourself.

Footnote fun

Always read the footnotes to any company announcement. Some interesting footnotes in the past few years include:

- **Enron:** Sketchy details on the off-balance sheet partnerships that hid Enron's debt

- **Tyco:** Pattern of huge restructuring costs

- **Worldcom:** Big increases in types of debt, including loans to executive officers

- **Adelphia:** Strange related-party transactions between family members

- **Healthsouth:** Huge increases in executive pay and perks, including stock options and related party transactions

What bankers do

In case you don't know it:

Investment banks traditionally have had three main sources of income: (1) corporate financing, issuance of securities, and merger advisory services; (2) brokerage services; and (3) proprietary trading. These three income sources may create conflicts of interest within the bank and with its clients. A firm's proprietary trading activities, for example, can conflict with its fiduciary responsibility to obtain "best execution" for clients.[2]

As the above authors explain:

A more frequent and more observable conflict occurs between a bank's corporate finance arm and its brokerage operation. The corporate finance division of the bank is responsible primarily for completing transactions such as initial public offerings (IPOs), seasoned equity offerings, and mergers for new and current clients. The brokerage operation and its equity research department, on the other hand, are motivated to maximize commissions and spreads by providing timely, high-quality (and presumably unbiased) information for their clients. These two objectives may conflict.[2]

But conflict is rife:

Many reports in the financial press also suggest that conflict of interest in the investment banking industry may be an important issue. One source of conflict lies in the compensation structure for equity research analysts. It is common for a significant portion of the research analyst's compensation to be determined by the analyst's "helpfulness" to the corporate finance professionals and their financing efforts (see, for example, *Wall Street Journal*, June 19 1997: "All Star Analysts 1997 Survey.")

At the same time, analysts' external reputations depend at least partially on the quality of their recommendations. And, this external reputation is the other significant factor in their compensation. When analysts issue opinions and recommendations about firms that have business dealings with their corporate finance divisions, this conflict may result in recommendations and opinions that are positively biased.[2]

Want more proof?

If more evidence were needed it's in the press. A Morgan Stanley internal memo (*Wall Street Journal*, July 14, 1992), for example, indicates that the company takes a dim view of an analyst's negative report on one of its clients:

Our objective ... is to adopt a policy, fully understood by the entire firm, including the Research Department, that we do not make negative or controversial comments about our clients as a matter of sound business practice. Another possible outcome of this conflict of interest is pressure on analysts to follow specific companies. There is implicit pressure on analysts to issue and maintain positive recommendations on a firm that is either an investment banking client or a potential client.

Be your own analyst

"The Pied Pipers of Wall Street" is what one commentator[3] calls investment bank stock analysts. The accusation: these stock researchers mislead investors by issuing flattering research reports to drum up other business for their bank.

The New York State attorney general apparently agrees. He launched an investigation (followed in 2003 by a probe by 12 U.S. state regulators) into leading U.S. banks' stock research departments.

So we're on our own when it comes to stock analysis then? That's no problem for online traders – they can improve on analysts reports anyway. The trick is to be your own analyst – and it's now a lot easier than it was, making analysts not just unreliable but increasingly outmoded.

Foremost, an analyst report can't tell you if a particular stock fits well within your existing portfolio. The author doesn't know your financial goals, risk appetite or other portfolio holdings. We could hardly do worse than bank analysts. Recent research[4] found that after transaction costs there was no point buying the strongest recommended stocks relative to the least favorably recommended ones.

Being your own analyst is straightforward. Most investors fail however, because they don't first ask what type of investments they are searching for. Do you want (in rough order of increasing riskiness) undervalued stocks, or growth companies (those that may be well valued but are growing in turnover and profits at a pace suggesting the share price will continue accelerating), or speculative recovery stories (relatively unhealthy companies that may be about to turn a corner and their share price follow)?

Knowing the type of company you are looking for, you can begin mimicking the analysts – but without the downside of any conflict of interest. The key is to be efficient. After all, with a portfolio of 15 stocks, and rejecting as many companies as you accept after your research, you could easily expend 30 hours in research. Undertake the research task only four times a year and a $20,000 portfolio achieving a 15% return only carries a $25 per hour "salary."

Efficiency means starting with research tasks which take the least time per company so you can rapidly narrow down the number of possible interesting companies and spend increasing research time as you zone in on the best candidates for inclusion in your portfolio.

Being your own analyst efficiently requires mimicking their research routine:

1. Produce a list of 30 stocks for further research using an online stock screen or independent stock research sites. A value investor will for instance narrow their search according to valuation measures such as price/earnings ratios.

2. An analyst's database of corporate history can be substituted by using the search facility on news and commentary sites to discover any problems about the company and whether it warrants exclusion from your list.

3. Fundamental data on a company for more detailed research to ensure the stocks meet your (value, growth, recovery) criteria are not the exclusive remit of the analyst but available freely.

4. Find out what the company you are researching is saying about itself. You don't need an analyst's report to access the company's annual report. Neither are analysts' reports needed any longer to provide access to company conference calls or webcasts. If small companies are your main interest, big bank analysts' reports are of little use anyway because they rarely cover such companies. Small company research sites provide an alternative.

5. Having bought the stock, monitor your holding using real-time quotes and online portfolio managers – something an analyst doesn't do for you.

But, being your own analyst means you can further improve upon what analysts' reports could ever tell you. You will want to know whether a particular stock should be added to your existing portfolio mix. For instance, is it likely to make you less diversified? Is your portfolio as a whole more likely to suffer from a market fall? Riskgrades.com is the best site to answer such questions, not an analyst's report.

Does this mean I only fill my bin with analysts' reports? No. They definitely have their uses for private investors, and I use them myself regularly. But they need handling carefully. Here's why:

1. I read them closely for reasons not to buy a stock after all my other research. Often the analysts with their access to company management may have discovered things of concern not discernible by private investors.

2. Sometimes I come across a particularly glowing report and use it as a starting point for my own research into the company.

3. Whilst a "buy" or "strong buy" is not a reason to purchase, a "hold" or "sell" is a reason not to.

4. Most importantly, they often usefully collect and summarize macroeconomic and sector data, giving a useful overview of which sectors look promising.

In the *Pied Piper of Hamelin* story, the piper rids the town of its rats by his pipe playing. Perhaps the implication that we private investors have been led a merry dance by the pied pipers of Wall Street is a little unfair to us. After all, it is not we private investors who are accused of being the rats.

My sites: Research

News/commentary sites with search facility
www.ft.com *****
www.digitallook.co.uk ****
www.citywire.co.uk ****

Company annual reports
U.K.: www.wilink.com *****
www.companiesonline.com ***
U.S.: www.wilink.com ****

Analysts research (banks and independent):
U.K.: www.multexinvestor.co.uk ***
www.equityinvestigator.com ***
www.moneyguru.co.uk ***
www.redskyresearch.com ****
U.S.: www.multexinvestor.com ****
www.zacks.com *****

Smaller company research
U.K.: www.t1ps.com ****
www.itruffle.com ***
www.investorinformation.co.uk ***
U.S.: www.smallcapcenter.com ***
www.pennypi.com ***

Fundamental company data
U.K.: www.hemscott.net ****
U.S.: Marketguide.com ****

Risk tolerance, asset allocation
www.warburg.com/portfolio.cfm ****
www.riskgrades.com *****

Online stock screens
U.K. stocks:
www.sharescope.co.uk *****
U.S. stocks:
http://moneycentral.msn.com/investor/finder/predefstocks.asp *****

Company webcasts/conference calls:
U.S.: www.fdfn.com ****
www.vcall.com ****
U.K.: www.wilink.com ****
www.rawfinancial.com ****

Is it time to trust the analysts again?

Preferably we would want stock ideas from highly trained, highly educated, full-time researchers who spend hundreds of hours tracking companies and meeting their management. So, is it time to trust equity research analysts from the big prestigious institutions again for stock ideas? Just as you cannot trust a bulldog without a leash, you cannot trust an analyst without a website to track his performance.

Do you remember the old accusations – that these analysts misled investors by issuing flattering research reports to drum up other business for their banks?

At the peak of the market boom just three years ago, of 28,000 analysts' recommendations on 6700 North American companies, less than 0.7% were sells, according to First Call – just at the point when the market started plunging and we needed analysts more than ever to tell us to sell.

The 2003 trust-building changes in the equity research industry have been significant: a $1.4 billion settlement in fines and Wall Street firms to spend $450 million to fund independent research.

So are equity analysts' stock picks performing outstandingly well under the new regime? Doesn't look like it. In 2003 Bloomberg tracked the picks of 459 analysts at the top investment banking firms. Only 18 analysts would have made or saved their clients money by outperforming the S&P 500. In fact these much publicized remedies, such as independent research departments, set to remove analysts' bullish bias miss their target altogether.

Research published in February 2003 notes three possible explanations for analyst bias: The "career concern perspective" (analysts are somehow rewarded for their optimism by their employers); the "selection bias" (analysts tend to cover the stocks they can recommend over stocks they cannot); and the "behavioral bias" (analysts tend to like the stocks they cover). "If you listen to the Enron debate," the researchers say, "all the senators and congressmen are going for the first reason; but the analysts point to the second and third explanations of this bias."[5]

Furthermore, U.S. companies still have a seemingly uncanny ability to beat earnings forecast set by 'expert' analysts who speak beforehand to the company management. A suspiciously high 82% of the companies that reported earnings by mid-February 2002 met or beat analysts' earnings estimates, according to First Call.

Beating analysts' figures was the most watched measure of corporate success in the booming late 1990s. The suspicion is that analysts are guided by companies to set beatable estimates, so when the real figure is released the stock receives a boost. Clearly, we cannot simply trust analysts because of recent investment banking changes.

So, what should the private investor do for his stock ideas? Forty pages of investment research will always be compelling to a private investor, whatever it says, and whatever warnings about your financial health are placed on the front cover; just as cigarettes are compelling to a smoker even if covered in warnings.

Instead, trust machine over man (or web over woman). Why would you want to follow an analyst whom you have never heard of, whose performance record you are not provided with, and whose human fallibility may lead to subconscious if not overt bias?

The alternative is far more compelling. Websites can crunch numbers of more companies than an analyst ever could and deliver stock picks based on the proven investment criteria of market legends such as Benjamin Graham (the man who taught Warren Buffett), Marty Zweig, Peter Lynch.

For instance, www.validea.com shows that if you followed its "Benjamin Graham" stock analysis, you would have outperformed the S&P 500 by 31% annually since 1999. We all know that past performance is not necessarily a guide to future performance, but if ever it could be, it would be in the case of proven performers like Benjamin Graham, not a thirty-something banker.

Furthermore, the outstanding www.investars.com ranks analysts' track records – something banks and the U.S. regulators shy away from. Which research house has the best track in a particular sector? Which analyst has the best track record for a particular stock? You won't get that in a stock research report.

Before the internet, such information would never have reached private investors. Unfortunately, private investors still do not know that they can reach it. Yes, these sites focus on U.S. stocks. But U.K. brokers allow you to buy U.S. stocks as easily as U.K. ones; invest in the U.K. and fly blind, or trade U.S. with better information. Doubtless much analyst research is excellent, but without web-tools investors just can't tell which. I relegate using analyst research for the data it provides, not the "buy" or "sell" rating. Focus on the serious fundamentals such as price/earnings. Use the tables comparing the stock to its peers. I discount the opinion and arguments that the analyst makes and focus on the data.

It is said a fool and his money are soon parted. What we learnt in the past few years is that a fool and his money are some party. We private investors have been made fools of by those we trusted who partied at our expense. Some of them refuse to believe the party is over.

My sites: Stock research

U.S. stocks

www.investars.com ***** (i)
www.standardandpoors.com **** (i)
www.multexinvestor.com ***
www.schwab.com **** (i)
www.valueline.com **** (i)
www.validea.com ***** (i)

U.K. stocks

www.stockcube.com (i) ****
www.redskyresearch.com (i)****
www.reuters.co.uk ****
www.hoovers.co.uk (i)****

(i) = provides research from sources who do not have
an investment banking division.

Conflicts remain

The problem will remain even in 2005. According to one report by
CBSMarketWatch:

> The central problem with the settlement is that it replaces investment banking
> conflicts with a new set of conflicts inherent in the independent research
> community, critics say. For instance, some independent research firms don't
> want their stock ratings or research made public because they worry their main
> clients – institutions such as mutual funds and hedge funds – may refuse to pay
> top dollar for analysis that quickly becomes common knowledge.

> That concern is shared by some of the independent consultants appointed by
> the regulatory agencies and the investment banks to select research. "The risk
> is that there will be cannibalization of independent research firms' institutional
> business," said Mark Fichtel, Lehman Brother's (LEH) independent consultant.
> "Some may decide to drop out of this settlement and I will have to find new
> firms to provide research." That kept some independent researchers, like
> Greenwich Investment Research, away from the settlement. "We'd have to be
> paid an awful lot of money to disseminate our research to what is basically the
> whole world," said Chris Hackett, Greenwich Investment Research's principal.
> "Right now we send it to a small group of clients, which they like because they
> get a chance to look at the research and act before everyone else."

Exacerbating the problem, companies that collect analyst ratings data, such as Thomson (TOC), limit the amount of information available to retail investors so they can sell full databases of recommendations history to institutional customers for more money, critics said. "Although institutional investors have been able to purchase access to a whole range of information, retail investors were limited to receiving information on those analysts that came out on top of Thomson's rankings," the CFA's Roper bemoaned in a letter to regulators last year. "Objective performance measurement can play an important role, but it will only do so if it is free from conflicts of interest." A spokeswoman for Thomson said the investment banks ask the company to restrict distribution of recommendation data in return for providing the information in the first place.

Independent research companies are not too bad

A study conducted by a trio of academics[6] found that the average annual returns of the independents' "buy" recommendations outpaced all the investment banks in the study by about eight percentage points a year during a prolonged time period. The study looked at how stocks performed from February 1996 through June 2003.

Some of the nation's largest investment firms – which include Merrill Lynch & Co., Morgan Stanley and Citigroup's Smith Barney unit – are now required to provide their clients with an independent source of research in addition to their own analysts' reports.

Based on the study, when there's a conflict, investors "would do better by following the recommendations of the independent research providers," says Brett Trueman, a professor of accounting at UCLA's Anderson Graduate School of Management, who co-authored the study with Brad Barber of the University of California, at Davis, and Reuven Lehavy of the University of Michigan.

According to the *Wall Street Journal*, "the independents'" edge was particularly striking after the Nasdaq stock market peaked in March 2000. "During the bear market, the independents slaughtered the investment banks," says Prof. Trueman. The authors think that the banks' performance had to do with the fact that they were reluctant to downgrade stocks because of investment banking ties:

> The study wasn't all bad news for major brokerage firms. All of the firms in the study and the independents did just about equally well during the bull market, the study found. The authors say that's not surprising because the banks were issuing "buys" at a time when shares were largely rising.

According to the study, the 10 investment banks that were part of the securities settlement turned in their worst performance between March 11, 2000, and June 2003, when stocks were performing poorly. The banks' picks underperformed those of the independents by an average of 18 percentage points a year during that period. The banks' track record was even worse for recommendations issued or outstanding after an initial public offering or follow-on stock offering during that period: Those picks underperformed by an average of 21 percentage points a year. The poor performance extended to firms with investment-banking business that weren't included in the settlement. (Under an agreement with Thomson Financial First Call, a unit of Thomson Corp. that provided the study's data, the authors agreed not to provide information about specific firms that they studied.)

The study doesn't directly answer investors' questions about how good the new research will be. That's because many of the firms that will provide research under the settlement aren't in the study. Among those that are: Buckingham Research Group, Cathay Financial and Green Street Advisors Inc.

Still, the findings suggest that it can pay to ask for a second opinion – and to carefully consider its findings. "The research reports investors will be getting can be quite useful supplementary information," says Prof. Trueman, who along with his colleagues looked at roughly 335,000 stock recommendations made by more than 400 securities firms.

Investors can obtain the reports via their brokerage firm's Web site or toll-free number. Trade confirmations and account statements must include the ratings given the stock by the firm's own analyst and an independent firm. The firms must offer the independent reports when they solicit an order for a domestic stock and certain foreign securities covered by their own analysts.

While the settlement means that many investors will now get access to independent research that was previously unavailable to them, there has been little information about the quality of this research – or the track records of its providers.

StarMine Corp., which rates analyst performance, says its data show uneven results on three independents providing research under the settlement: Argus Research, Buckingham Research and Fulcrum Global Partners. None "really stand out in a way that I can commend their performance overall," says David Lichtblau, StarMine vice president. "While the firms have some standout analysts," he says, the overall "results are mixed, both in terms of accuracy of earnings estimates and stock-picking performance ... [and] more or less in line but slightly worse than" the average brokerage firm.

Others suggest that the independents may be losing some of their edge. "Over the past year, as the market has gone up, independents haven't performed as well," says Kei Kianpoor, chief executive of Investars.com, which tracks analyst research. One reason: Independents tend to issue more "sell" recommendations than firms with investment-banking ties, which means they do worse when share prices are rising. The settlement and media scrutiny may have also played a part.

No – EBITDA[7] does not mean "earnings before I tricked damn auditor"

So every time we interview these slick CEOs and CFOs – what on earth are they talking about. Are they being "straight-up" or slippery as an eel? The aim of this section is to ensure that you understand the most important aspects of what CEOs are speaking about.

Growth rates

TABLE 6.1 Growth rates (%)			
Company	Industry	Sector	S&P 500
Sales (MRQ) vs qtr 1 yr ago	9.08*	7.92	19.47
Sales (TTM) vs TTM 1 yr ago	8.88*	8.30	26.89
Sales – 5-yr growth rate	9.85	13.15	22.43
EPS (MRQ) vs qtr 1 yr ago	–13.79*	5.39	25.44
EPS (TTM) vs TTM 1 yr ago	–3.92*	3.84	23.49
EPS – 5-yr growth rate	12.66	14.13	21.84
Capital spending – 5-yr growth rate	14.20	15.81	28.30

Sales growth

A company can perform well over the short term with rising earnings even if sales are dropping. This can occur if profits (earnings) are being increased due to cost cutting. However, there will come a time when costs cannot be lowered any further and decreasing sales growth feeds back into lower earnings. For that reason examining sales growth is important.

Earnings per share growth

EPS growth is a key factor feeding into company growth. The year-to-year comparison for the most recent quarter (MRQ) represents the most up-to-date growth information available to the financial community and is always an important determinant of near-term stock price performance. Assume that strong MRQ growth rates will be accompanied by strong stock price performance and vice versa. If that is not the case, then examine the news reports to find out why.

The website Market Guide explains that when examining company-to-industry capital spending comparisons, remember that it is normal for a business to spend at least some money for capital projects year in, year out. But at times capital spending can mushroom to especially high levels as a major project ramps up and then slides to a lesser pace as the newly completed project allows the company to trim down to basic "maintenance" levels.

If you see that a company's capital spending growth was significantly higher than that of its industry, that could suggest that the company's needs should moderate, relative to its peers, in the next few years. That would give the company more flexibility regarding the use of its cash flow (dividends, share buybacks, acquisitions, and so on). If you see that growth in spending trailed the industry average, that might suggest pent-up capital needs (and increased spending) in the years ahead.

Finally, compare the five-year growth rates for capital spending and sales. This can be important since there's usually a relationship between the value of a company's assets and the amount of sales that those assets can generate. A rate of sales growth that exceeds the rate of capital spending growth might indicate that a company is finding new ways to generate more revenues from existing plant. But it could also mean that capacity is getting tight and capital spending increases are just around the corner.

Valuation ratios

These are essential. They give me an idea of whether I am picking up a bargain, a fairly priced stock or an expensive one. For me the key is price trend, so valuations do not veto a stock selection but if all other things were equal, I would want a lower valued stock. Alternatively some investors focus purely on valuations and this can be a useful gauge of a company's potential.

Price to earnings

The p/e ratio shows you the multiple you're paying for each dollar of earnings of the company. One would normally prefer a company with a lower p/e to one with higher p/e. However, note that there can be little wrong with paying a higher p/e multiple for a rapidly growing company because you expect its future earnings rate to be higher.

A good rule of thumb is that a stock is attractive if its p/e ratio is lower than its long-term compound growth rate in EPS. Conversely, a company with a low p/e ratio is not necessarily a good thing. It may be because its outlook is more uncertain due to factors such as competition, a lawsuit, or a cyclical downturn. I tend to look for p/e lower than the industry average.

As well as p/e, examining other similar ratios is always very useful (and definitely impresses the opposite sex at bars – go ahead and try it); these are price to sales (which is especially useful for early-stage growth companies that might not have reached profitability), price to book value, and price to cash flow. Each provides a slightly different perspective and I look on them as an artist not as a scientist; in other words, I try to get a broad, general feel for the figures rather than requiring them to be very exact.

Beta

Beta measures stock price volatility relative to the overall stock market. So, for instance, if we use the S&P 500 as a proxy for the market as a whole and we automatically define its beta as being 1.00, then a higher beta indicates that a stock is more volatile while a lower beta indicates stability. For example, a stock with a beta of 0.90 would, on average, be expected to rise or fall only 90% as much as the market. So if the market dropped 10%, such a stock might rise or fall 9%.

Price to sales

Price to sales is generally used to evaluate companies that don't have earnings and don't pay dividends – in recent times this has often meant internet companies. For these companies, you may consider that high multiples of sales and high growth rates suggest optimistic future earnings expectations on the part of investors. Where earnings have wild swings in any particular year, for instance due to one-off items, price to sales can be a good indicator of the underlying health of the company.

Price to book

Price to book is a theoretical comparison of the value of the company's stock to the value of the assets it owns (free and clear of debt). This is probably of less importance in practice than in theory. The idea behind it is that book value is a proxy for the proceeds that would be realized if the company was to be liquidated by selling all its assets and paying all its debt.

In reality, though, assets are valued on the books at the actual prices the company paid to acquire them, minus cumulative depreciation/amortization charges. The idea behind these costs is gradually to reduce the value of the assets to zero over a period of use in which they approach obsolescence. However, this is based on specific accounting formulas that may not resemble "real world" time to obsolescence. And remember that for a services company, the 'book value' does not produce the revenue. So all in all, I tend to ignore this.

Cash flow and net income

Net income gives us some idea of "how much money the company is generating" which in turn may give us an idea of the health and wealth of the company. To calculate net income, we subtract all expenses from revenues. Unfortunately things are never quite that simple.

For instance, a manufacturing firm spends $10 million to build a factory that will help it create products for a period of ten years. We would recognize factory construction expenses of $10 million in year one, and zero in each of years two to ten. This would suggest one unusually poor year for profits, followed by nine very good ones.

The preferred practice is to match revenues as closely as possible to the expenses incurred to generate those revenues. In our example, we assume that the $10 million factory generates ten years' worth of revenues so we apportion one-tenth of the $10 million outlay in each of those ten years. This one-tenth charge is known as depreciation (amortization is a similar annual charge for a different sort of one-off expenditure that is matched against more than one year's worth of sales).

So, how should an investor assess all of this? Well, keep on reading. As well as net income we would want to look at cash flow as an indicator of corporate health and strength. If you want to know how much the company can afford to pay in dividends or use for other investments, you would look to the cash flow, which is calculated by adding noncash depreciation and amortization charges back to net income.

But cash flow alone doesn't give us the full story. Free cash flow looks at the cash the company's operations actually generated in a given year and subtracts important "nonoperating" cash outlays, capital spending, and dividend payments. Accordingly, free cash flow is the purest measure of a company's capacity to generate cash.

Cash flow is a less pure number, but also less susceptible to wide year-to-year swings as capital programmes periodically build up and wind down.

Clearly, we are looking to compare price to cash flow and price to free cash flow relative to other companies in the same industry and also to see how cash flow and free cash flow change year on year for the company in order to gauge a measure of its growth and valuation. We want price to cash flow ratios to be low relative to other companies in the same industry and we want cash flow to be rising year on year.

Let's take a closer look at cash flows (yes, it may feel tedious – but it's good for you).

Table 6.2 (Statement of cash flow) from Market Guide is divided into three sections. As Market Guide explains:

The *operating* section tells you how the company's basic business performed. The *investing* section will highlight capital expenditures, purchase of investment securities, and acquisitions. This is how the company has invested its money for the future. The *financing* section shows if the company borrowed

TABLE 6.2 Selected statement of cash flow (CF) items (indirect method)					
	Annual			Year to date	
	12 months ending 31/12/95	12 months ending 31/12/96	12 months ending 31/12/97	9 months ending 30/09/97	9 months ending 30/09/98
Net income	1,427,300	1,572,600	1,642,500	1,231,600	1,201,600
Depreciation and amortization	709,000	742,900	793,800	557,000	648,300
Noncash items	–4,200	32,900	–110,700	0	0
Other operating CF	164,100	112,600	116,700	–68,400	147,500
Total operating CF	2,296,200	2,461,000	2,442,300	1,720,200	1,997,400
Capital expenditures	–2,063,700	–2,375,300	–2,111,200	–1,444,000	–1,350,100
Other investing CF	–45,300	–195,000	–106,000	–102,200	–50,100
Total investing CF	–2,109,000	–2,570,300	–2,217,200	–1,546,200	–1,400,200
Dividends paid	–226,500	–232,000	–247,700	–186,300	–179,500
Sale (purchases) of stock	–314,500	–599,900	–1,113,100	–568,400	–1,049,100
Net borrowings	445,100	779,300	1,001,500	415,000	390,100
Other financing CF	63,600	157,000	145,700	146,000	204,200
Total financing CF	–32,300	104,400	–213,600	–193,700	–634,300
Exchange rate effect	0	0	0	0	0
Net change in cash	154,900	–4,900	11,500	–19,700	–37,100
Note: Units in thousands of U.S. dollars.					

money, or if the company issued or repurchased shares. The *net change in cash* is equal to the net effects of what the company generates in operations, spends to invest for the future, how it finances itself, and the impact of foreign currency adjustments.

You want to see a company in which *net income plus depreciation are greater than capital expenditures plus dividend payments*. This is the definition of *free cash flow*. If a company has free cash flow, then it can finance its growth and finance its dividend payments from internal sources. If a company doesn't have a positive free cash flow, it may have to sell equity which will dilute your holdings, borrow money, sell assets, or use its working capital more efficiently. The cash flow statement provides insight into which of these sources funded the company's activities in the period(s) in question.[8]

Some of the items to look for in the statement of cash flows include:

- Positive and growing cash from operations.

- Large and growing capital expenditures meaning that the company is investing in its future.

- Repurchase of stock represented by a negative number (as it is a use of cash) is generally positive. Sales of stock (positive values) are generally negative unless explained by rapid growth which often requires additional equity capital.

- A negative number for net borrowings indicating a repayment of debt is generally positive. A profitable company with low financial leverage taking on some new debt may also be positive. A highly leveraged company taking on more debt can be dangerous.

Share-related items

For me *market capitalization* just provides an idea of how big the company is that I am investing in: it is not a trade-breaker. It is the stock price multiplied by the number of shares outstanding. This is the benchmark upon which a company is classified as:

- large cap (capitalization greater than $5 billion)
- mid cap (capitalization between $1 billion and $5 billion)
- small cap (capitalization between $300 million and $1 billion)

- micro cap (capitalization below $300 million).

Larger companies tend to be safer to invest in than small companies, although several studies indicate that, while riskier, the smaller companies as a group tend to outperform larger companies over long periods of time. I tend to focus more on smaller and some micro cap companies, sprinkled with a few safer large caps like Telecom Italia, Cisco, Sun, Oracle, TelMex, Apple, and Nokia.

The *shares outstanding* is the number of shares issued by the company less any shares the company has bought back. The *float* indicates the number of shares held by everybody other than officers, directors and 5% or more owners. If there is little float, there's generally very little trading volume and anybody wishing to buy or sell the stock may impact the price significantly.

Dividend information

The *annual dividend* is the total amount of dividends you could expect to receive if you held the stock for a year and there was no change in the company's dividend payment. It is based on the current quarterly dividend payment rate projected forward for four quarters. Since I look for growth companies, I prefer it if the company reinvests its dividend rather than paying it to shareholders.

There was a time when a company not paying a dividend could expect to have its share price punished by virtue of the fact that many conservative funds looking for income rather than capital growth from their stocks would steer clear of such companies. Higher yields on stocks can suggest Wall Street expectations of sluggish growth.

The *dividend yield* is the indicated annual dividend rate expressed as a percentage of the price of the stock, and could be compared to the coupon yield on a bond. It allows you to see how much income you can expect per $ or £ investment from this stock, so allowing you to compare it with other stocks you may be looking at. Some prefer high yield, others low. If you are looking for high-growth companies as a general rule, all other things being equal, you will prefer low-yield companies.

The *payout ratio* tells you what percentage of the company's earnings have been given to shareholders as cash dividends over the past twelve months. I look for stocks with a low payout ratio, which indicates that the company has chosen to reinvest most of the profits back into the business.

There are a few sectors whose stocks are regarded as income vehicles – utility and real estate in particular. Investors in these sectors focus more on yields than those in other sectors.

Management effectiveness

The management effectiveness is about *return on capital*. If you invest in government bonds, you would know you are going to get a certain return: the "risk-free rate of return." Since investments in businesses are riskier, you would be expecting a better return than the risk-free one.

Return on equity
The shareholders of a company can be thought of as having given a company capital – or equity. The *return on equity* (ROE) is a measure of how effectively the company has managed this equity. *Equity* represents that portion of the company's assets that would be distributed to shareholders if the company were liquidated and all assets sold at values reflected on the company's balance sheet, so it is what the company itself and therefore the shareholders own and does not include, for instance, money loaned from a bank.

Return on investment
Since *return on investment* (ROI) only relates to capital provided by shareholders, it is a limited measure of management effectiveness since we also want to know how the company is performing with the other sources of money at its disposal. Return on investment shows how effective management is in utilizing money provided by the company's owners (equity) and long-term creditors.

Return on assets
As well as shareholder capital and long-term money granted to the company, there are also shorter term loans of capital, and so *return on assets* (ROA) is a broader measure than the above two of how a company is handling funds provided to it. For example, an internet company may borrow money to purchase some Sun Microsystems routers for its website. The lender may be providing short-term (that is, less than one year) credit. Return on assets measures management's effectiveness in using everything at its disposal (equity, long-term credit and temporary capital) to produce profits.

Profitability

Profitability ratios relate to how much of the revenue the company receives is being turned into profit.

Gross margin shows you what percentage of each revenue dollar is left after deducting the direct costs of producing the goods or services which in turn bring in the revenue. For a services company, the most common direct costs would be employees' salaries.

The money left at this stage is called gross profit. Gross margin expresses the relationship between gross profit and revenues in percentage terms. For example, a gross margin of 10% means that ten cents out of every revenue dollar are left after deducting direct costs.

Operating profit and *operating margin* follow the progress of each revenue dollar to another important level. From gross profit we now subtract indirect costs, often referred to as overheads. Examples of over-heads would be the costs associated with headquarters' operations: costs that are essential to the business, but not directly connected to any single individual product manufactured and sold by the company.

Finally, *net profit* and *net margin* show you how much of each revenue dollar is left after all costs, of any kind, are subtracted, such as interest on corporate debt and income taxes. High margins are better than low margins, and this applies equally when comparing companies in the same industry.

Tax rates

Profitability is also affected by tax rates. A company may have an unusually low tax rate because of losses carried forward or other temporary issues. These will vanish in the future and could sharply affect the profitability of the company. Consequently, it is a good thing to see if the company has an unusually low tax rate.

Recommendations

Ultimately, everything you do when you analyze a stock boils down to what you'll find in this report: **specific investment decisions**. The **Recommendations table** tells you exactly what professional securities' analysts who cover the company have decided to do regarding its stock (Table 6.3).

The table contains five possible investment recommendations: strong buy, buy, hold, underperform and sell. They are based on the five recommendation categories used by most investment advisory organizations. The terminology may vary from one firm to another (for example, some might

TABLE 6.3 Analyst recommendations and revisions			
	As of 22/04/1999	As of 4 weeks ago	As of 8 weeks ago	As of 12 weeks ago
1 Strong buy	1.6	1.5	NA	NA
2 Buy	1.8	1.7	NA	NA
3 Hold	1.7	1.7	NA	NA
4 Underperform	1.0	1.0	NA	NA
5 Sell	1.0	1.0	NA	NA
Mean rating	2.0	2.1	NA	NA

label the third recommendation "neutral" instead of "hold"). But whatever set of labels you see, you can assume that *the investment advisors are ranking stocks in a five-step, best-to-worst sequence.*

Critics of Wall Street research point out that brokerage firm analysts are quick to recommend purchases of stock, but almost never advise customers to sell. You can evaluate this by examining Market Guide's recommendation tables for a large number of stocks.

If you do that, you are very likely to find that *"underperform" and "sell" recommendations are extremely rare; "neutral" ratings aren't quite so scarce, but they do appear far less frequently than do "strong buy" and "buy" recommendations.* Fortunately for you, I/B/E/S compiles and Market Guide presents additional information that enables you to derive worthwhile real-world Wall Street recommendations despite the fact that analyst ratings tend to cluster towards the top of the scale.

The last row of the table presents the mean rating. This is a weighted average of all the individual ratings. The best possible score would be 1.0 (to achieve that, every analyst would have to rate the stock a "strong buy") and the worst possible score would be 5.0. Realistically, given the aforementioned top-of-the-rating-scale bias, you should expect most mean ratings to fall in the 1.00–3.00 range. But within that context, you still can, and should, *compare a stock's mean rating to those of others you are considering and favor those with better (that is, lower number) scores.*

Also, *look at the columns showing the recommendations four, eight and twelve weeks ago.* If you are a momentum investor, you will want to favor stocks for which there are a gradually increasing number of top recommendations or improving mean rating scores. Those who prefer out-of-favor stocks may take a different approach. Such investors would prefer stocks for which the mean rating has been deteriorating.

A mean rating that is stable (or modestly better) from the four-week-ago period to the present after having deteriorated from the twelve- to eight- to four-week-ago intervals might be especially interesting. This trend could be signalling the early stages of a turnaround. A gradual increase in the number of recommendations over the past twelve weeks would indicate that Wall Street is turning its eye toward a company that had previously been ignored or undiscovered.

Performance

Excellent sites like Market Guide provide data allowing you to compare the price performance of stocks relative to major indices and the industry they are in. You can also get a feel for this from sites with graphing facilities. These are mainly viewed in two ways by most people.

Value investors may look for underperformers on the basis that these stocks will eventually "catch up" with the rest of the index, even if in the short term they will underperform and drag down a whole portfolio. *Growth investors* may well look for those that lead the market in terms of performance.

For instance, Table 6.4 (**market guide price performance table**) shows you the stock's percentage price movements over each of five measurement periods: 4 weeks, 13 weeks, 26 weeks, 52 weeks, and year to date (YTD). Large percentage changes, as shown in the second (actual %) column, will obviously catch your eye. But the other three columns are the ones that can add important depth to your understanding of the stock's recent performance.

TABLE 6.4 Price performance vs rank in industry				
Period	Actual (%)	S&P 500 (%)	Industry	Rank
4-week	5.2	−1.1	71	64
13-week	21.3	8.7	78	78
26-week	54.9	19.9	86	83
52-week	69.4	40.2	95	89
YTD	13.6	6.1	74	83
Note: Rank is a percentile that ranges from 0 to 99, with 99 = best.				

Column three compares the stock's price activity with that of the bench-mark S&P 500 index. It shows the percentage point differential between your stock and the index. Column four shows you how the stock performed relative to the average for the industry in which the company operates. This is a "percentile" rank. Looking at this sample, we see that the four-week tally is 71.

This means that the stock performed better than those of 71% of the companies in its industry. Now look at the fifth column, which contains an industry rank. It shows a percentile score of 64. This tells us that the industry performed better than did 64% of the industries in the Market Guide universe (viewed from a different perspective, 36% of the industries in the Market Guide universe performed better).

Institutional ownership

Institutional ownership tables show the extent to which institutional investors (pension funds, mutual funds, insurance companies, and so on) own a stock.

Traders take account of institutional ownership for several reasons, one of which is that if the major institutions are buying, with all their high-flying analysts backing a stock and their millions of dollars vested in these companies, then perhaps we should be more assured in our own decisions.

There is also another way that institutional ownership can back or provide trading ideas. If an institution that owns a position in the company is small, it would indicate that the company has been noticed a little by institutions, with a potential for greater recognition. But the stock may rise as it gets better known and more institutions decide to buy in.

Many believe it is best to own a company that is 5–20% owned by institutions. Such a level would suggest that there is some institutional interest and some knowledge of the company, and that there's also ample room for more institutional interest in the future.

Insider trading

Who knows a company even better than institutions? Maybe the company's executives and senior officers do. These are the insiders. If they are buying, perhaps we should be too, or at least be reassured. And not only their buying, but also their level of holding can be an important sign.

However, when insiders own a very large and controlling percentage of the company, they may not feel responsible to outside shareholders. This is particularly visible in companies with multiple classes of stock, with insiders/management retaining voting control over the company.

Insider selling can, and often does, reflect little more than a desire on the part of key employees to convert part of their compensation (for example stock options) to cash for other uses. So it need not automatically be bearish. However, this is what makes insider trading a difficult gauge of a good or bad stock.

But buying by insiders could be a different story. Here, people are putting new money into the stock of their corporations, and possibly reducing the diversification of their personal assets. It's highly unlikely that any insider would do this unless he/she had a favorable assessment of the company's prospects.

But of course insiders could be buying after a big fall in the stock price in an effort to show faith in the company – and that may be a desperate attempt to encourage outsiders to invest, who, if they do not, could mean that the stock keeps falling. Also, insiders could simply be wrong in their assessment about the future prospects of the company. Nevertheless, it is a useful indicator to take note of.

No – EBITDA[7] is not "earnings before I tricked damn auditor"

Other things you need to know about the markets:

EBITDA:	earnings before I tricked damn auditor
EBIT:	earnings before irregularities and tampering
CEO:	chief embezzlement officer
CFO:	corporate fraud officer
NAV:	normal Anderson valuation
FRS:	fantasy reporting standards
P/E:	parole entitlement
EPS:	not earnings per share but eventual prison sentence. As in Enron is trading at an EPS of 6 (6 years that is)
Bull market:	a random market movement causing an investor to mistake himself for a financial genius
Bear market:	a 6–18-month period when the kids get no allowance, the wife gets no jewelry, and the husband just gets "no"
Standard & Poor:	an accountant's life in a nutshell

- If you had bought $1000.00 worth of Nortel stock one year ago, it would now be worth $49.00.

- With Enron, you would have $16.50 of the original $1000.00.

- With Worldcom, you would have less than $5.00 left.

- If you had bought $1000.00 worth of Budweiser (the beer, not the stock) one year ago, drunk all the beer, then turned in the cans for the 10 cent deposit, you would have $214.00.

Based on the above, my current investment advice is to drink heavily and recycle.

What all those charts mean

You see them all the time, on TV, in magazines. Here is what all those charts mean.

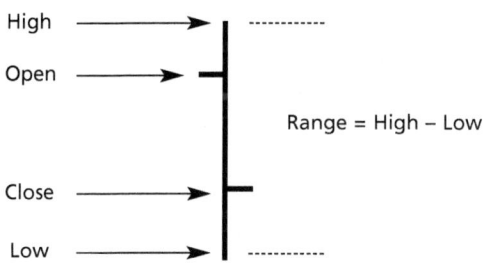

Figure 6.1 Open, high, low, close price bar

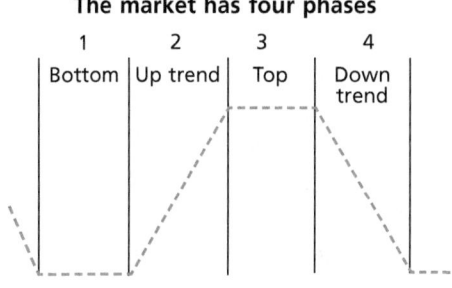

Figure 6.2 Trends

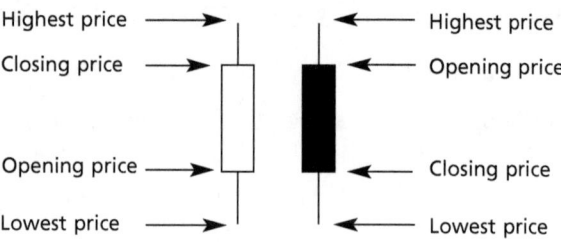

The body is filled if the open is higher than the close

Figure 6.3 Candlestick charts

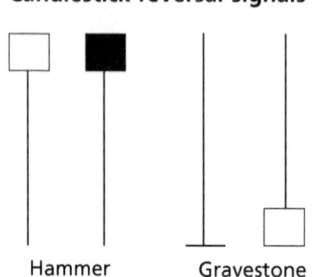

Candlestick reversal signals

Hammer   Gravestone

Figure 6.4 Patterns in Japanese candlesticks suggesting price reversal

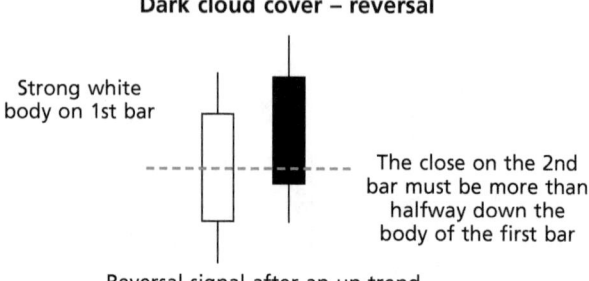

Dark cloud cover – reversal

Strong white
body on 1st bar

The close on the 2nd
bar must be more than
halfway down the
body of the first bar

Reversal signal after an up trend

Figure 6.5 Another Japanese candlestick reversal pattern

Morning star – reversal

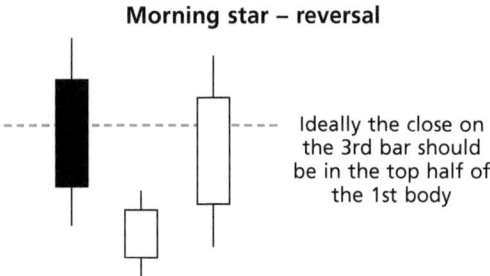

Ideally the close on
the 3rd bar should
be in the top half of
the 1st body

Figure 6.6 Price reversal pattern

Evening star – reversal

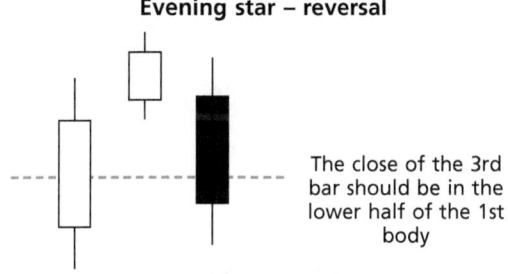

The close of the 3rd
bar should be in the
lower half of the 1st
body

Figure 6.7 Price reversal

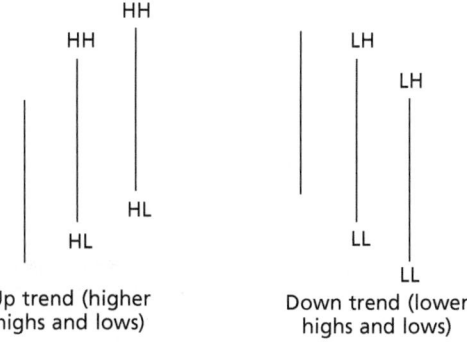

Up trend (higher
highs and lows)

Down trend (lower
highs and lows)

Figure 6.8 Trends

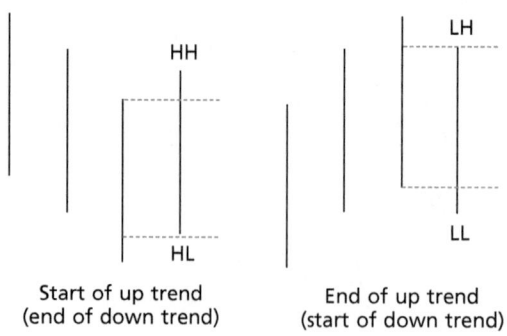

Start of up trend   End of up trend
(end of down trend)   (start of down trend)

Figure 6.9 Trends: start and end

Trading head and shoulders

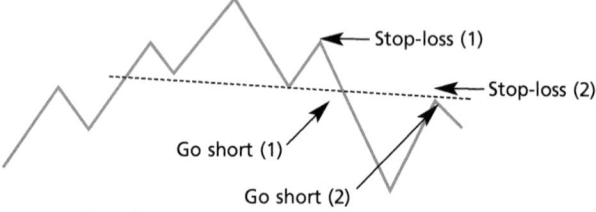

(1) Go short when price breaks below the neckline. Place a stop-loss above the last peak. (2) If price rallies back to the neckline, go short on a reversal signal and place a stop-loss above the resistance level

Figure 6.10 A popular price chart pattern

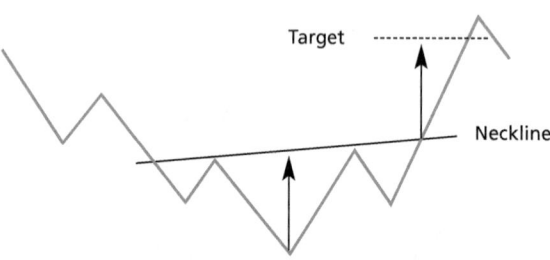

The target is measured vertically from the lowest trough to the neckline (drawn through the peaks on either side). It is then projected upwards from the breakout above the neckline.

Figure 6.11 Inverted head and shoulders pattern

Support level

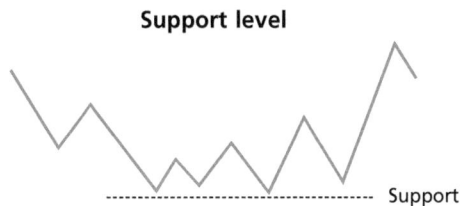

-- Support

The support level is stronger every time that price respects the support
line and/or if high volumes are traded at the support level

Figure 6.12 When TV talking heads talk about "support"

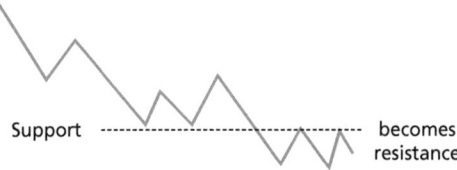

Support ----------------------------------- becomes
                                            resistance

Once penetrated, the support level may act as a resistance level.
Stockholders who bought at the support level will be inclined to sell
when the price rallies back to that level to recover their losses

Figure 6.13 Support and resistance

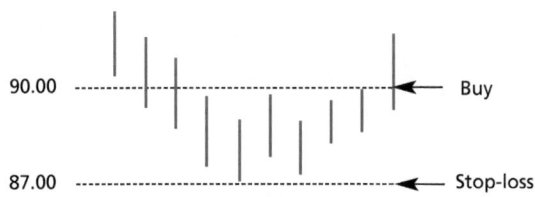

90.00 -----------------------------------◄── Buy

87.00 -----------------------------------◄── Stop-loss

Example of a stop-loss: stock purchased at $90.00 and
stop-loss placed at $87.00 (below the recent low)

Figure 6.14 What analysts mean by stop-loss

Our secret cheat sheets – exclusively for you

At Bloomberg, staff have access to lots of functions on the Bloomberg
terminal which are not open to the public. Some which are open to the
public, however, include those which list data you probably will want to
look at as a trader.

Below is a list of such data, but since most readers will not own a $1500 per month Bloomberg terminal, I have also listed some websites as alternative sources of information.

Today's top business and financial headlines	Pathburner.com Ft.com Marketwatch.com
Search news by keyword	Pathburner.com
Global stock market news	Ft.com Pathburner.com
Earnings analysis	www.firstcall.com
Mergers and acquisitions news	http://www.alpeshpatel.com/ News/Category.asp?id=18
Economic news	www.alpeshpatel.com/News/ Overview.asp
Broad market perspective ■ World equity indices ■ Stocks and sectors moving an index	www.forexnews.com www.adr.com www.alpeshpatel.com
Equity analysis ■ Company specific news ■ Financial ratios ■ Company graphs	www.yahoo.com www.bigcharts.com

Notes

1 "Conflict of Interest and the Credibility of Underwriter Analyst Recommendations", Roni Michaely of Cornell University and Kent Womack of Dartmouth College. (February 1999) Oxford University Press, *Review of Financial Studies*, **12**.
2 AOL company accounts.
3 *The Pied Pipers of Wall Street: How the analysts sell you down the river,* Benjamin Cole (Bloomberg Press 2001).
4 "Can investors profit from the prophets? Security analyst recommendations and stock returns", Brad Barber, Reuven Lehavy, Maureen McNichols, Brett Trueman, *Journal of Finance*, April 2001.
5 "Analyzing the Analysts: Career Concerns and Biased Earnings Forecasts," Harrison Hong and Jeffrey Kubik, *Journal of Finance*, Feb 2003 www.stanford.edu/~hghong/analysts-Jf.pdf.
6 Brett Trueman, Brad Barber and Reuven Lehavy (2001) *Prophets and Losses*.
7 Earnings before interest, tax, depreciation and amortization.
8 Market Guide – marketguide.com.

CHAPTER 7

What the viewer never sees from this side of the camera

You must abide by the highest standards of journalistic ethics and perform your duties with objectivity and without intent to achieve financial gain for yourself, directly or indirectly. **Bloomberg Code of Ethics**

Understanding how financial news is made is essential to understanding how markets move. The news is impacted by events and events are impacted by news. It is the latter that concerns the investor. After all, investors watch CNBC and Bloomberg to get financial news. If that news is not simply reporting, but interacts with events to shape the story as you interpret it, you need to understand what is going on in order to understand how the markets may react and ultimately how you should react to that.

- Bloomberg and the *Financial Times:* probably the last great honest financial source with integrity, and why that's scary
- Why we're pretending to be sad

Bloomberg and the *Financial Times:* probably the last great honest financial source with integrity – and why that's scary

I trust the *Financial Times* and I trust Bloomberg. I know editors and journalists there. But, trust all financial journalists everywhere?

Two examples suffice. In 1995, the *Columbia Journalism Review* reported: "As a businessman, I decided that if Bloomberg is perceived as credible, that credibility will help us sell more terminals." As soon as Bloomberg made its terminal available to *The Times*, other newspapers requested them. "We decided that if a paper had a certain circulation or was a flagship paper, we'd make it available to them, too," says Winkler, founder of Bloomberg News.

"The company now has terminals at nearly 150 papers, [many of which] will be paying only a minimal fee for installation and telephone service. Meanwhile, the *New York Times* Syndicate will soon include a selection of Bloomberg stories (not real-time data or charts and graphs) in its feed to some 600 newspapers."

As a Bloomberg employee I was forbidden from taking gratuities. As a Bloomberg supplier, each Christmas my company, which provided my services to Bloomberg, would receive a letter threatening that Bloomberg would cut off all relations if the company offered any gifts at Christmas to any Bloomberg staff, including myself presumably.

The reason for no gifts was obvious. *The Bloomberg Way* (given to every Bloomberg News staffer) states it clearly:

> We don't accept gifts, gratuities, travel expenses or lodging, from people, institutions or other entities. We make every attempt to pay our way in every story we cover. Free lunches also discouraged.

> Imagine the PR man for XYZ Corp. takes you to a cozy dinner at 21 Club with filet mignon, two bottles of Chateau Rothschild, a glass of Remy Martin in your hand and a gold-plated Cross pen with your name embossed on the side – a gift next to your dessert fork. Now that the company has flattered you for two hours, it wonders whether you might consider doing a big story on the unveiling of its RTD2 switching device that you know has no track record … Oh, that Remy tastes so good with the Cuban cigar, and that pen will look so nice in your breast pocket, and XYZ will fly you to Bermuda for the weekend for a three hour conference on the RTD2 … Gotcha.

This last point is important for private investors to realize too. Financial journalism, is journalism. And since journalists have power, companies try every way to encourage them to offer publicity. Offers I have refused include a flight to Paris for a press launch, a day at Ascot, a day playing golf at Wentworth and so on.

But, what about other writers. They cover a product and a company's share price shoots up. You can't trust the company to tell the truth. If you read a "soft" piece from a journalist, work under the presumption that I do: someone gave the journalist a nice lunch.

But what is a "soft" piece. It is one without probing insight and critique. It is one which praises incessantly. It is one which could have been written by the company itself!

Let me give more examples from inside financial journalism.

The journalist who "got it"

I was interviewing the CEO of a major technology company in 2000 from Bloomberg TV. Of course at that time all tech companies were major. But this one had promised shareholders revenues of $1 billion in 12 months. Obviously its share price reacted accordingly.

Now, the CEO was clearly disappointed that the interview was going to be conducted by me, my having taken the role of Bloomberg tech expert, and not my predecessor who although not from the TV side, but the Bloomberg News side, used to do such interviews on TV – and do them really badly (for which read boringly).

But the reason for his obvious disappointing expression when we met only became apparent after the interview. Now, my practice in interviewing any CEO is to put on my attorney hat. I look to cross-examine and grill the CEO. The way I prepare for such interviews is by looking at what is on the Bloomberg terminal, what the company itself says about itself and what any web news sources say. I will then, as any good attorney does, concede the good points, and attack on the poor. That I felt was the best way to add value to viewers.

So, for instance, a typical question to a CEO may be: "Your sales are up 25% quarter on quarter. But given that your profit margin is down and so is your profitability, clearly you are selling more by cutting your profits – you're cutting your own throat, aren't you?"

Sure, I could have added, "I put it to you that …" if I were in court, but you get the idea. And to the credit of Jack Reed, my immediate editor, and Katherine Oliver – his line manager – it is the way they liked it. All this was pre-Enron too.

On this one occasion after the interview the CEO asked if BCD (I have concealed the name of the previous colleague) was around because "he really got what this company was about." I knew exactly what he meant. BCD told it the way the company wanted it told. Was I being overly suspicious? You could say my suspicions were confirmed when, firstly, this company's shares plummeted and today it is worthless. And secondly that BCD jumped fence, as he surely had planned, with a fat Rolodex from his times as a Bloomberg journalist, to now advising tech companies on raising finance to resuscitate their ailing selves. Perhaps the most unconvincing suspicion was that this former employee had a mean and hungry look.

On my first day at Bloomberg BCD took me to one side, eyed me up and down and said: "So how did you get this job?" I explained I was the author of a financial bestseller, CNN interviewed me, the head of TV at Bloomberg thought it would be a good idea to have me on air and then called up to meet and offered it to me.

"So the book's the secret. I want to write a book," he proclaimed. Now, I can sense when someone is insecure about their job and worried that I might be a threat. And the best way to deal with such people is to reassure them that you are no threat. Anything else and it gets messy, political, and they tend to have a penchant for knives and an eye on your back.

Equally, I knew that if I was invited here and this guy already does some of what I was asked to do, then he can't be that good. "Sure, let me know how I can help you. I can put you in touch with my publisher if you wish." That last line is usually the clincher to everyone who thinks you write a book and hey presto your life is better. Actually, they like the idea of a book, but not the idea of the late nights, the exhausting typing, researching and work.

In life such people finish second because they never see a bigger picture. For them it is win–lose. You must lose for them to gain. There can never be any win–win. And they console themselves that their lives too would be better but they just didn't take that shortcut.

Sure, they could be Richard Branson, it's just that they never had a rich pushy mother … and … so on. There are always excuses.

Such people exist in journalism as everywhere else. These journalists use the profession to make contacts for when they can jump ship. You, the poor investor, do not know, when the journalist is writing a piece about a particular company, whether it is because he is thinking of moving into PR, investor relations, venture capital, or investment banking. Or does he plan to always stay a journalist. So you do not know how 'fluffy' the piece is. And the danger? Well, look at Enron. How many journalists were sleeping on the job?

We can be bought. It's not cash, it's not even the prospect of a future job. You the investor suffers a direct loss in your investments. I won't say "the truth" is the victim. No, something far less philosophical is the victim – your bank balance. However, even in the litigious U.S., no one has sued the journalists over not uncovering poor management and accounts. There's a thought.

The supreme irony is that Matt Winkler, the founder of Bloomberg News did a piece on Mike Bloomberg, then Mike hired him some months later to start Bloomberg News. And so it goes on.

Inside baseball

Of several thousand columns I have written for various media, only twice have editors exerted editorial pressure. The first time was when I was interviewing Kelvin McKenzie, former editor of the *Sun* newspaper (the most widely read paper in the U.K. – *The National Enquirer* and *USA Today* rolled into one) in his capacity as promoter of a dot-com company typical in 2000; this one charged for online horoscopes. Jack Reed, editor, reminded me (knowing my direct style) that Kelvin was also responsible for deciding Bloomberg's contract with a major radio station. He need not have worried, Kelvin was classless and hung himself with his second-rate performance and justification for taking money from the insecure who paid for horoscopes.

The second was my editor at FTMarketWatch. A piece about taking care with stories by financial journalists who basically recycle company press releases means we as investors need to be very careful. I was told it was "too inside baseball." I wasn't sure what that meant, but I knew I had to submit a new piece.

The problem was it was probable my editor felt it might not be of interest to the broader public. I will give the benefit of the doubt that it was not because I was criticizing journalists.

Wide-boys who claim to be financial journalists

Then there are the dishonest. It does not take long for a scribe to work out that their opinions influence other opinions and that means there is money to be made. Personal gain. One of the worst examples of this was reported by the BBC about journalists at a British tabloid paper in 2000:

> *Mirror* editor Piers Morgan breached the newspaper industry's code of practice in the recent share dealing scandal, the Press Complaints Commission has ruled. The PCC said Morgan had fallen short of the high professional standards demanded by the code. The commission's report also found against journalists Anil Bhoyrul and James Hipwell, who had written and edited the paper's City Slickers column. The PCC launched its inquiry into share dealing by journalists at the *Mirror* after it emerged that a number of staff had bought shares tipped in the City Slickers column.

> The code of practice prohibits journalists from:
> - Making personal gain out of financial information before it is published
> - Writing about shares which they own without informing their editor
> - Buying or selling shares about which they have written recently or intend to write about in the near future.

My disclaimer, which I crafted myself, for my editor at the *Financial Times* is:

> Disclosure: I do not have any financial interest in any of the websites. I do not directly or indirectly, through family/derivatives, have interest in any of the securities mentioned (except where expressly clear in the face of the document) although as an active trader could do in the future (but only at least two weeks post publication) and may have done in the past. I have not disclosed the names of the securities mentioned in this column to any 3rd parties and will not do so before publication.

Here is something all financial journalists should know: Bhoyrul and Hipwell were charged by the Department of Trade and Industry with conspiring to contravene section 47(2) of the Financial Services Act 1986. Section 47(2) of the 1986 Act states: "Any person who engages in any course of conduct which creates a false or misleading impression as to the price of any investments is guilty of an offence if he does so for the purpose of inducing another person to acquire those investments." The trial is some time this year.

Watergate and financial journalism

"And money was increasingly becoming the mother of all stories. For those who can recall Watergate, the best advice any two reporters received in the 20th century was: 'Follow the money!'" – So wrote Matt Winkler, the founder of Bloomberg News whom Michael Bloomberg appointed for the job.

So where is the financial Watergate? Why did financial journalists not break the Enron story before it got to the stage it did? Why are financial journalists not uncovering financial scandals as big as the political scandals that other journalists do. We know they exist.

Two *Wall Street Journal* journalists broke the Enron story. As they congratulate themselves in their book *24 Days* – one is left wondering why it took ten years to get to the bottom of it. This was not so much breaking a story in the sense of advance warning, as getting to the scene of a crime, seeing a dead body and saying "here it is." That's not breaking a story, not prevention, not early detection, not 'if we don't know, no one will' – as in the case of Watergate.

Is financial investigative journalism dead, sleeping on the job, or too scared of law suits? What is to be done? One thing is for sure, it's the little guy, the private investor who gets royally cheated.

Why we're pretending to be sad

Was it a good or bad day on the market today? You look at the news, maybe a website or financial TV to get an idea. We would go on air and talk about the market. After a long day, a 7pm show was the final hurdle and we were usually quite happy to be going into the studio. In an hour we would be free. But the market is down 100 points.

"Okay people, let's not look so happy. A lot of people will have lost money there today," the presenter would say.

Hang on a minute. This example illustrates a broader issue. First, if we're glum, isn't that going to affect how some viewers decide what to do with their investments. Second, since when did presenters become stock pickers? Third, short-term falls will have benefited those who are short stocks, so not everyone is glum. Fourth, it is only a day – are we not exacerbating a short-termist view of the market which is exactly what we're criticized for.

I mention this illustration because it depicts a broader problem: *the messenger is the message.*

Consequently, like many hedge fund managers, when looking for trading ideas and stock picks, I will do a news word search. There are certain key words in financial news stories I will hunt for. Those words allow me to determine that I have a good starting point for investigating further whether the stock is likely to rise or fall.

I used the stocks associated with news stories containing those words to pick stocks on the program on Bloomberg, where each week I would have to give a six-month "buy" and "sell." When a Bloomberg intern went through my picks – they outperformed all other stock pickers on the channel.

Of course the names of stocks associated with stories containing those words were only the beginning. If 10 stocks were thrown up, I would narrow them down to the best candidate, based on share price trend, fundamentals, earnings, and so forth.

So, what were those words and where and how did I search the news for them? Where and how is easy – I used www.pathburner.com to search news stories for the words. What were the words?

For bullish stocks they were:	*For stocks expected to continue to fall:*
share soars	share plummets
earnings rise	earnings drop
exceed expectations	met expectations
beat expectations	in line with market expectations
director buys	director sells
upgrade	downgrade

Note the words used by financial journalists can be divided into three types: industry terms (for example upgrade), descriptions (for example director buys) and, most interestingly, journalist opinion (for example "soars").

It is the latter that potentially shapes opinion. And the latter that feeds back into other market perceptions. That is why I am after such words.

Let's blame ourselves: investors get the markets they deserve

Now I do not want to be seen as a whiner not taking responsibility for our weaknesses but seeking to blame financial journalists for all that is wrong with our portfolios.

"I don't come to work to earn a living, I come to make money." So said David Kyte, the largest independent trader on the LIFFE (London's derivatives exchange). Make no mistake, we trade and invest to make money.

And that's good. It means we're loved by God. After all, God must love the money makers, why else would he divide so much among so few of them.

Investors get the markets they deserve. Let me explain.

Meet the "loser-genius." He comes from the subcategory of investor defined by *Encyclopaedia Britannica* as 'dumb-ass, moronic-ass'. He thinks he's cracked the market because if a stock falls, you should buy even more of it. Why? Well, he argues in deep tones of sincerity, whilst scratching his overgrown brow, because it has a lower "average purchase price" then. So if you bought some at 100p and more at 80p, it only needs to go up somewhere between 80p and 100p for you to break-even. Oh, "genius-boy" will also tell you the stock's cheaper now.

He deserves what he gets. And he gets losses. Trading is not about the number of "wins" but about how much money you make in total. Seldom does buying more of a falling stock represent the best place out of 3000 listed U.K. stocks to put your money and become even more undiversified. Novice investors confuse price with value. I know my wife does when shopping.

When this urge does overcome you, take my advice. Lie down, have a Scotch, read a book. The urge to make a bad losing decision will soon pass with a bit of thought.

Or take the closely related cousin (closely related due to some inbreeding I might add) of "dumb-ass, moronic-ass" and that's "investorsaurus ignoramus." He piles into rising stocks a bit too late (because he wants to be absolutely sure it's going to keep rising) and then stays after everyone else has left the party (actually he doesn't get party invites so that analogy goes right over his head) and the stock is plummeting (oooh, because that short-term trade suddenly looks attractive as a long-term investment – now that it's halved in value: think of all the potential). For any Americans reading this – that last bit was irony.

Why do investors end up holding too long or getting in too late? Basically, why do they mistime? Investors have overly optimistic expectations about the prospects of future earnings growth for stocks trading at high-valuation multiples, and when these expectations are not met, it results in lower subsequent stock returns.

Skinner and Sloan, from Michigan University, observed the "earnings torpedo" effect on Oracle and Rainforest Café in the late 1990s.[1] The two researchers used a sample of 103,000 firm quarters between 1984 and 1996 as the basis for their study and tracked stock return behavior over 20 quarters. The price of high-flyers stocks climbed steeply to a maximum of

10% when the earnings news was positive, but fell rapidly, losing 10% to as much as 20% of their value when they disappointed on earnings.

Guess what bad investors do? They ignore the negative news and hold on, remembering old glory days. They do not readjust their expectations as quickly as professionals. They deserve what they get: a falling stock.

Other research by Barber and Odean[2] examining 700,000 individual investors found they were more likely to be net buyers of attention-grabbing stocks (that is, those stocks in the news) than institutional investors, even after an earnings warning. In other words, not only would many stay in long past a sell-by date, others would actually get in!

Good traders will tell you it's not what happens in the markets that matters but how you react. When I interviewed Pat Arbor in Chicago for my book *The Mind of a Trader*, he was chairman of the world's largest derivatives exchange and had been a floor trader for many years and he told me about one old hand who would take new traders under his wing by taking them into the nearest trading pit, telling them to buy a contract, of, say, corn futures, and then he would tell them immediately to sell it.

Why? So they knew what it felt like to take a loss.

Investors who can't take losses definitely get the markets and the results they deserve. It is definitely not true that Chris Gent, CEO of Vodafone, in an effort to keep shareholders holding the stock as it fell from 400p to 100p, said: "Don't worry, we may be worse off than we were yesterday, but we're better off than we will be tomorrow." No, he didn't say that. By the way, under his stewardship, the company wiped off £300 billion from the market cap – and the CEO still didn't go to prison. Nick a mobile phone and you're in the clanger.

So how do others join the species, "smart-ass investorsaurus"? You know the answer. It's genetic modification. No, the real answer is independence of mind, achieved by following your own research and the discipline to get in and out when you think it is right. Don't stay in too long as the price falls. Remember that when you're in a hole, digging faster doesn't help you to get out.

Finally, if you are unsure about what next year will bring, take solace from two pointers. If this year was an "annus horribilis", never mind, there are creams for those things. And secondly, take solace: there is one thing that differentiates humans from animals – financial worries.

So let's get adventurous

Why are we so much more adventurous about the food we put in our stomachs than we are about the stocks we put in our portfolios? Some have portfolios akin to the Atkins diet – overdosing on one particular sector, or size of company, such as blue chips. But offer a tasty little morsel of energy stock from China, up 35% by the spring of 2004, undervalued relative to its peers, strong revenue growth? Oh no, I'll stick to Marks & Sparks. Is it little wonder our portfolios are bloated with stodgy stocks held in rather dreary, old-fashioned combinations. What you need is a little bit of "fusion" investing. Of course you have to be aware of your appetite for risk, so deal accordingly.

Fusion cooking involves mixing ingredients from several countries, but it's important to get the *combinations* right. At one end of the spectrum you get cinnamon almonds with deep fried squid, at the other something that looks disappointingly like goulash.

Fusion in your portfolio means a liberal sprinkling of that essential ingredient for profitability – diversification. First, add a smidgen of international stocks using American depository receipts (ADRs) – foreign stocks traded on the New York Stock Exchange in dollars. You use exactly the same broker and processes as for buying Microsoft or Apple. For instance, you can use Barclays stockbrokers online CFD service.

These international stocks spread risk and offer access to some of the world's strongest growing regions and largest companies – like Gazprom, Ericsson, Elan – each up 138%, 55% and 204% if you look at the year to May 2004. The free www.adr.com gives you as much data about them as you will get on any U.K. company.

Effective diversification often comes from holding international securities because they are less correlated to domestic ones. Investments with low correlations (whose prices move less in tandem with each other) reduce "portfolio risk" – the chance that all your investments will fall together – while maintaining returns. Harry Markowitz won a Noble prize for that discovery – confirmed by recent research.[3]

Second, to improve your diet and your financial health, you have to look at the methods you are using for picking stocks. You don't always go to the same grocer, do you? Well, do you use charting as well as fundamentals? Do you know your MACD from you p/e, your halibut from your cod? Incidentally, the MACD (moving average convergence divergence) is an indicator measuring when a stock is gaining momentum – and, together with the stochastic and the relative strength index, is one of my favorites. The Barclays website homepage has a "guide to technical analysis."

As any chef will tell you, it's not just about the ingredients you use, but also how you prepare and serve them. In investing that translates into "Are you using the full array of stock orders for getting the best price. Have you checked out limit orders and stop orders?" Each of these improves your portfolio by potentially improving the price at which you buy and sell.

Third, consider "going short." One form of diversification for traders is cross-hedging. I always try to simultaneously hold various "long" (buying in anticipation of a price rise) and "short" positions (selling in anticipating buying back more cheaply to close the trade). Contracts for difference (CFDs) make this as easy as buying a stock.

Fourth, add sizzle and spice by broadening the size of companies you invest in. Have you looked at small caps and AIM recently? AIM is up 54% over the year to spring 2004, the FTSE 100 only 15%. So stop sticking to your favorite restaurants – there's a lot more on the menu.

Notes

1   Skinner and Sloan (2002) "Earnings Surprises, Growth Expectations, and Stock Returns", *Review of Accounting Studies,* **7**: 289–312.
2   Brad Barber and Terence Odean (2003) "All that Glitters", University of California.
3   "Smooth Transition Regression Models in U.K. Stock Returns" Nektarios Aslanidis, University of Crete. September 2002 www.soc.uoc.gr/econ/seminars/ Aslanidis_2002a.pdf.

Page numbers in **bold** type refer to figures; those in *italic* to tables or boxes